Pragmatic Illusions

Bruce Miroff

PRAGMATIC ILLUSIONS

The Presidential Politics of
JOHN F. KENNEDY

DAVID McKAY COMPANY INC.

New York

Pragmatic Illusions:
The Presidential Politics of John F. Kennedy

COPYRIGHT © 1976 BY David McKay Company, Inc.

MANUFACTURED IN THE UNITED STATES OF AMERICA

Development Editor: Edward Artinian
Editorial and Design Supervisor: Nicole Benevento
Interior Design: Bob Antler
Cover Design: Lawrence Ratzkin
Production and Manufacturing Supervisor: Donald W. Strauss
Composition: Adroit Graphic Composition, Inc.
Printing and Binding: Haddon Craftsmen

Library of Congress Cataloging in Publication Data
Miroff, Bruce.
Pragmatic illusions.
Includes bibliographical references and index.
1. United States—Politics and government—1961-1963.
2. United States—Foreign relations—1961-1963.
3. Kennedy, John Fitzgerald, Pres. U. S., 1917-1963.
I   Title.
E841.M54   973.922'092'4   76-7554
ISBN 0-679-30298-0
ISBN 0-679-30299-9 paper.

To Martin and Sophie Miroff

Acknowledgments

Many friends, teachers, and colleagues aided me in writing this book. My work was strengthened by the critical acumen of those who read and commented on the manuscript: Norman Jacobson, Hanna Pitkin, Thomas Leatherwood, Joel Rosenberg, Ira Katznelson, Victor Navasky, and Alfred Watkins. I am particularly grateful to those who gave me detailed editorial assistance: Lawrence Levine, Greil Marcus, and Sue Miroff. My principal intellectual debt is to Michael Rogin, who supervised the original version of this study as a doctoral dissertation in political science at Berkeley. Rogin's supervision was exemplary; never imposing his own perspective when it clashed with mine, he combined incisive criticism with encouragement to help me fulfill the goals I had set for myself.

Others, too, deserve mention for their roles in the genesis of this book. I am grateful to the staff of the Kennedy Library, especially Sylvie Turner, for their assistance during my research visit in 1973. Edward Artinian, my editor at David McKay, has done a great deal to get this book published. Finally, I want to thank a dear friend, Lillian Rubin, and to pay tribute to my uncle, Harry Ratner, who died in 1974; both have shown me the worth of a life committed to social and political change.

The author wishes to thank Harper & Row, Publishers, Inc. for their permission to reprint material from *The Strategy of Peace* by John F. Kennedy and Houghton Mifflin Company for permission to reprint material from *A Thousand Days: John F. Kennedy in the White House* by Arthur Schlesinger, Jr.

Contents

Introduction

The Presidency, only a few years ago the pride of the American political system, has today become its most problematic feature. The fall from the presidential grace of the post–New Deal era has continued to accelerate throughout the last decade. Lyndon Johnson, with credibility blasted and power squandered in Vietnam, conducted a prudent retreat by refusing to stand for reelection in 1968. Richard Nixon lacked even that saving prudence; he drained his office of much of its remaining prestige before he resigned. Nixon's hand-picked successor, Gerald Ford, now occupies the White House, continuing the Nixon policies while searching for a public image that will link him to the more halcyon days of the Presidency.

Political scientists and historians, who were themselves rapt in admiration for the strong Presidency of the post–New Deal era, have not failed to heed these developments. Their glowing accounts of the Presidency contradicted by the egregious administrations of Johnson and Nixon, these scholars have responded with a new and more critical analysis of the presidential office. In the words of Erwin C. Hargrove, "we are in the midst of a time of revisionist thinking about the Presidency." [1]

One of the most popular of the "revisionist" studies attributes contemporary presidential woes to personality problems. In the language of James David Barber's *The Presidential Character*,[2] it was their "active-negative" personalities that brought Lyndon Johnson and Richard Nixon to grief. Compelled to furious activity yet doomed by his personality to frustration in that activity, Johnson rigidly pursued his Vietnam policy far beyond the restraints of reason. Nixon, Barber predicted in 1972, was susceptible to a similar fate. He would probably be unable to let go of a failing course of action if his fragile sense of self ever became deeply invested in it.

Another approach has emphasized the organizational problems of the White House, particularly the problem of presidential isolation. George Reedy's *The Twilight of the Presidency*[3] introduced the subject of isolation into the presidential literature, where it has been echoed and expanded by a host of others. Reedy pointed out that Presidents were no longer democratic politicians with insights into common American realities; rather, they lived like monarchs, surrounded by deferential advisers who filtered and tailored information about the world to accord with their sovereign's desires. The results could easily be read in recent events: decisions that took account of neither popular sentiments nor historical constraints were pressed relentlessly on the country by Presidents who had little grasp of their real consequences.

Arthur Schlesinger, Jr.'s *The Imperial Presidency*[4] added a historical dimension to the new "revisionist" literature. According to Schlesinger, it was the expansion of the presidential war power, especially during the Cold War, which had paved the way for executive usurpation.

> The Imperial Presidency was essentially the creation of foreign policy. A combination of doctrines and

> emotions—belief in permanent and universal crisis,
> fear of communism, faith in the duty and the right of
> the United States to intervene swiftly in every part of
> the world—had brought about the unprecedented
> centralization of decisions over war and peace in the
> Presidency. . . . So the imperial Presidency grew at the
> expense of the constitutional order. . . . And, as it
> overwhelmed the traditional separation of powers in
> foreign affairs, it began to aspire toward an equivalent
> centralization of power in the domestic polity.[5]

"Revisionism"—whether in these or in other variants—now dominates the literature on the Presidency. Having nearly fallen into the role of White House adjunct, presidential scholars seem at last to have established their critical distance.[6] That distance is, however, far more narrow than it first appears. For mixed in with the ringing criticisms and elaborate analyses of recent presidential abuses are some barely hidden, nostalgic yearnings for presidential power. This supposedly "revisionist" literature is soft at the core; despite their disillusionment, most presidential scholars cannot conceal the fact that they are still in love with the Presidency.

Examples of this unextinguished love abound in current works. For James David Barber, the dangerous propensities of the "active-negative" President are ultimately overshadowed by the creative potential of the "active-positive" presidential character. The conclusion of Barber's book looks longingly to this figure: "A Presidential character who can see beyond tomorrow—and smile—might yet lead us out of the wilderness." [7] Emmet John Hughes is a more sensible and balanced commentator than Barber, yet he too ends his book on the Presidency with an invocation: "A Presidency of 'honest and wise men,' wearing the armor of this confidence, may go on to answer . . . the hope of the Republic." [8] Even Arthur Schlesinger, Jr., despite apologies for his own earlier presidential worship, cannot completely renounce that worship; his final chapter dismisses proposals for basic changes in the presidential office in favor of a "constitutional" Presidency which could nonetheless remain "a very strong Presidency indeed." [9]

Most of these scholars, it is clear, assume that the fall from presidential grace is reversible. They believe that the Presidency, once it has been chastened and constrained by Congress, the media, and the public, can again become what they assume it once was under Roosevelt, Truman, and Kennedy: the source of progressive change in the American political system. These Chief Executives, presidential scholars argue, took the leading role in reshaping America into a more rational and just polity. And when the United States is ready to advance once more in a progressive direction, only another President of their type, the argument goes, will be able to supply the necessary leadership.

It is their view of the past that allows most presidential scholars to cling to hopes for a brighter presidential future. The anguish of recent events is relieved by glances at a more distant presidential history. But the glances are superficial, and the history romanticized. The "revisionist" literature on the contemporary Presidency relies upon completely conventional accounts of earlier presidential history; few of its contributors have bothered to reexamine that history in any depth or with any critical motives.

Given presidential scholars' idealization of Roosevelt, Truman, and Kennedy, this failure is not surprising. A critical examination of their careers would produce a host of questions about these presidential heroes. More important, it would cast doubt upon any easy assumption that the nature of the modern Presidency has been progressive. A number of existing studies indeed point to a very different view: that the role played by twentieth-century Presidents has been characteristically conservative.[10] "Liberal" as well as "conservative" Presidents, these studies indicate, have bent their strongest efforts, not to alter, but to preserve America's dominant institutions. Whatever their professed sympathies, their actions have served, not to redistribute wealth and power, but to perpetuate existing inequalities. And as central figures in the maintenance of established socioeconomic arrangements, the same Presidents have been granted—or taken for themselves—an extraordinary panoply of powers.

The steady accumulation of power in the White House throughout the century has, in this view, been neither an excrescence upon the American political system nor an arbitrary creation by ambitious Presidents. Rather, it has chiefly come about as a response to the enormous demands placed upon the Presidency—demands to ensure American predominance abroad, to stabilize the corporate economy, to contain social disorder. It is understandable that in this process presidential ambitions have increasingly become distorted. It is also predictable that if the functions of the modern Presidency remain what they have been in this century, presidential ambitions will continue to be distorted.

So long as presidential scholars adhere uncritically to the "progressive" interpretation of presidential history, their already limited separation from the office will remain tenuous. Analyses of personality disorder, isolation, or imperial mentality notwithstanding, they will remain susceptible to seduction by the first Chief Executive who can cloak himself in the mantle of FDR, HST, or JFK. Unless presidential scholars disabuse themselves of the illusions of the past, unless they come to terms with the continuity of twentieth-century presidential history, their "revisionist" theories will survive no longer than the arrival of the next liberal in the White House.

A genuinely "revisionist" theory must, therefore, reexamine fully and critically the politics of earlier Presidents. The subject of this book is the Presidency of John F. Kennedy, and the brand of pragmatic liberal politics that Kennedy practiced. In the chapters that follow, I shall study Kennedy's mode of presidential leadership in depth, looking in turn at each major focus of that leadership: United States–Soviet relations, Latin American and Vietnam involvement, economic policy, civil rights.

The Kennedy Administration is particularly crucial to any new perspective on the Presidency. For while Kennedy's foreign policy has been subjected to serious criticisms in the last several years,[11] his image as a progressive and creative leader remains potent among academic as well as popular audiences. For both, the temptation is great to perceive a break in presidential history after Kennedy's death. That temptation must be overcome.

Kennedy is even more important as a subject for "revisionist" work on the Presidency because of his centrality to those who write about and interpret the office. If Franklin Roosevelt was the inspiration for the worshipful presidential literature of the 1950s and early 1960s (such as Richard E. Neustadt's *Presidential Power*), John Kennedy was the self-conscious inheritor of that literature. It was he who first translated its tenets into action; it was his Presidency, as much as those which followed, that revealed their unanticipated consequences.

Although Kennedy's career exemplified all of the strong Presidency themes that the "revisionist" writers have now supposedly renounced, he remains curiously untarnished in the eyes of these writers. None of them have applied their critical strictures to Kennedy. Indeed, he remains a model for many writers of the kind of President we still require.

James David Barber, for instance, finds Kennedy's Presidency a model of "active-positive commitment." [12] Kennedy's vigorous, open, optimistic personality enabled him, in Barber's view, to grow in the White House, to mature from the uncertain grasp of power displayed during the Bay of Pigs affair to the confident and controlled statesmanship of the Cuban missile crisis. It also enabled him to overcome his own earlier detachment toward the problem of civil rights, and to plunge into the racial turmoil of 1963 with decisive and courageous action. If some observers had doubted whether the cool, self-possessed Kennedy cared deeply about any political issue, for Barber his civil rights stance in 1963 conclusively banished such doubts. In this case, "Kennedy's commitment was complete." [13]

Erwin C. Hargrove assesses Kennedy in similar terms in *The Power of the Modern Presidency*. Hargrove is more sensitive than Barber to disturbing elements in Kennedy's foreign policy; he draws attention to the tone of aggressiveness and the preference for military options which were characteristic of that foreign policy even through the Cuban missile crisis. But Hargrove too sees 1963 as the year when Kennedy overcame his earlier flaws. Not only did Kennedy's foreign policy take on a new orientation toward peace in 1963; he had also come, by this time, to abandon his previous caution in domestic affairs. "He was," Hargrove writes, "developing a strong personal, emotional, and moral commitment to a series of related domestic programs, and it seems likely that he would have been a second-term President of great achievement in domestic reform had he been able to sustain strong personal idealism as the chief resource for leadership." [14] Kennedy is not, in Hargrove's analysis, a subject for "revisionist" criticism. Rather, he is "more nearly the kind of man we can expect and hope to find in the Presidency most of the time—a democratic character who is a political man by virtue of role as much as personality." [15]

If John F. Kennedy is "the kind of man we can expect and hope to find in the Presidency most of the time," we had better look a bit more closely at the meaning of his Presidency and his politics. Reliance upon Kennedy myths—whether the original myths of the post-assassination period or the revised myths of the post-Vietnam period—will not do. For the sake of clarifying not only Kennedy's historical role, but also the role of the modern Presidency in general, a critical analysis of the Kennedy Administration is essential.

1

An Existential Hero?

John F. Kennedy still possesses a secure hold on the American imagination. The awkwardness of his presidential successors has served only to highlight Kennedy's charm, grace, and wit, and to intensify the pain of their loss. In an era of widespread disillusionment with public figures, Kennedy's personal appeal is hardly dimmed. To gauge that appeal, we need only notice how, more than a decade after his death, affectionate remembrances of Kennedy are guaranteed a place on the bestseller lists.

Preoccupation with his personal attractiveness has, unfortunately, done more to obscure than to clarify John Kennedy's political record. It has also tended, ironically, to obscure what might be termed his "political personality." Numerous friends and associates have shown us why Kennedy was an appealing figure. Numerous commentators have explained to us why he was a politically popular one as well. But what have remained elusive, in most of these accounts of Kennedy, are the connections between personal traits and presidential beliefs, between personal impulses and policy directions. We have enough portraits already of the charismatic hero; we need to look more intently at the political man.

As a preface to an examination of his presidential politics, this chapter sketches John Kennedy's political personality and conception of leadership. The picture of Kennedy that I draw is hardly a flattering one. The purpose of that picture is not, however, to deny Kennedy's genuine charm, nor to question his personal virtue. Rather, it is to reveal the congruence between personality and policy in his Presidency. It has increasingly been argued that much of what Kennedy did as President was forced upon him by political pressures—especially from Congress, the military, and the right wing in general. I suggest the opposite: that most of Kennedy's actions as President were fully in accord with his deepest values, beliefs, and ambitions.

John Kennedy's political personality was shaped, above all, by his intellectual stance, his ambition, and his preoccupation with courage. Kennedy's intellectual powers are a favorite topic of his chroniclers. Theodore C. Sorensen * marvels at Kennedy's detachment, objectivity, and candor. Kennedy's keenly analytical intellect, he relates, slashed through conventional prejudices and myths to seize upon the essential facts of any issue. [1] Arthur Schlesinger, Jr., is equally impressed: "Self-criticism was a vital strength in his luminous and rational intelligence, so consecutive and objective, so lucidly in possession of his impulses and emotions." [2]

We are also shown by Kennedy's chroniclers the boundaries of his intellectual field. Foremost among intellectual irrelevancies for Kennedy was the realm of abstractions. He had neither time nor inclination to dabble in economics, political theory, social criticism. And toward political ideologies he harbored an attitude bordering on contempt. "He never took ideology very seriously, certainly not as a means of interpreting history and even not as part of the material of history." [3] Kennedy valued ideas only if they promised results, only if they

* Quotations from Theodore C. Sorensen's *Kennedy* have had to be paraphrased or summarized. We could not obtain permission from Mr. Sorensen to reproduce material from his book.

could work for him. He was, in short, a classic American pragmatist.

If objectivity ostensibly ruled out theorizing or ideology for Kennedy, detachment similarly ruled out passion. "Coolness" was the keynote of the Kennedy style in both thought and action. Displays of passion had, with few exceptions, no place either in private or before the public. Here is Schlesinger again: "What was forbidden were poses, histrionics, the heart on the sleeve. . . . What was required was a tough, nonchalant acceptance of the harsh present." [4] Such "coolness" was not universally admired; some critics found Kennedy cold, even doubted his capacity for emotional response. But his admirers scorned this charge. As Schlesinger put it, Kennedy refused to show emotion not because he felt too little, but "because he felt too much and had to compose himself for an existence filled with disorder and despair." [5]

In Schlesinger's words there are—probably by intention—echoes of a fashionable postwar Existentialism, but Kennedy's intellectual and emotional posture can, I think, be explained in less dramatic terms. His skepticism toward abstractions, his resistance to visible passion—these stemmed from both deep-seated personal proclivities (as Schlesinger elsewhere acknowledged) [6] and a not untypical American faith in the power of the "fact." For Kennedy, facts were the authentic stuff of political understanding. Facts were objective and unadorned; they were free of partisan bias, without ideological taint. Besides, as President, Kennedy had at his disposal a rich profusion of facts, far more than any of his assorted critics. This gave him the superior vantage point; facts were power.

Kennedy was brilliant in his mastery of facts. He absorbed them relentlessly and employed them with a telling instinct. He was superb at impressing an audience—whether businessmen, reporters, even his own aides—with his grasp of details. At times it almost seemed as if his claim to presidential authority rested upon his demonstration that he knew more facts about America than anyone else in the country.[7]

But for all his riches of facts, Kennedy lacked something more essential: a sense of nuance, and of depth. As Norman Mailer observed at the time, there was in the Kennedy Administration "a total and depressing lack of attention for that vast heart of political matter which is utterly resistant to categorization, calculation, or statistic." [8] While the measurable and the tangible were avidly gathered up by Kennedy and his associates, the underlying, unquantifiable social reality continually eluded their grasp. Educational or job discrimination could be seen in the figures; the intensity of white racism was imperceptible to Kennedy until it began to turn against *him* during the summer of 1963. Educational crisis was marked by the superiority of the Russians in turning out quantities of engineers and scientists; that American schools might also be growing more authoritarian and irrelevant was a possibility that hardly occurred to Kennedy and his New Frontiersmen, occupied as they were in seeking greater "investment" in educational "resources." Facts filled John Kennedy's political understanding—and simultaneously bounded it. The problems with which he dealt were defined by statistics, as were their solutions: a more rapidly advancing GNP, additional funds for school construction and teachers' salaries, increased voting rights suits and more blacks in the federal service.

Kennedy's objectivity limited him to the facts; his detachment divorced him from the emotional dimension of events. Whether it was a question of temperament or of intellectual choice, John Kennedy seemed singularly devoid of political passion. Few of the great political events of his maturity—the Great Depression or rise of Fascism in the 1930s, Cold War hysteria and persecution of dissenters during the McCarthy era—appeared to have touched him very deeply.[9] Although he had picked a career dedicated to public affairs, he always maintained an emotional reserve toward those affairs.

In the White House Kennedy kept his emotional distance. As we shall observe in a later chapter, throughout the accelerating civil rights struggle of his Presidency he seemed relatively immune from feelings of anger or outrage. While many of his supporters grew increasingly anguished at the injustice and repression exposed in the course of the black freedom struggle, Kennedy persisted—at least until Birmingham—in treating that struggle as a conventional (though particularly troublesome) issue. Consequently, the extraordinary passions that fired the civil rights movement into action scarcely registered in his political calculations. Kennedy never seemed fully to comprehend the depth or significance of the great domestic event of his Presidency, not because he lacked the facts, but because he could not feel its emotional urgency.[10]

I have stated that John Kennedy's intellectual stance was premised upon objectivity and detachment, upon freedom from the distortions of both ideology and emotion. To maintain this stance, a bit of self-deception was necessary. For along with the wizards of fact, like Robert McNamara, and the "tough-minded" operationalists, like McGeorge Bundy, with whom Kennedy surrounded himself, there was an ample supply of ideologists and theoreticians swarming around the President. Men like Walt W. Rostow, Maxwell Taylor, and Walter Heller did not *appear* as theoreticians or ideologists in Kennedy's eyes; *their* abstractions were couched in a "hard" social science language, and were sufficiently close to conventional American beliefs that they escaped the pragmatic censure which so often fell upon the Administration's critics. As subsequent chapters will demonstrate, these men helped to provide Kennedy with a broad ideological framework, a framework that was particularly harmful because it was never recognized as such.[11]

Kennedy's "objectivity" was, consequently, rooted in a conventional set of assumptions—modernized, of course, and decked out in the latest jargon ("stages-of-growth" theory of economic development, "neo-Keynesian" approach to fiscal policy, "flexible response" military strategy)—about the virtues of American society and the beneficence of America's role in the world. Kennedy accepted all the givens of liberal ideology: the Cold War struggle against international communism, the regulated growth of a corporate economy, the process of domestic reform through incremental legislation. Nothing he read, no one he talked to, really challenged those givens. For all the talk about cutting through prevailing myths and biases, Kennedy was a prisoner of the most fundamental American myths and biases. Ironically, among the myths that served to conceal from him the traditional liberal context in which he operated was the pragmatic myth itself—the myth of his own objectivity.

These words might seem rather harsh in view of Kennedy's favorable attitude toward the American intelligentsia. On the New Frontier long-suffering American intellectuals at last were accorded official recognition. As the media tirelessly reported, intellectuals were assiduously courted by the Kennedy Administration. Artists, writers, social critics were invited to private lunches or to glittering formal dinners, and treated to generous helpings of Kennedy charm and wit. Many were visibly impressed by Kennedy, and grateful for the attention he paid to them.

Others, however, continued to have their doubts. Robert Lowell, for example, recalled his feelings after attending the dinner for André Malraux:

> Then the next morning you read that the Seventh Fleet had been sent somewhere in Asia and you had a funny feeling of how unimportant the artist really was; that this was sort of window-dressing and the real government was somewhere else. . . .[12]

Kennedy, as Lowell and a few others perceived, did not really pay all that much attention to the ideas of "outside" intellectuals. Toward such intellectuals, particularly those who were critical or radical, the New Frontier attitude was, in fact, tinged by an underlying scorn. Arthur Schlesinger, Jr., himself one of the Administration's chief links to the intellectual community, was not immune from this "insider's" scorn. In *A Thousand Days* intellectual critics of Kennedy's policies were christened the "utopian" left. In contrast to the pragmatic New Frontiersmen, these "utopians" were, according to Schlesinger, addicted to total solutions in foreign affairs and fuzzy manifestos on domestic change. Worst of all, they had nothing immediate and practical to recommend. "They acted as if they were crying out great ideas in the wilderness which the political leaders studiously ignored. In fact, the political leaders themselves were begging for usable ideas—and not finding any." [13]

The New Frontier was a hospitable place for intellectuals, if they accepted the same liberal orthodoxies as Kennedy. But the Kennedy Administration was hardly an "intellectuals' administration." The men under Kennedy with real power—e.g., the Secretaries and Assistant Secretaries of State, Defense, and Treasury—were not, in the main, from the academic or scientific world. John Kennedy recruited for these positions in the same place his predecessors had: the top echelons of the corporate structure. Academics such as Walt W. Rostow, Arthur Schlesinger, Jr., and Walter Heller gave the Kennedy Administration a distinctively intellectual flavor, but its solidity and its authority came from its corporation executives and lawyers, from men like Robert McNamara, C. Douglas Dillon, Roswell Gilpatric, and George Ball. [14]

His mastery of facts and his underlying adherence to conventional values were vital sources of strength to John Kennedy in his role as politician—but they placed an equally crucial limitation upon him as a political leader. He was knowledgeable and incisive when it came to existing political realities— but almost completely devoid of fresh ideas. Kennedy had nothing new to teach to the American public. Those disgruntled liberals who periodically complained that he displayed plenty of style but little substance (that, for example, his domestic reforms were merely warmed-over New Deal and Fair Deal proposals) were mistaken only in their hope that somewhere he might, out of exaggerated caution, be hiding such substance. For Kennedy could offer only an intensified Cold War struggle abroad and a further rationalization of corporate capitalism at home. Nor could he respond creatively to the great domestic event of his Presidency, the emergence of the mass-action civil rights movement. Primarily through its style and rhetoric, the Kennedy Administration managed to convince much of the nation that it represented genuine novelty in American political life. What it really presented, Ronald Steel observed, were "tired cliches in vinyl wrappings." [15]

Contemporary critics noted the absence on the New Frontier of any vision or design for the future of American society. James Reston recounts, in this regard, a revealing story about Kennedy:

> I once asked him in a long private talk at Hyannis Port what he wanted to have achieved by the time he rode down Pennsylvania Avenue with his successor. He looked at me as if I were a dreaming child. I tried again: did he not feel the need of some goal to help guide his day-to-day decisions and priorities? Again a ghastly pause. It was only when I turned the question to immediate, tangible problems that he seized the point and rolled off a torrent of statistics about the difficulty of organizing nations at different levels of economic development.[16]

Kennedy's response to Reston can be seen, as it has been by Schlesinger, as a reflection of the pragmatist's disdain for impractical questions. But it also can be seen as hinting at something far more significant—that Kennedy possessed so thoroughgoing an acceptance of the American social and economic order that he could not begin to think of why or how it might need changing.

The conventionality of Kennedy's thought permitted little insight into the deeper problems of American society; it similarly impaired his perception of other societies. The Kennedy Administration was largely free of the glacial chauvinism with which its predecessor had confronted the world; toward such phenomena as nationalism or neutralism Kennedy and his aides displayed considerable understanding and flexibility. But there were strict limits to that understanding and flexibility. When it came, for instance, to a question of social revolution John Kennedy could be as uncomprehending and moralistic as John Foster Dulles. Kennedy's inability to come to grips with the revolutionary process transforming the Third World is readily apparent in his counterinsurgency venture in Vietnam. It will be made equally plain when we consider his futile attempt at nation-building in Latin America.

Kennedy's cautious approach to domestic problems and aggressiveness in international affairs has been explained by his defenders largely in terms of a conservative mood in the country during his Presidency—and a shrewd sense of timing that awaited the expected mandate of a second term. Yet the preceding pages suggest that it is misleading when liberals attribute the disappointments in his record to circumstances. Kennedy's accomplishments, particularly in domestic affairs, did not fall short of his purportedly lofty dreams; rather, they were a mark of how meager those dreams really were. He was scarcely a reformer, much less a political visionary; rather, as I. F. Stone bravely observed at the height of the canonization process immediately following the assassination, "Kennedy, when the tinsel was stripped away, was a conventional leader, no more than an enlightened conservative, cautious as an old man for all his youth, with a basic distrust of the people and an astringent view of the evangelical as a tool of leadership." [17]

Stone judged Kennedy to be an "enlightened conservative"; such a term is not too far removed from what I mean by "pragmatic liberal." Indeed, the word "conservative" may be instructive, for it points to Kennedy's paradoxical relationship with the dominant, corporate institutions in American society. Kennedy fought running battles with the business community, the military, and the conservative politicians throughout his

Presidency; it was precisely through this combat that his liberal credentials were established. Yet, though it was seldom evident at the time—especially to the participants—such battles always remained on the level of means. The ends Kennedy sought were essentially the same as the ends of his conservative adversaries. If anything, he pursued these common ends more vigorously than his adversaries.

Though Kennedy, as a pragmatist, professed disdain for all ideology, the nature of his pragmatism inevitably led him to become a spokesman for the kind of ideology that is usually termed "corporate liberalism." Having nothing new to teach, nothing fresh to offer in the way of social change, Kennedy could only present the existing corporate world in more fashionable garb. His skill was such as sometimes to clothe that world with grace, and even drama. But in the end his most celebrated utterances boiled down to its clichés. Kennedy thus shared the fate of so many American liberals: to tend to the needs of the established powers while claiming to serve society's underdogs, and to mistake the uncomprehending abuse of those powers for proof of the legitimacy of his claim. Kennedy was actually to serve the status quo far better than its avowed champions; it is here, in fact, that we shall discover the true character of his achievement.

I have dwelt upon Kennedy's intellectual limitations at some length, for if we fail to grasp those limitations we cannot accurately recapture the dilemma of Kennedy's political ambition. The subject of Kennedy's ambition is a crucial one. It sheds considerable light on the actions of a figure more elusive than his chroniclers originally led us to believe.

As might be expected, Kennedy's ambition is hardly a favorite topic for his chroniclers. They relate to us extensive anecdotes about his lucid mind, coolness in action, courage under pressure, but when it comes to the question of ambition the accounts become rather meager. Kennedy himself sometimes spoke of the Presidency as the center of action in the American political system, the field where a political man

not correct

might fully express whatever excellence he possessed. But beyond this, he and his admirers are guarded. If we are to gauge the nature and extent of his ambition, we must turn to more indirect evidence.

Reviewing such evidence, a familiar if rather intensely held ambition become apparent. Kennedy wanted, it seems, to be a hero, a great President and political leader whose deeds would be acclaimed by those arbiters of greatness, the historians. Numerous writers have told of the powerful family pressures toward a political career which molded (or warped, depending on the author's point of view) all the Kennedy sons. Much— probably too much—has been made of the demands of a patriarchal father and competition from a dynamic older brother. But in John Kennedy's case at least, the fascination with heroism seemed to be nurtured as much by some inner fantasy as by an aggressive family circle.

As a boy, the rather sickly John Kennedy loved to read. And the subject which most excited him was heroism.

> He spent hours in his room at Riverdale or Hyannis Port absorbed in history and biography—King Arthur, *Scottish Chiefs, The White Company,* Cooper, and later Churchill's *Marlborough* when he was in his teens. History was full of heroes for him, and he reveled in the stately cadences of historical prose.[18]

This boyish enthusiasm for heroism never left Kennedy. As a Senator and President he still preferred to read (and write) history and biography; the books that Arthur Schlesinger, Jr. lists as Kennedy's favorites include biographies of Marlborough, Lincoln, John Quincy Adams, Calhoun, Talleyrand.[19] Kennedy was well aware that economic and social factors shaped history, but he tended to regard those factors largely as background for the deeds of great political actors. He devoured the stories of these actors, noting down whatever lessons they might contain for his own story.

Given this view of history, Kennedy as President kept a

watchful eye on the judgment of future historians even as he grappled with immediate concerns. Everything said or written during his Presidency hence bore the stamp of historical data. Indeed, he did not wait for future judgment; he stocked his Administration with scholars (including historians like Schlesinger and Rostow) who sought to establish its renown even before it had ended. "Everywhere Kennedy looked, he could see the historians; he was already in the books, on the great stage." [20]

Kennedy yearned for greatness. But he was hemmed in by his own limitations. He possessed no novel or powerful political vision to offer the American people. Nor was he identified with any social movement whose success might be equated with his own. He was bright and attractive, but his obvious charm scarcely amounted to the kind of personal depth (such as that of Lincoln) which stamped its character upon a time. Kennedy was a relatively conventional American politician longing to be an unconventional political hero; in this disparity between the man and his ambition lay the precise nature of his dilemma.

Even history seemed ranged against Kennedy's ambition. The times were unpropitious for political heroics. Greatness, Kennedy believed, required a crisis in order to manifest itself. As he had written in *Profiles in Courage,* "Great crises produce great men, and great deeds of courage." [21] But no crisis was perceptible, at least to a majority of Americans. They appeared to share the sentiment of the Eisenhower Administration that this was an era of relative peace and prosperity.

History, however, proved more pliable than ambition. Kennedy found his call to greatness. He found it in a theory which enjoyed popularity in some liberal circles during the late 1950s—the theory of the post-Sputnik Soviet world offensive. Kennedy's elaboration of the thesis that the Soviet Union would employ its superiority in missile technology and economic growth rate in a coordinated campaign to communize the world will be examined in the next chapter. The consequences of this grievously distorted view of contemporary history will indeed form one of the major themes of this work. I do not mean to suggest here that Kennedy adopted this thesis simply, or even primarily, because it fit in with his personal needs. But it *did* answer his problem perfectly. It denied emphatically the absence of crisis; it asserted instead the onset of the supreme crisis. "Each day we draw nearer the hour of maximum danger." [22] It proclaimed the Kennedy Presidency the period of perhaps the most critical ordeal in American history; at stake was nothing less than the nation's survival. "Before my term has ended," Kennedy informed the American public when he assumed office, "we shall have to test anew whether a nation organized and governed such as ours can endure. The outcome is by no means certain." [23]

In the ubiquitous Soviet challenge, and in the determined effort by his administration to repulse that challenge, John Kennedy found his hero's role. The call to an intensified Cold War struggle supplied his Presidency with the aura of purpose and passion it otherwise lacked. The struggle would be hazardous, Kennedy proclaimed; yet America would thereby conclusively affirm its greatness. "While no nation has ever faced such a challenge, no nation has ever been so ready to seize the burden and the glory of freedom." [24] The summons to dedication and sacrifice was not a novel theme in American history, but it certainly was a heroic one; while most Americans were actually called upon to do or sacrifice very little during Kennedy's Presidency, still they knew that great events were at hand.

Russia's challenge to the American nation was, above all, a challenge to its leadership. In the vast, yet often subterranean contest which characterized this new phase of the Cold War the decisive factor would be neither troops nor weaponry, but the strength of leadership, its foresight and courage. The times, in John Kennedy's eyes, demanded heroic statesmanship—and he felt ready and eager, despite widespread criticisms of his youth and inexperience, to assume the statesman's role.

In fact, the role was assumed well before he became President. Perhaps the dominant theme of Kennedy's numerous speeches in the years 1958–60 was an attack upon the weakness and indecision of the incumbent President. Eisenhower, he charged, was at heart a sentimentalist in foreign affairs, constantly deceived by "the illusion that good intentions and pious principles are a substitute for strong creative leadership." [25] But Kennedy, the presidential aspirant, had in mind a different model of statesmanship. Frequently in these speeches he drew parallels between Winston Churchill's attempts in the 1930s to warn a complacent Britain of the Nazi threat and his own efforts to awaken an equally complacent America to the enormity of the Soviet challenge. At times, as in the concluding words of his celebrated "missile gap" speech to the Senate in 1958, Kennedy's identification with Churchill became complete:

> No Pearl Harbor, no Dunkirk, no Calais is sufficient to end us permanently if we but find the will and the way. In the words of Sir Winston Churchill in a dark time of England's history: "Come then—let us to the task, to the battle and the toil—each to our part, each to our station. Let us go forward together in all parts of the [land]. There is not a week, nor a day, nor an hour to be lost." [26]

That the Soviet Union was not Nazi Germany did not deter Kennedy from identifying himself with Churchill. That the Soviet leadership might even prefer détente to conflict was hardly admissible into his historical analogy. For Kennedy was absorbed in these years in trying on his new mantle; he was the prophetic statesman in a period where those in power possessed none of the attributes of statesmanship.

When Kennedy became President many commentators voiced the expectation that he would seek to follow in the footsteps of Franklin Roosevelt. But his chief historical model, from all indications, continued to be Churchill.[27] Lacking both the ideas and the interest to be a domestic reformer, he sought greatness in the realm of world affairs. As he had followed the out-of-power Churchill in warning of an extraordinary foreign threat, so would he follow the wartime Churchill in mobilizing and inspiring his countrymen to overcome that threat. Kennedy had read the heroic history books and mastered their lessons. Now he would apply those lessons and make history.

Kennedy's Presidency was to be highlighted by global crises; indeed, his entire term was often couched in the language of crisis. He had forecast that crisis in his prepresidential speeches, but once in office his emphasis shifted from the exercise of foresight to the manifestation of courage. Courage was, in the eyes of Kennedy and his associates, the supreme mark of statesmanship. While critics, unhappy with the President's timid domestic program, gibed that he displayed more profile than courage, New Frontiersmen understood that the courage was there where it really counted, in foreign affairs. That Kennedy had little passion for social reforming would scarcely prove a hindrance to his greatness. America's survival was at stake; at such a moment, the nation's leader had, in the Churchill mold, to be brave.

Courage was the human quality that John Kennedy had always cherished most. In his book *Profiles in Courage* he had described it as "that most admirable of human virtues."[28] Kennedy's personal courage was indisputable, whether it was revealed in wartime bravery, stoic disregard for physical suffering, or audacity in defying the taboo against a Catholic running for President. But courage in his eyes was not simply a matter of an inner steeling to adversity. It was also a political virtue, which needed to be exhibited on a public stage. Like the indomitable Churchill, Kennedy saw his mission as awakening his countrymen from complacency and softness and summoning them to a demonstration of nerve and will in the face of a global challenge. The courage they would show in the coming crisis would determine their stature and worth as a people—and his stature and worth as well.

Courage became a preoccupation of the Kennedy inner

circle, and at times an obsession. Consider, for example, the question of negotiations. There was no dogmatic intransigence here about entering into negotiations with the Soviet Union; the official attitude of the Kennedy Administration toward negotiations was, in contrast to that of its predecessor, a prudent one. The trouble was, before negotiations could commence, American bravery and determination had first to be proven to the enemy. A willingness to go "all the way" had to be demonstrated before the talk could turn to accommodation and compromise.

A peculiar assumption crops up throughout Kennedy's foreign policy record: that every important international conflict was a test of America's (and his) nerve and will. In Berlin and Cuba, Laos and Vietnam, nuclear testing and space exploration, the fundamental point at issue for Kennedy was always American courage. At no point could America waver or show signs that it feared the risks of the conflict, for this would only spur the Soviet offensive on to further advances. Only unfaltering courage could persuade the Soviets to halt their drive and relinquish their designs upon the Free World.

For a man who prided himself on his "realism," the obsession with courage provided events with a coherence that was dangerously unreal. Political, economic, historical particularity were seen by Kennedy only as background for the incessant Soviet probing of American mettle; the complexity of foreign affairs was repeatedly reduced to the simplistic imagery of a rite of *machismo*. The Kennedy Administration knew, for example, that the Berlin question involved festering problems for the Soviet Union: the status of East Germany, the cohesion of its Eastern European empire. But it would not recognize Khrushchev's announcement that he would sign a separate peace treaty with East Germany at the end of 1961 as an attempt to deal with those problems; instead, Berlin was proclaimed "the great testing place of Western courage and will." [29] Guerrilla warfare in South Vietnam was never understood as a response to the authoritarianism and repressiveness of the Diem regime; instead, it was regarded as a challenge to the United States to demonstrate its determination and endurance in combating "wars of liberation." In the theory of the Soviet offensive almost every significant occurrence in the world, it seemed, represented a reckoning for the American spirit.

Distortion of perception was not the only unfortunate consequence when courage was elevated to the supreme place in American foreign policy. Courage itself became deformed in the process; it turned into bellicosity and arrogance. When President Kennedy asserted American courage in Berlin or Cuba or Vietnam, he bore scant resemblance to the lonely senatorial heroes of *Profiles in Courage,* who had risked personal disaster by following the dictates of their conscience against the demands of their constituency. *He* was the leader of the most powerful country on earth, flexing its enormous military muscle and insisting upon the primacy of its national will. His words may have spoken of bravery, but Kennedy's tone sounded, especially to foreign ears, more like belligerence. Since his chief adversary was himself prone to belligerent outbursts, the mixture was highly explosive. It was to be a chilling era in international relations.

Some commentators detected a note of self-doubt in Kennedy's repeated avowals of American courage. After the fiasco at the Bay of Pigs and his unimpressive performance in his meeting with Khrushchev at Vienna, Kennedy seemed preoccupied, they suggested, with proving his mettle to the Soviet Premier. A posture of toughness thus had to be consistently maintained in American foreign policy until Kennedy's triumph in the missile crisis finally permitted him to relax. Only then, this interpretation goes, could he begin to explore avenues of peaceful cooperation with the Soviets.[30]

This line of interpretation may well be correct, yet I think it overlooks the extent to which "toughness" was a preoccupa-

tion of the Kennedy circle. It was a fundamental maxim of
Kennedy and his associates that their enemies got as far as they
did primarily because they were tough. As W. W. Rostow posed
the problem:

> In a sense, the men in Moscow have had to establish
> whether the nerve and will of the West matched their
> own. . . . The Cold War comes down to this test of
> whether we and the democratic world are
> fundamentally tougher and more purposeful in the
> defense of our vital interests than they are in the
> pursuit of their global ambitions.[31]

Rostow's view, despite the characteristic hyperbole of its expression, was endemic to the New Frontier.[32] Kennedy and his
associates were out to prove from the start that they, as pragmatic liberals, could be tougher than the heirs of Lenin and
Stalin.

The great emblem of this toughness was the Green
Berets.[33] They were a pet project of Kennedy's. Against opposition from the top brass he expanded Army Special Forces
some sixfold; in addition, he overrode Pentagon objections to
bestow the elite green beret on Special Forces troops.[34] The
emergence of the Green Berets exemplified Kennedy's deep
fascination with the idea of counterinsurgency. In the American venture at counterinsurgency they were to be the military
personification of the Kennedy virtues: intelligence, élan, and
above all, toughness.

The romantic image of the Green Berets has faded these
days; it is hard to make heroes out of men trained in the cruel
arts of counterrevolution. But in Kennedy's time the underside
of the Green Berets was carefully hidden from the American
public. They were depicted in terms that made them almost
sound like a second Peace Corps.[35] That they carried out tor-
ture and destroyed villages was never mentioned; it was a vital
part of the Kennedy Administration's conception of toughness

not to expose the more squeamish public to the actual methods of counterinsurgency. The courage that Kennedy admired ceased to be so admirable when it was transformed into the posturing of toughness. In the case of the Green Berets it became something far more frightening than a posture; the emblem of bravery had now become a disguise for brutality.

So far I have described some of the ways in which John Kennedy's Presidency was distinctively colored by his personality. I have indicated how Kennedy's ambition, though lacking a basic reference point in the exigencies of American society, found its outlet in global crisis, how courage became a substitute for social vision and transfigured a conventional politician into a would-be political hero. This portrait of Kennedy has been drawn from both his public record and the recollections of his close associates. Yet, under the pressure of later developments, particularly in Vietnam, some of those same associates have begun to warn us that we should be wary of any impression that Kennedy was a militant Cold Warrior. They distinguish between the Kennedy of public record and Kennedy in the privacy of the White House; the real, private Kennedy, they maintain, held to a far more skeptical and far less apocalyptic position than that which he publicly exhibited. Since this argument runs counter to my interpretation in the preceding pages, it deserves to be answered.

The image of a cool and skeptical Kennedy behind the public persona of the committed and combative leader is most cogently presented in David Halberstam's *The Best and the Brightest*. In Halberstam's view we must not take Kennedy's public utterances or official positions too straightforwardly. If he seemed on the surface to be totally immersed in a global struggle against communism, be it in Berlin or South Vietnam, underneath, so Halberstam tells us (after interviewing Kennedy intimates), the President was troubled by doubts about the wisdom of his course. His advisers may have been almost unreservedly hawkish, but Kennedy never lost his skeptical bent. Hence he remained, in Halberstam's account, superior to the biases or delusions of his subordinates, managing (most of the time) to restrain and balance off Rusk's Cold War orthodoxy, McNamara's statistical imperatives, Rostow's apocalyptic contingency plans, Stevenson's diplomatic caution. While Kennedy sometimes followed his counselors into important errors, in private he gave repeated indications that he was learning from his mistakes—and that he was on the verge, when he died, of correcting the most decisive of them.

> In the last few weeks of his life he had talked with some aides, such as Kenny O'Donnell, about trying to paper it [Vietnam] over through 1964, keeping the commitment away from Goldwater as a target, and then trying to negotiate his way out. He had spoken similar words to Mike Mansfield, though omitting the reference to the 1964 election, simply talking about de-escalating, letting out his misgivings about our involvement. The men who were close to him in the White House felt that these doubts were growing all the time.[36]

How are we to evaluate such an account of Kennedy? It is not difficult, of course, to believe that Kennedy was more skeptical in private than in public. But to assert that there was an *essential* difference between the public and the private man is another story altogether. One consequence of this assertion is that we must set aside most of what Kennedy said in public (and what his defenders lauded at the time) in favor of testimony from his aides, several years later, about his innermost doubts. We must abandon publicly accessible evidence in favor of privileged accounts by men whose impartiality on this subject is highly suspect. Of course, the "insiders" might be right. But there are obvious dangers whenever history is written from the insiders' point of view.

Nor is the problem here solely one of evidence. For on matters other than Vietnam, the available record on Kennedy—both public *and* private—discloses little skepticism. Kennedy adhered to a "hard line" throughout the Berlin crisis of 1961. During the Cuban missile crisis of 1962, he dismissed out of hand explanations that would have limited the dimensions of the affair, and carried confrontation with the Russians to the brink of nuclear war. Even in the Alliance for Progress, he stuck to an overblown scheme of counterrevolutionary liberalism through repeated failures. Kennedy may indeed have been skeptical about the details of key policies; but in the end, when he made his decisions, he almost invariably came down as hard as his hawkish advisers.

Besides, why did Kennedy have such a preponderance of hawkish advisers? He selected these men in the first place, retained them, consulted them. It seems a bit farfetched to claim, as Halberstam does, that he was much more reserved or dubious about his policies than all his hand-picked advisers.[37]

The insiders' version of a skeptical John Kennedy hemmed in by circumstances and bad advice but privately preparing to break with Cold War orthodoxy is at bottom a belated, post-Vietnam revision of the original Kennedy myth. Throughout this book, therefore, I shall judge Kennedy by the positions to which he publicly committed himself—those his defenders wish to forget as well as those which they continue to applaud.

But Kennedy's commitments extended beyond the policies of his administration; they covered the office of the Presidency itself. He had a well-developed conception of presidential leadership, a conception that profoundly influenced the positions he was to take. That conception is worth exploring.

When John Kennedy's electoral victory brought to a close eight years of a grandfatherly and rather dull Presidency, it excited widespread hopes and fantasies of a renaissance in American political leadership. Kennedy obviously had the potential stuff of leadership; he was young, dynamic, bright, brave. His personal popularity had grown steadily throughout the 1960 campaign; as he took office many cherished the hope that his popularity would soon be transformed into popular leadership in the authentic, democratic sense.

Norman Mailer reflected the exhilaration of these times in a dramatic campaign portrait of Kennedy. American society, wrote Mailer, was sinking in a slough of conformism, as Americans found themselves out of touch with their own deepest traditions of adventure and change. The country sorely needed a hero to electrify it, to embody a life of challenge and uncertainty so vividly that it would be jolted free of its desperate yearning for security. Only such an "existential hero" could lead the nation back to life—and in John Kennedy's youth, courage, and élan, Mailer thought he perceived the makings of this hero. "I knew that if he became President, it would be an existential event: he would touch depths in American life which were uncharted. . . . We as a nation would finally be loose again in the historic seas of a national psyche which was willy-nilly and at last, again, adventurous." [38]

Such bright hopes were to go unfulfilled. Kennedy was a popular President, a star of the media unlike any President before or since, but his Presidency fell far short of any national political reawakening. His personal popularity always remained oddly apolitical, divorced from policy or program. He continually frustrated his original well-wishers with his cautious leadership, ignoring, for example, their pleas for "fireside chats" on controversial domestic legislation in favor of working the traditional congressional pathways. Mailer soon lost faith, commenting sadly that "a President is supposed to enrich the real life of his people—the mind which looks out from this President's eyes has lost the way." [39] A more orthodox critic, James Reston, likewise bemoaned Kennedy's limited impact upon American political consciousness: "He never really exploited his considerable gifts as a public educator." [40]

These charges were disputed by the President's most able defender, Arthur Schlesinger, Jr. In *A Thousand Days* Schlesinger devoted considerable space to rescuing Kennedy's reputation as an educator. Complaints about Kennedy's reticence in addressing the nation rested, Schlesinger argued, on an inaccurate historical memory of the educational prowess of Woodrow Wilson and the Roosevelts. They had not, in reality, appealed to the nation any more frequently than did Kennedy. Like his great predecessors, Kennedy understood that the key to public education was timing.

> In the absence of visible crisis Presidents had to wait for some event to pierce the apathy and command the nation's ear; experience was a more potent teacher than exhortation. At moments one felt that it was nearly impossible to change people or policies in advance of disaster. . . .[41]

To seek the public's attention in the absence of domestic or foreign crisis was, in this view, almost inevitably a fruitless course. A President would squander his political capital thereby—and probably succeed only in boring the public.

Schlesinger's defense of Kennedy as educator was skillful, but at bottom it was a rationalization. A review of Kennedy's speeches and other public appearances bears out the critics' charge that he was inattentive to the educational opportunities of his office. No doubt he did possess an acute sense of the difficulties of political education in America. But he lacked an accompanying concern for overcoming those difficulties. Kennedy was simply not all that interested in being a public educator—and to understand this lack of interest is to begin to understand the essence of his conception of leadership.

The critics wanted Kennedy to talk more about domestic problems, particularly those before the Congress, but legislative matters were seldom the focus of his concern. His preoccupation—and his pleasure—was with foreign affairs. Here he did try to communicate to the American people an interpretation of events, but one so sweeping that few outside his own immediate circle could grasp it in its entirety. On domestic matters, though, his educational efforts were limited. He tended to make one legislative proposal central (the trade expansion bill in 1962, the tax cut in 1963) and devote a high-pitched campaign to securing its enactment; other proposals were generally treated as peripheral. If they were controversial and likely to be defeated in Congress, his legislative liaison staff would work dutifully for them, but intensive efforts to win public backing were avoided. In the entire span of his Presidency he gave just one major address on medical care for the aged (to a national rally of senior citizens) and none at all on aid to education.

The idea that congressional conflicts might be instructive in themselves never appealed to Kennedy. He was largely indifferent to the educational value of any congressional battle fought before the public as long as that battle was likely to be a losing one.[42] Deepening public consciousness of an issue such as Medicare, or sharpening the lines of debate on it, weighed little when compared to the need to conserve popularity and power for the key bill or the situation of national emergency. Kennedy expended his store of power cautiously.

Kennedy's political objectives did not orient him toward public education. More important, neither did his conception of politics itself. Genuine political education requires leadership that takes ordinary people seriously, that cares about their level of political consciousness and aims to improve their opportunities for political participation. But Kennedy, though possessing great ability to gauge public opinion and calculate electoral sentiment, regarded the American people more as spectators than participants in the political drama. He wanted their approval and their support, but not their judgment or their action. These were the province of the political elite.

On any level of political life, Kennedy believed, it was not the mass, but its leaders, who really mattered. As Theodore White observed of him during the 1960 campaign: "Politics, in his conversation, were groups of men led by other men. To know who the leaders were and understand them was to know and understand how the group worked." [43] Thus, Kennedy preferred to woo, conciliate, or compromise with recalcitrant Congressmen rather than appealing over their heads to the populace, because it was the interests and opinions of those Congressmen, and not an amorphous public opinion, that would settle the fate of his legislative program. The pragmatist's understanding of American politics as bargaining and adjustment within a pluralistic political elite, joined to a temperament that felt "genuine mistrust of mass emotion as a tool in politics," [44] left Kennedy with a skeptical view not only of the possibility, but even of the utility, of political education.

The elitist strain in Kennedy [45] was particularly evident in the way he listened to others' political views. From members of the political elite—inside or outside government—Kennedy patiently solicited criticisms and judgments; he was, Walter Lippmann recalled, "a great listener." [46] But if the criticisms came from more untutored voices, Kennedy was no longer so ready to listen. When John Lewis attempted, at the March on Washington, to articulate the passionate vision of the young civil rights workers in the South, Kennedy would not hear it; instead, members of his administration worked behind the scenes to censor Lewis's speech. (This incident is described in the chapter on Kennedy and civil rights.) Leaders from the "respectable" civil rights organizations were periodically consulted at the White House, but not these angry young blacks fresh from the southern struggle.

Mass political participation was a prominent theme in Kennedy's rhetoric. Perhaps the most widely quoted sentence from his Inaugural Address had been his challenge to the public: "And so, my fellow Americans, ask not what your country can do for you; ask what you can do for your country." [47] But aside from the Peace Corps, the Kennedy Administration was hard pressed to cite outlets that it had opened for citizen involvement in politics. When, for example, the President was questioned at press conferences as to what *specifically* Americans

might do for their country, he could never come up with anything that sounded very elevating. Beyond requesting generalized support for his demonstrations of American courage
around the globe, Kennedy was reduced to suggesting such sacrifices as acceptance of higher postal rates and a curb upon
expense accounts.[48]

Instead of facilitating greater popular involvement, Kennedy, in line with his conception of politics as the province of an
elite, ruled out mass participation in the key areas of public
policy. Foreign policy, the great preoccupation of the Kennedy
Presidency, was reserved as the domain of a handful of men.
This was dramatically symbolized by the Kennedy Administration's moment of glory, the Cuban missile crisis, when fifteen
or twenty men (the "Ex-Com") deliberated the fate of the
American nation and indeed the world. It was evident too in
the conduct of the Vietnam War, as the nature and extent of
American involvement were kept a tightly held secret and the
public repeatedly fed misleading information. Before an elite
forum, the American Foreign Service Association, Kennedy
made explicit an assumption which underlay his entire approach to foreign policy: that the mass of Americans lacked the
qualifications for comprehending the complexity of the nation's
foreign relations. He told these foreign-service officers that
questions of foreign policy "are so sophisticated and so technical that people who are not intimately involved week after
week, month after month, reach judgments which are based
upon emotion rather than knowledge of the real alternatives." [49]

Economic policy, the prime domestic concern of the Kennedy Administration, demanded similar expertise. Kennedy
described his "New Economics" to a White House Conference
on National Economic Issues in the following terms:

> The fact of the matter is that most of the problems, or
> at least many of them, that we now face are technical

> problems, are administrative problems. They are very
> sophisticated judgments which do not lend
> themselves to the great sort of "passionate
> movements" which have stirred this country so often
> in the past.[50]

It was hard enough for Kennedy to grasp the computations of his economic advisers; to throw open economic issues to the unschooled and emotional public was out of the question. Few Americans outside the government (with the important exception of businessmen) had any part to play in the construction of Kennedy's "sophisticated" economic policy. The management of the economy, like the management of foreign affairs, rested in the hands of a few.

There *was* one great surge of citizen politics in these years—the mass-action civil rights movement. Although Kennedy is sometimes credited with establishing the political climate which made such a movement possible, it had actually erupted into American politics before he acceded to the Presidency, with the "sit-in" campaigns of 1960. Kennedy's campaign pledges and electoral victory did help the movement, now hopeful of federal backing, to pick up momentum. Still, it received little direct encouragement from the White House. For Kennedy and his aides did not really welcome this form of participation in public affairs. Rather, they made persistent efforts to channel or blunt the actions of the civil rights movement, to shift the struggle from mass demonstrations to the quieter and more restricted forums of the courts and Congress. Kennedy feared, as we shall see, that the independent actions of a mass movement would result in his loss of control over the issue of civil rights; the course and intensity of the issue would then be defined by others, often in a manner incongruent with his own political purposes. Kennedy may have wanted Americans to serve their country, but the definition of that service was to be left up to him.

The Kennedy myth has, in not so many years, obscured
John Kennedy's relationship with the American public. Kennedy did succeed in drawing public attention to politics—but
that attention did not, in most cases, lead to involvement. His
style and glamour provided a vicarious identification for millions of Americans; but when it came to real participation, little
was either wanted or achieved. The Kennedy Administration
presented to the nation a far more colorful spectacle than its
predecessor. After Kennedy's death, it was fondly remembered
in the image of Camelot. It was more apt an image than most
people suspected. The king and queen and knights of the new
Camelot had pursued their celebrated adventures while the
populace had looked on with admiration and awe. It may have
been good pageantry, but pageantry was a far cry from a
politics of democratic participation.[51]

Public education remained for John Kennedy a secondary,
and often troublesome, element of political leadership. The
essence of leadership, in his view, did not reside in instructing
and energizing masses of people, but in exercising power over
the relative few who counted in political life. The centrality of
power in Kennedy's concept of leadership was explained by
Theodore Sorensen. According to Sorensen, Kennedy's philosophy of the Presidency emphasized power, as a matter of
national duty rather than as a goal of personal ambition. Kennedy believed that the White House should dominate the executive branch, and that the executive branch should have
primacy in the federal government; further, the federal
government was to lead the United States and the United
States was to lead the international community.[52]

Kennedy, Sorensen was quick to add, was never exces-
sively self-conscious about power. He seldom spoke of it, and
viewed it as neither an exalted prize nor an anguishing burden.
Power was simply a tool to be employed in the pursuit of
presidential goals. Sorensen was particularly anxious to dis-
parage any suggestion that Kennedy had been following Richard E. Neustadt's recipe for presidential success, that Kennedy

had deliberately pursued personal power in the fashion recommended by Neustadt's *Presidential Power*. Kennedy had enjoyed reading the book and had employed its author in 1960 for a study of presidential staffing—but he needed no political science professor, Sorensen insisted, to teach him about the nature of power.[53]

But if Kennedy did not seek power as his paramount goal, if he did not hunger for personal power in the manner of Neustadt's hero, FDR, still Kennedy passed all of Neustadt's major tests. Kennedy's executive style could have been used to illustrate many of the maxims in Neustadt's book. Kennedy did not, for example, like to wait for data or proposals to be placed before him. Often he preferred to reach into the middle levels of administration and ferret out information for himself; staff members of the various agencies were thus surprised by telephone calls direct from the President. He insisted too that he always be furnished with options. He did not wish to receive any of the prepackaged solutions Eisenhower had favored; policy choices were to remain in *his* hands. Further, he calculated carefully the effect of supporting unsuccessful measures in Congress, sensitive to a possible decline in prestige which would diminish his store of power. These features of his presidential style may not amount to a preoccupation with power; indeed some might be of value to any President. Yet they do suggest that Kennedy spent a considerable amount of his time ensuring that he retained as much power as possible.[54]

Concern with presidential power shaped not only Kennedy's own work methods, but those of the entire executive branch. For years political scientists had focused upon techniques for increasing presidential efficiency and power. Kennedy and his associates took up their work. The bulky organizational apparatus that the Eisenhower Administration had installed in the executive branch was largely dismantled by Kennedy. Reliance was placed less on formal structures than on new, flexible organizational techniques, such as the ad hoc task force. Robert McNamara was the great organizational hero;

his streamlining of the Defense Department, carried out with the aid of civilians armed with the latest innovative methods, was regarded almost with awe on the New Frontier. The accomplishments of Kennedy and his men in the field of organization were substantial, and sometimes brilliant. Yet in retrospect it is difficult not to regard them with some ambivalence. The streamlining of the Pentagon, for instance, turned out to be more significant in enhancing the President's confidence in his war-making abilities than it did in ensuring civilian control over the military.

Kennedy's executive style was plainly keyed to power. But his concern with power ran deeper than the operational techniques that fascinated political science devotees of the "strong" President. The primacy of power was integral to Kennedy's whole pragmatic conception of politics. To attain the results he wanted—and to escape the results he feared—there was no substitute for power.

The pragmatic leader conceives of the political realm as a conflux of competing elites. For such a leader to operate successfully within this realm, the power resources of each of these elites must be considered, their opinions weighed, their interests at least partially satisfied. Above all, it is a realm of limits, of maneuvering within multiple constraints for largely incremental improvements in one's power position. Kennedy held to such a view throughout his Presidency. Indeed, indications are that his sense of constraint grew with his experience as President. As a presidential aspirant, Kennedy had exuberantly characterized the office he sought as the "center of action" in the American political system. In 1963, however, in a foreword he contributed to Theodore Sorensen's *Decision-Making in the White House,* his characterization of presidential power was more restrained.

> Many things have been written about the conditions
> of presidential decision. The President, for example, is
> rightly described as a man of extraordinary powers.

> Yet it is also true that he must wield these powers
> under extraordinary limitations—and it is these
> limitations which so often give the problem of choice
> its complexity and even poignancy. Lincoln, Franklin
> Roosevelt remarked, "was a sad man because he
> couldn't get it all at once. And nobody can." Every
> President must endure a gap between what he would
> like and what is possible.[55]

Kennedy accepted not only the reality, but also the ines-capability of existing constraints. He never attempted to change the political context in which he operated, to open up the political process to new possibilities or develop alternative sources of power. He remained uninterested, for example, in the concept of party reform, much to the disappointment of liberal academics like James MacGregor Burns. More significantly, he resisted the new form of politics emerging with the civil rights movement: mass action, argument on social fundamentals, appeals to considerations of justice and morality. Moving the American political system in such a direction would necessarily have been long range, requiring arduous educational work and promising substantial political risk. The pragmatic Kennedy wanted no part of such an unpragmatic undertaking.[56]

Instead, Kennedy adapted his presidential course to the existing structure of power. This did not mean that he abandoned his quest for power; on the contrary, it led him to devote even more energy to the quest. What it did require was that he accommodate important power-holders (e.g., southern Congressmen or corporation executives) on matters close to *their* hearts in order to have his power intact and formidable when *he* really needed or wanted it. Where Kennedy especially wanted power was in foreign affairs; to have leeway in this area he was willing to leave substantially unchallenged the power of established forces over much of domestic policy. Presidential power during Kennedy's term hence rested on a delicate balance within the political elite. Even when Kennedy sought innovation he was careful—as we shall observe when we consider his 1963 tax reduction proposal—to preserve that balance.

If Kennedy's power in domestic affairs was limited, in foreign affairs his writ was largely unchallenged. So too was his ambition: to assert control over not only the American global establishment, but also the course of events around the globe. The pluralism of power was to give way here to a breathtaking assertion of global primacy. For Kennedy believed that the United States (and its leadership) *could* determine the basic content of contemporary world history, and therefore *should* determine it.[57]

I need not go into the nature and fruits of that belief here; they will occupy us throughout much of the book. Yet it is somewhat misleading to leave the impression that Kennedy and his fellow New Frontiersmen pursued global power with unchecked arrogance. Their search for power had its under-side—the nagging fear of loss of control.

Early in his Presidency, in the planning for a Cuban invasion, Kennedy had lost control over his administration. Sorensen emphasizes this fact in his narrative; the President had never been able, he explains, to get a grasp on the Cuban project as it progressed toward execution.[58] While Kennedy was hardly as innocent as Sorensen makes him out to be, he had been seduced by his desire of overthrowing Castro into accepting the CIA's pet scheme for accomplishing that end. The power of conception and implementation had basically remained with the CIA as Kennedy responded uncritically to their plans. And he had been burned badly. False information had been piled onto absurd premises to create the picture of a general uprising sparked by the invasion force; at the Bay of Pigs that picture was exposed as pure fantasy. Kennedy thus had to watch helplessly while the invasion was crushed.

He responded to the Cuban disaster by placing his own men (e.g., Robert Kennedy and Maxwell Taylor) in the key positions controlling major operations. These men gave him a greater sense of security; decision and execution were now in his hands and in the hands of his most trusted associates, to be shaped by their objectivity and realism. (Ironically, Vietnam proved that they were just as susceptible to fantasy as the CIA had been.) And this power was not to be relinquished. In every subsequent crisis, Kennedy and his inner circle retained tight control even over operational details.

Yet the fear of losing control did not disappear, in foreign affairs and even in domestic affairs. That fear was evident in the 1963 debates over whether the United States should continue to back Ngo Dinh Diem in Vietnam. As conflict between the Buddhists and Diem intensified through 1963, the Kennedy Administration faced an unsettling prospect: not only would its military strategy be undermined by continued civil strife in South Vietnam, but the justification for American military involvement itself, the nationalist aspirations of Diem, would crumble in light of his regime's obvious unpopularity and brutality. That prospect was temporarily warded off by the coup against Diem, but it was almost immediately apparent that this was only a stopgap measure.

Similarly, the proliferation of protest demonstrations after Birmingham threatened to take the civil rights question out of Kennedy's hands even as he moved to reassert control with new legislation. His surprisingly harsh criticism of demonstrations suggested an underlying apprehension that racial conflict might develop too rapidly to be resolved on the basis of the Administration's modest proposals. Growing black militancy —and reciprocal white fears—might create a situation where Kennedy would be helpless, out of his depth.

I can only speculate here, but perhaps Kennedy's fear of loss of control reflected some awareness of his own limitations, personal as well as institutional. He may have sensed that if he could not define these situations on his own terms, he might not be able to act in them or even to comprehend them. If questions cut too deeply and passions grew too intense, reality might slip away from the calculations of the pragmatic rationalist. Power was thus insurance for Kennedy, insurance against the loss of that settled political reality upon which his whole political career had been premised.

Kennedy's fears were not realized; it was his successor who would lose control both in Vietnam and over the black struggle at home. In his final days in office Kennedy expressed considerable satisfaction over his administration's contribution to American power. "Our adversaries have not abandoned their ambitions; our dangers have not diminished; our vigilance cannot be relaxed. But now we have the military, the scientific, and the economic strength to do whatever must be done for the preservation and promotion of freedom." [59] The Kennedy Administraion had magnified American power—and identified that power with its own.

2

Creating History

"**O**ur frontiers today are on every continent. . . . For our future and that of the rest of the people of the world are inseparably bound together, economically, militarily, politically." [1] John F. Kennedy wrote these words in 1960, on the eve of his successful campaign for the Presidency. With such words Kennedy signified his intention of extending the boundaries of American, and especially presidential, politics. More than any previous American President, he was to assume responsibility for nearly the totality of world events. His self-defined field of action was to be the entire globe.

All Kennedy's chroniclers note his preoccupation with foreign affairs. Sorensen's remarks on the subject are typical. Kennedy, he states, was considerably more interested in foreign policy than in domestic affairs. He devoted much more of his time and energy to foreign policy; he immersed himself in its details and involved himself in foreign policy projects from their inception to their implementation. [2] But such remarks, while accurate, are too pallid to capture Kennedy's conception of his own world-historical role. Closer to that conception (and to his yearning for the status of "great" President) are the words of his Inaugural Address: "In the long history of the world, only a few generations have been granted the role of defending freedom in its hour of maximum danger. I do not shrink from this responsibility; I welcome it." [3]

Succeeding chapters will examine the major landmarks of Kennedy's foreign policy: the Berlin confrontation, the Cuban missile crisis, the nuclear test ban, the Alliance for Progress in Latin America, the effort at counterinsurgency in Southeast Asia. But before turning to those events it is important first to consider the conception of world politics which Kennedy held (and which most of his advisers shared). The present chapter is devoted to an elaboration and an analysis of that conception, particularly its central theme—the existence of a menacing new Soviet offensive aimed at world domination, and the determined American effort to engage and defeat that offensive.

Kennedy's view of world affairs merits extended discussion for several reasons. That view established the basic context within which the politics of the New Frontier took place. Not only did it shape the international undertakings of the Kennedy Administration; but it also had considerable impact upon domestic programs, affecting Kennedy's approach to economic growth, to education, even to race relations. Further, it was in Kennedy's image of world affairs that the essence of New Frontier ideology was embodied. Examination of that image will show how deeply the pragmatic liberalism of the Kennedy Administration was rooted in the dogmas of the Cold War.

But it is not only to set the scene for a discussion of Berlin or Cuba or Vietnam, or to provide a sample of New Frontier ideology, that I focus on Kennedy's view of the world. The central argument of the chapter is that this view, and the actions it dictated, far more than any Soviet intentions or actions, actually shaped events in the early 1960s. Through his presidential words and deeds John Kennedy largely created his own history, forcing events into the mold of a historical theory that he had articulated well before he took office.

Kennedy's conception of world affairs received its first

expression in the late 1950s, in a series of speeches attacking the foreign and defense policies of the Eisenhower Administration. These speeches were collected in a campaign volume entitled *The Strategy of Peace*. It is highly instructive to review Senator Kennedy's "strategy of peace," for it was to become the fundamental program of the Kennedy Presidency.

In Kennedy's eyes the launching of *Sputnik I* in October of 1957 marked a watershed in the history of the Cold War. Soviet success in propelling a satellite into space indicated that the Russians now held a significant lead over the United States in missile technology. And the Soviet Union could be counted on to take advantage of this "missile gap." Bent as always upon world domination, the Soviets would, in Kennedy's view, use the Sputnik launching as the first salvo in a new and coordinated offensive aimed ultimately at the destruction of the West.

Kennedy thought it unlikely that the Soviet Union would test its missile superiority in nuclear combat with the West; the means of assault would undoubtedly be more complex and more subtle. Kennedy in 1958 visualized the "post-Sputnik Soviet offensive" in terms that were to remain unchanged through the rest of his career:

> In the years of the gap, the Soviets may be expected to use their superior striking ability to achieve their objectives in ways which may not require launching an actual attack. Their missile power will be the shield from behind which they will slowly, but surely, advance—through Sputnik diplomacy, limited brush-fire wars, indirect non-overt aggression, intimidation and subversion, internal revolution, increased prestige or influence, and the vicious blackmail of our allies. The periphery of the Free World will slowly be nibbled away. The balance of power will gradually shift against us. The key areas vital to our security will gradually undergo Soviet infiltration and domination.[4]

In the face of this extraordinary challenge, the Eisenhower Administration remained frozen in positions that had permitted major Soviet gains even before Sputnik. Eisenhower's foreign policy, Kennedy argued, was a mélange of "piecemeal programs, obsolete policies, and meaningless slogans." [5] Eisenhower's defense strategy, Kennedy charged, had sacrificed military strength to the dogma of balanced budgets. Most shocking of all, the Eisenhower Administration could not even comprehend the new dimensions of the crisis. As W. W. Rostow, another adherent of the theory of the Soviet offensive, wrote in 1960:

> ... the leadership within the Executive Branch did not fully agree concerning the character of the crisis that was faced; and there was even disagreement as to whether the nation faced a major crisis. In fact, the President used a part of his influence to deflate the nation's sense of urgency in the face of the flow of events.[6]

The bulk of criticism against the Eisenhower Administration fell upon its defense strategy. Kennedy joined a growing chorus of critics (most notably Army Generals Matthew B. Ridgway, James Gavin, and Maxwell Taylor, the Gaither and the Rockefeller Panels) in assaulting the Eisenhower-Dulles doctrine of "massive retaliation." The Eisenhower Administration, seeking to combat communists and balance budgets at the same time, had fixed upon a military "New Look" that promised, in its reliance on nuclear weaponry, the most deterrent for the least cost. But this strategy, its critics charged, had proved a total failure. It had permitted the erosion of American capacities for conventional warfare, while failing even to maintain American security against nuclear attack, due to the rapidity of technological change.

Advocated as a replacement for "massive retaliation" was the strategic doctrine of "flexible response." This doctrine called for a step-up in American military capabilities at all levels, from preparation for guerrilla war to nuclear delivery systems, so that the President would have at his disposal flexible and appropriate tools to deal with any type of communist aggression. No longer, it was argued, would the communists be able to penetrate Free World defenses by conventional attacks or guerrilla infiltration, secure in the knowledge that American power, contained almost exclusively in nuclear weaponry, would not be used. Now the United States would be able to engage the communist offensive on any military level it chose.

The critics were basically correct in characterizing "massive retaliation" as a clumsy and dangerous strategy. Yet it should be noted that the strategy they proposed as a replacement was in many respects even more dangerous. By creating an American capacity for involvement in armed conflict anywhere in the world, they went a long way toward ensuring that involvement. But perhaps this was, in large part, what they foresaw and desired. Consider, for example, General Maxwell Taylor's comments (in 1960) on the American failure to intervene in the battle of Dienbienphu in 1954:

> The need was apparent for ready military forces with conventional weapons to cope with this kind of limited-war situation. Unfortunately, such forces did not then exist in sufficient strength or in proper position to offer any hope of success. . . . This event was the first, but not the last, failure of the New Look to keep the peace on our terms.[7]

In these years Kennedy, as we have seen in the previous chapter, adopted the role of political prophet, comparing himself to Winston Churchill in his warnings of peril to a complacent public. But Kennedy's speeches went beyond warnings; they also set forth a plan for dealing with the crisis. Kennedy proposed to confront the systematic Soviet offensive with an equally systematic American "strategy of peace"—"a long-range, coordinated strategy to meet the determined Soviet program for world domination." [8] He had, he told the Senate in

June of 1960, a twelve-point agenda for America; upon the fulfillment of that agenda rested America's future success, and even its survival.

Many of the foreign policy undertakings of the Kennedy Presidency were contained in embryonic form in that twelve-point agenda. The first two points were the most significant. The massive nuclear buildup of 1961, which was to have critical implications for U.S.–Soviet relations, was predicted in Kennedy's initial proposal, aimed at "stepping up development and production of the ultimate missiles that can close the gap." [9] Even more important in foreshadowing Kennedy's presidential policies was his second point. "We must regain the ability to intervene effectively and swiftly in any limited war anywhere in the world—augmenting, modernizing, and providing increased mobility and versatility for the conventional forces and weapons of the Army and Marine Corps." [10]

The rest of Senator Kennedy's agenda spoke sweepingly of new approaches in other areas of American foreign policy, such as Latin America and Africa. But Kennedy's "strategy of peace" was, in its essentials, scarcely distinguishable from the military strategy of "flexible response." What came through most clearly in his major proposals was a desire to gear up the nation for the new modes of warfare which the theory of the Soviet offensive had foreseen. Kennedy was proclaiming in this speech, indeed in all his speeches in these years, that America faced the likelihood of losing the Cold War unless it readied itself to engage the communists on every level—economic and ideological as well as military—on which they operated.

His tone in these speeches was seldom warlike; often he spoke of the need for negotiations with the Soviet Union, and expressed hopes for a thaw in the Cold War. While critical of summit diplomacy, he affirmed that "it is far better that we meet at the summit than at the brink." [11] These remarks no doubt reflected Kennedy's own deep-seated hopes for peace;

they also were designed to gain the support of the Stevenson liberals in the Democratic party. However sincerely he meant them, they were not the central message of Kennedy's speeches from 1958 to 1960. That message was, unmistakably, a call to intensify America's Cold War efforts, to mobilize the nation against "a peril more deadly than any wartime danger we have ever known." [12]

Perhaps the most revealing feature of these prepresidential speeches was Kennedy's judgment of Eisenhower. Plenty of blunders could be found in Eisenhower's record in foreign affairs, and Kennedy picked out most of them. But his critique of Eisenhower went well beyond mistakes in policy; it was fundamentally an attack upon Eisenhower's personal style. The old General was, in the eyes of the young politician, a captive to the illusion of good intentions. Having allowed the crusading spirit of the early 1950s to wane, Eisenhower now dreamed of peace through personal diplomacy. His conciliatory approach toward the Soviet Union—capped by the Khrushchev visit to the United States in 1959—exuded a naive and dangerous softness which only lulled Americans more deeply into complacency.

> Attitudes, platitudes, and beatitudes have taken the place of a critical and vigilant intelligence marching in advance of events, and by the measures taken, producing the events we want. We have allowed a soft sentimentalism to form the atmosphere we breathe. And in that kind of atmosphere, a diffuse desire to do good has become a substitute for tough-minded plans and operations—a substitute for a strategy.[13]

While Kennedy saw weakness in Eisenhower's character and style, others understood these same qualities in Eisenhower as valuable for the maintenance of peace in these years. The contemporary historian John Lukacs, for example, wrote of Eisenhower: "With all of his shortcomings, the benevolence and temperateness of his character together with his knowledge of the horrors of war were, and still are, important factors in the balance." [14] Kennedy's failure to appreciate Eisenhower's temperateness was ominous; it prefigured the "tough-minded" and often bellicose stance that he himself was to assume as President. There was to be little room on the New Frontier for the benevolence of an Eisenhower—or a Stevenson. The Kennedy Administration never fell victim to the illusion of good intentions; its own illusion, we shall see, was very nearly the opposite.

The same Cold War theory that his senatorial speeches had presented could be illustrated by statements and actions throughout Kennedy's Presidency. The first six months of his presidential term, however, saw a particularly dramatic and important presentation of this theory, a presentation that would set the tone for most of the Kennedy years. New lines of global confrontation between the United States and the Soviet Union were laid down in these months—in large part, the record suggests, by John F. Kennedy.

Kennedy did not wait long, after taking office, to expose the American public—and Nikita Khrushchev—to the sweep of his historical theory. Sorensen relates that Kennedy's Inaugural Address had been intentionally crafted to stress positive themes: the possibility of cooperation with the Soviet Union, the hopes for conquering poverty and disease. But ten days later, in his first State of the Union Address, Kennedy dropped the tones of optimism. In language that repeatedly verged on the apocalyptic,[15] he painted a picture of world conflict so chilling that it surprised even those familiar with his prior warnings to the nation.

At stake in the next four years, Kennedy told the American people, was nothing less than the survival of the Republic. Domestic problems, especially economic recession, were troublesome.

> But all these problems pale when placed beside those
> which confront us around the world. No man entering
> upon this office . . . could fail to be staggered upon
> learning—even in this brief 10 day period—the harsh
> enormity of the trials through which we must pass in
> the next four years. Each day the crises multiply. Each
> day their solution grows more difficult. Each day we
> draw nearer the hour of maximum danger, as weapons
> spread and hostile forces grow stronger. . . . Our
> analyses over the last 10 days make it clear that—in
> each of the principal areas of crisis—the tide of events
> has been running out and time has not been
> our friend.[16]

Kennedy went on to specify the crises that were building
up toward that "hour of maximum danger." There was the
chaotic situation in the Congo, which threatened to issue in a
Soviet base in the heart of Africa. There was the unrelenting
pressure of the Chinese Communists upon the noncommunist
states of Asia, pressure extending from the mountains of India
to the jungles of Laos and South Vietnam. And there was a
grave new danger in the Western Hemisphere itself. "In Latin
America, Communist agents seeking to exploit that region's
peaceful revolution of hope have established a base on Cuba,
only 90 miles from our shores." [17]

The initial response to this menacing worldwide communist offensive was to be an immediate American military
buildup. The main points of Senator Kennedy's twelve-point
agenda were reiterated as the new presidential program, as
Kennedy requested additional appropriations for the development of Minuteman and Polaris missiles and for improvement
of air-lift capacity for conventional warfare. There was also to
be a new initiative in America's foreign economic programs,
stressing more flexible and long-range aid projects. But even
these undertakings did not relieve the pessimism of Kennedy's
message. The speech ended upon the same grim note with
which it had begun. "The tide is unfavorable. The news will be
worse before it is better." [18]

What produced this remarkable speech, which even some of Kennedy's admirers found unduly "alarmist"? The speech can in part be attributed to rhetorical excess, a vice to which Kennedy would frequently fall victim. There was also a hint of calculation; Kennedy may have been attempting, in advance, to preserve some political leeway in case of foreign policy reverses.[19] But in the main, the speech must be taken as expressive of his view of the world at that historical moment, a view which he very strongly wanted to impress upon the American people. Kennedy firmly believed that the United States was approaching the "hour of maximum danger"; the world looked extremely threatening to the new American President in January of 1961, well before confrontation over Berlin, the Cuban missile crisis, or large-scale fighting in Vietnam. The onset of the Kennedy Administration is thus a good period to use in assessing the crisis Kennedy had proclaimed, and the historical theory which explained that crisis.

The specific evidence Kennedy produced to back up his gloomy prognostications was rather scanty. The Congo, Laos, and Cuba may have presented problems for American foreign policy makers—but they hardly constituted a threat to American security, much less to American survival. It was ludicrous to imagine that jungle warfare in Laos, or even socialism in Cuba, posed any immediate danger to the United States. The danger was only credible if all these events, and others, were part of a pattern, if they all represented the stealthy advance of a single enemy whose aim was the defeat of America.

Kennedy's crisis thus rested, not on immediate circumstances, but on what had become by 1961 the hoariest of Cold War myths: the idea of a monolithic communist drive, headed by the Soviet Union, to achieve world domination. Ignoring the significance of the Yugoslav breakaway, the Chinese and Vietnamese revolutions, and numerous other signs of diversity in the communist bloc, as well as the continual manifestation of Russian national and great-power aims,

Kennedy and his advisers persisted, as had their predecessors, in seeing the specter of Soviet Communism behind almost every world development that they found troubling. They added to the Cold War tradition, however, with their theory of the post-Sputnik Soviet offensive. This theory accounted, in their eyes, for the rash of (what they perceived as) anti-American occurrences in the years after 1957. Kennedy's 1958 prediction—of accelerating Soviet advances behind a shield of missiles —had, they argued, been borne out by succeeding events.

> It was only after the launching of Sputnik in October, 1957 that the second great Communist offensive of the post-war years was fully launched. It was in 1958 that Moscow laid down its ultimatum on Berlin. It was in 1958 that the Communist party in Hanoi announced it would undertake a guerrilla war in South Vietnam. Soon afterward the Pathet Lao, with the active help of Communist North Vietnam, resumed their effort to take over Laos. It was in these first post-Sputnik years that the Soviets sought to exploit the potentialities for acquiring in the Congo a Communist base for operations in central Africa. . . . It was also at the end of 1958 that Castro took over in Cuba.[20]

It should scarcely be necessary, in the 1970s, to disprove once again the idea of a monolithic world communism, or to refute the claim that Castro's Cuba was a product of Russian machinations and the war against Diem in South Vietnam an offensive by the "Sino-Soviet" bloc. It should not even be necessary to point out that American policy had played a substantial role in bringing about the very events it abhorred—e.g., the part played by the United States in the renewed outbreak of guerrilla warfare in Vietnam through its support for Diem's refusal of reunification elections. What *is* necessary to consider about the Kennedy version of the late 1950s and early 1960s is its obfuscation of the many signs that the Soviet Union was, in these years, basically seeking, not defeat for the United States, but détente. For the theory Kennedy held could not help but distort any conciliatory moves on the part of the Soviet Union. Holding on to the imagery of world revolution long after Moscow had abandoned that dream, Kennedy's theory transmuted Soviet gropings toward a modus vivendi with the West into subtle stratagems for communist advancement.

Thus, Kennedy (and his fellow believers in the post-Sputnik missile-gap offensive) placed great emphasis on Khrushchev's Berlin ultimatum in 1958, but downgraded the importance of his abandonment of that ultimatum for inconclusive talks and a promise of a summit meeting. They responded coldly to Khrushchev's extraordinary visit to the United States in the fall of 1959. Kennedy himself warned against any relaxation of tensions in light of the "Spirit of Camp David": "A more careful reflection on Mr. Khrushchev's visit, it seems to me, is cause for redoubled efforts, not relaxation." [21] The collapse of the Paris Summit in 1960, after the U-2 incident, they took as proof of Soviet perfidy, and as a final demonstration of the futility inherent in Eisenhower's attitude of personal goodwill toward the Soviets. Their theory told them that the Soviet Union was again pursuing world mastery; they could not grasp the possibility that Khrushchev's repeatedly expressed eagerness to consult with Eisenhower suggested more limited aims, most likely "a Russian-American accommodation, preferably to be based on the prevailing territorial status quo." [22]

Kennedy's suspicion of peaceful gestures on the part of the Soviet Union was continued into his Presidency. Shortly before his inauguration, he told George Kennan of several recent Soviet overtures, all of which had "stressed the urgency of negotiations and invited exchanges looking toward a summit meeting." [23] Upon his inauguration, Khrushchev and Leonid Brezhnev sent Kennedy a particularly cordial message. And a few days later the Russians, as another signal of friendship to the new administration, released two American fliers who had been shot down over the USSR in a RB-47 reconnaissance plane six months earlier. Kennedy, however, did not seem to pay much heed to these gestures. He thought he perceived a far more revealing intimation of Soviet intentions in a speech which Khrushchev had delivered in Moscow on January 6, 1961.

In that speech Khrushchev had announced that the world was inexorably moving toward socialism, and that "wars of national liberation" were the decisive factor in this historical process; consequently, the Soviet Union would give its whole-hearted support to such wars. Kennedy considered the speech a definitive rendering of Soviet policy; he believed it to be so important that he had all his staff read it. But where Khrushchev had spoken of Russian *support* for "wars of national liberation," Kennedy, with his theory of the Soviet offensive at hand, translated these words into Russian *direction* of such wars. Khrushchev's optimistic, bombastic oratory (a kind to which he was prone) became in Kennedy's eyes a blueprint for world conquest. (According to David Halberstam, the misinterpretation ran even deeper: "Years later very high Soviet officials would tell their counterparts in the Kennedy Administration that it was all a mistake, the speech had been aimed not at the Americans, but at the Chinese." [24]) The speech confirmed the new President in his belief that the Russians were still on the attack; the aforementioned Soviet gestures toward conciliation could therefore be safely disregarded. Kennedy's initial response to the Soviet Union, which was to set the tone for U.S.–USSR relations in the coming months, was thus his State of the Union Address.

One final point needs to be made about that State of the Union Address and its relationship to Kennedy's theory of the post-Sputnik Soviet offensive. Notably absent from Kennedy's portrayal of the crisis facing America was his earlier emphasis on the "missile gap." For Kennedy had learned upon entering office that there was no "missile gap," that the United States in fact possessed a marked advantage over the Soviet Union in ballistic missiles. The first premise of Kennedy's theory—that the Soviet Union possessed a superior nuclear shield, from behind which it could confidently advance by both overt and surreptitious means—had turned out to be fallacious. Yet, for Kennedy, this fact seemingly did not matter. The theory of the Soviet offensive could not be disproved by Russian weakness just as it could not be disproved by Russian gestures of good-will. Nothing testifies more clearly to the sway of ideology over Kennedy and his associates than this adherence to a theory of contemporary history even after the key premise that had given rise to it had been completely exploded.

Kennedy's reaction to the first foreign "crisis" his administration faced—over Laos—seemed on the surface to belie the crusading tone of his initial presidential speeches. He moved to head off a potential takeover of the country by the Pathet Lao guerrillas by calling for an immediate cease-fire and negotiated settlement. While he backed up that call with a threat of American military intervention, he made it clear that the United States was willing to see a neutralist coalition government emerge from negotiations. Since the Eisenhower Administration had, with remarkable ineptitude, supported a right-wing anticommunist regime, the position Kennedy took represented a new flexibility in U.S. policy toward Laos.

But if his acceptance of a compromise settlement in Laos appeared to signal a retreat from the idea of global struggle, that appearance was deceptive. Kennedy knew that with the history of American blundering and right-wing incompetence there was no hope for any anticommunist regime in Laos; thus he could accept communist participation in a coalition government as a political necessity. The same thinking did not hold true, however, with regard to South Vietnam. South Vietnam was far larger and more strategically vital than Laos. Also, it had a huge American-trained army and a strongman as President whom Kennedy greatly admired. In South Vietnam there would be no compromise settlement; in the same months that Kennedy sought negotiations over Laos he began to construct the apparatus for a major counterinsurgency effort in Vietnam.

The handling of Laos in 1961 did not represent a precedent for Vietnam; nor did it represent much of a triumph for diplomatic over military methods. Kennedy did not want to send American troops into Laos—the military conditions there were highly unfavorable—but he came quite close to doing so. Marine units in Japan and Okinawa were prepared in March of 1961 for transfer to Thailand; one unit was actually landed there. And the possibility of their introduction into Laos seemed strong—until the Bay of Pigs. Only that disaster, according to Sorensen, finally set Kennedy's mind firmly against military intervention. He simply could not afford the chance of a Laotian disaster following so swiftly after the Cuban one.

Two months after the State of the Union speech, in the midst of jockeying with the Soviet Union over the question of Laos, Kennedy sent to the Congress his Special Message on the Defense Budget. In what was to be only the first of three 1961 requests for additional defense expenditures, Kennedy asked on March 28 for $2.4 billion beyond the budgetary figure that the Eisenhower Administration had deemed sufficient for American security. The bulk of the money—about $1.8 billion—was to go for large-scale increases in the production of the Polaris, Minuteman, and Skybolt missile systems—this despite the knowledge in Washington of the substantial lead in strategic weapons which the United States already held over the Soviet Union. New funds were also to be directed toward improving American capacities in conventional and unconventional warfare. To justify this expenditure the President recited his by now familiar litany of communist tactics: "subversion, infiltration, intimidation, indirect or non-overt aggression, internal revolution, diplomatic blackmail, guerrilla warfare, or a series of limited wars." [25] With this message to Congress, Kennedy, who at other times would speak perceptively of the folly of the arms race, began what Sorensen described as the most rapid and large-scale military buildup in America's peacetime history. An additional $17 billion would be appropriated over the span of three years to provide the United States with the most powerful armed force in history. [26]

In the face of mounting evidence detailing the Soviets' strategic inferiority, President Kennedy had an important chance to slow down the nuclear arms race. A few of his experts in the field of strategic weaponry (notably Science Adviser Jerome Wiesner and Carl Kaysen of the National Security Council) were indeed pressing for the Administration to take that chance, to hold back on missile expansion and initiate new talks with the Soviets on disarmament prospects. But Kennedy and his top advisers were decidedly skeptical about disarmament in 1961. And they were intent, regardless of the level of Soviet strength, on a massive buildup of American strategic power.

Several possible explanations have been adduced for the buildup: that Kennedy was locked into it by campaign promises and Pentagon pressures; that he wanted to replace vulnerable Titan and Jupiter missiles with "hardened" (against nuclear attack) Minuteman and Polaris missiles; that he hoped to increase American strength to such a point that the United States could face down the supposed communist offensive and, in effect, dictate peace terms to the USSR. Whatever the rationale, what was remarkable was that Kennedy and his chief advisers apparently gave little thought to the repercussions that such an action would inevitably have in Moscow. That the Soviet leadership would feel threatened by an American buildup, that they would feel compelled to respond with their own buildup in order not to be left far behind in the arms race—these obvious and immediate consequences were ignored by Washington. [27] But the consequences of Kennedy's massive increase in strategic weaponry were to go beyond Khrushchev's announcement, on July 8, of the Soviet decision to increase its military expenditures as a response to the American move. They extended, as will be shown, to the Soviet resumption of nuclear testing and the Cuban missile crisis.

The defense message of March 28 signaled Kennedy's determination to best the Soviets decisively in strategic weapons competition. On April 17, the invasion of Cuba by a force of exiles organized, trained, and armed by the CIA seemingly marked the first step in Kennedy's effort to take the initiative in the Third World as well. The Bay of Pigs affair will be treated in a later chapter, in connection with Kennedy's approach to Latin America. What should be noted here is that, in tandem with the announced arms buildup, it presented to the world (and particularly to the Soviet Union) the image of a new aggressiveness in Washington. That image was perhaps somewhat blurred by the clumsiness of the invasion attempt; nevertheless, these early foreign policy undertakings of the new Administration seemed to indicate that Kennedy, operating upon the theory of the Soviet world offensive, was intent upon launching a major counteroffensive of his own.

As revealing as the Cuban invasion of Kennedy's thinking in this period was the remarkable series of speeches he delivered in its aftermath. The bitterness of failure seemed momentarily to penetrate his usual coolness; as David Horowitz observed, "a very central Kennedy nerve was laid bare here." [28] He took the responsibility for the failure of the invasion attempt upon himself; yet the real culprits, he insisted in an impassioned address to the American Society of Newspaper Editors on April 20, were the communists. By a strange twist of logic, the defeat of an invasion backed by the United States became for Kennedy yet another proof of the communist drive to take over the world. The explanation for the Bay of Pigs, and beyond that the picture of the world which Kennedy offered on this occasion, are so striking that, even if their intensity is partially attributable to the emotions of the moment, they deserve full reproduction:

> . . . it is clearer than ever that we face a relentless struggle in every corner of the globe that goes far beyond the clash of armies or even nuclear armaments. The armies are there, and in large number. The nuclear armaments are there. But they serve· primarily as the shield behind which subversion, infiltration, and a host of other tactics steadily advance, picking off vulnerable areas one by one in situations which do not permit our own armed intervention.
>
> Power is the hallmark of this offensive—power and discipline and deceit. The legitimate discontent of yearning people is exploited. The legitimate trappings of self-determination are employed. But once in power all talk of discontent is repressed, all self-determination disappears, and the promise of a revolution of hope is betrayed, as in Cuba, into a reign of terror. . . .
>
> We dare not fail to see the insidious nature of this new and deeper struggle. We dare not fail to grasp the new concepts, the new tools, the new sense of urgency we will need to combat it—whether in Cuba or South Vietnam. And we dare not fail to realize that this struggle is taking place every day, without fanfare, in thousands of villages and markets—day and night—and in classrooms all over the globe.
>
> The message of Cuba, of Laos, of the rising din of Communist voices in Asia and Latin America—these messages are all the same. The complacent, the self-indulgent, the soft societies are about to be swept away with the debris of history. Only the strong, only the industrious, only the determined, only the courageous, only the visionary who determine the real nature of our struggle can possibly survive.
>
> No greater task faces this country or this administration. No other challenge is more deserving of our every effort and energy. Too long we have fixed our eyes on traditional military needs, on armies prepared to cross borders, on missiles poised for

flight. Now it should be clear that this is no longer
enough—that our security may be lost piece by piece,
country by country, without the firing of a single
missile or the crossing of a single border.

We intend to profit from this lesson. We intend
to re-examine and reorient our forces of all kinds—our
tactics and our institutions here in this community.
We intend to intensify our efforts for a struggle in
many ways more difficult than war, where
disappointment will often accompany us.

For I am convinced that we in this country and in
the free world possess the necessary resources, and
the skill, and the added strength that comes from a
belief in the freedom of man. And I am equally
convinced that history will record the fact that this
bitter struggle reached its climax in the late 1950's and
the early 1960's. Let me then make clear as the
President of the United States that I am determined
upon our system's survival and success, regardless of
the cost and regardless of the peril! [29]

A week later, speaking to the American Newspaper Publishers Association, Kennedy spelled out to the press its role in
this global conflict. In the face of what he termed a danger
greater than any declared war, it was time for the press to begin
exercising "self-restraint" in matters touching upon national
security. The President was not proposing any new machinery
of government censorship, but he did hope to enlist the press in
his battle against "a monolithic and ruthless conspiracy . . . a
system which has conscripted vast human and material resources into the building of a tightly knit, highly efficient
machine." [30]

The menace of a disciplined and ruthless army of communist agents was invoked once more to a dinner of Cook
County Democrats on April 28. More noteworthy in this
speech, however, was an image to which Kennedy would frequently return—the image of a beleaguered but proud America,

virtually alone among the major democratic nations in its recognition of and commitment to the global struggle.

> Now our great responsibility is to be the chief
> defender of freedom, in this time of maximum danger.
> Only the United States has the power and the
> resources and the determination. We have committed
> ourselves to the defense of dozens of countries
> stretched around the globe who look to us for
> independence, who look to us for the defense of
> their freedom.[31]

Kennedy was seldom again to present his Cold War theory
in such a complete (and extreme) form as in these post–Bay of
Pigs speeches, but their themes remained a constant feature of
his rhetoric. These speeches are difficult to reconcile with the
claim of Kennedy's admirers that he was notably free of the
stale dogmas of the Cold War. Even a cursory examination of
them turns up a host of such dogmas.

The Manichean world-view of the Dulles era, these
speeches show, still dominated Kennedy's thought. If he declined to attach adjectives like "godless" and "atheistic" to the
word communism, communism as a force remained for him
unqualifiedly evil. It appeared here as a dehumanized, ma-
chinelike apparatus, searching relentlessly after power and dominion simply for their own sake. It was a "monolithic and
ruthless conspiracy," whose goal was not a new social order, but
only the ancient dream of world empire. America, on the other
hand, represented freedom and justice everywhere in the world.
If communist motives were sinister, American motives, Kennedy insisted after the United States had sent an invasion force
against a neighboring nation, were spotless.

In the face of a challenge by this global, implacable enemy,
almost the entire responsibility for defending the cause of freedom fell upon the United States. Only America, in Kennedy's
view, held back the communists from their global ambitions; as

he put it in a 1963 speech, "if the United States were to falter, the whole world, in my opinion, would inevitably begin to move toward the Communist bloc." [32] Perhaps no word appeared so often in John F. Kennedy's speeches as the word "burden." But if the imagery of the Cold War shifted somewhat from the moralistic and quasi-religious vocabulary of Dulles to Kennedy's more subdued language of obligation, the change was not necessarily for the better. That language of obligation became a convenient guise for the practice of American interventionism; it was to be in the name of commitment and responsibility that the United States now projected itself into the internal affairs of other nations.

Kennedy's admirers insist that he recognized the pitfalls of American interventionism. They cite in support of this view his words to a University of Washington audience on November 16, 1961:

> . . . we must face the fact that the United States is neither omnipotent nor omniscient—that we are only 6 percent of the world's population—that we cannot impose our will upon the other 94 percent of mankind—that we cannot right every wrong or reverse each adversity—and that therefore there cannot be an American solution to every world problem.

These are perceptive words, but they fly against the bulk of Kennedy's statements and actions as President. Consider, for instance, his statement to an Arizona audience *on the very next day:*

> Other countries look to their own interests. Only the United States has obligations which stretch ten thousand miles across the Pacific, and three or four thousand miles across the Atlantic, and thousands of miles to the south. Only the United States—and we are only 6 percent of the world's population—bears this kind of burden.[33]

The routing of the invasion force at the Bay of Pigs had not shaken any of his views, but strengthened them in Kennedy's eyes. He did not draw from Castro's success any lesson about the evident mass support for the Cuban leader; instead, he stepped up his attacks upon Castro as a tyrant and a Russian puppet. He did not learn much about the limitations of American interventionism in the affairs of other nations; instead, he determined to control future interventions more tightly with his own people (rather than the CIA). The Bay of Pigs, an invention of his own government, became for Kennedy one more piece of evidence for the existence of a Soviet offensive —and one more spur for an intensified American effort to counter that offensive.

The slighting of Soviet gestures of conciliation, the massive American arms buildup (Kennedy requested additional defense spending once again on May 25), the Cuban invasion, the fierce rhetoric of "relentless struggle"—these provided the background for Kennedy's meeting with Khrushchev at Vienna in June of 1961. Since the meeting was to inaugurate one of the most tense and dangerous phases in the entire history of the Cold War, it is well to keep in mind that background. Kennedy went to Vienna expecting an encounter with a global foe; not surprisingly, he found what he was expecting.

As far as can be gathered from the unofficial accounts we have of their conversations, Kennedy and Khrushchev spent a good deal of time at Vienna debating Kennedy's theory of the Soviet world offensive. Kennedy expressed the hope that the two great powers could prevent direct confrontations in the future; this would not be difficult if the Soviet Union concentrated on its internal affairs and ceased its attempts to subvert the nations of the Free World. Khrushchev responded that it was not the agents of the Soviet Union but the powerful idea of communism that sparked revolutionary change around the globe. Kennedy then reiterated the need for both sides to avoid situations that might lead to war. "All right, said

Khrushchev, but how could we work anything out when the United States regarded revolution anywhere as the result of Communist machinations?" [34] Kennedy remarked that he did not oppose the fall of corrupt or reactionary governments, but, he insisted, "social changes must take place peacefully and must not involve the prestige or commitments of America and Russia or upset the balance of world power." [35]

After this revealing collision of views discussion turned to specific issues—and it was on the subject of Berlin that the future lines of confrontation began to emerge. With Khrushchev's insistence that the "intolerable" German situation be ended by a peace settlement, with or without the participation of the Western powers, and with Kennedy's expression of opposition to changing the Berlin status quo, began an eighteen-month period in which the United States and the USSR twice stood near or on the brink of nuclear war.

This period of confrontation seemingly represented that "hour of maximum danger" which Kennedy had so often predicted. But, it is time to ask, was that prediction a clear-sighted perception of the movement of events, or was it somewhat closer to being a self-fulfilling prophecy?

I have emphasized the first six months of Kennedy's Presidency because I believe they suggest an answer to this question. Kennedy in this period spurned friendly gestures, rhetorically prepared the nation for global conflict, and instituted a series of actions that the Soviets could not help but regard as hostile. The Soviet Union was hardly blameless in these months. Indeed, Khrushchev was continually oscillating between declamations of peaceful intent and threatening words about Russian nuclear might. He was intransigent in his demands for an unwieldy "troika" system to revamp the United Nations Secretariat. And he was, when he finally presented to Kennedy his plans on Berlin, somewhat harsh and bellicose. Yet, Kennedy's words and actions were the dynamic factor in this period. It was Kennedy who announced that the Cold War had entered a new and more intensive phase; it was his military buildup and invasion of Cuba which in reality initiated that phase.[36]

Events of the next eighteen months—the tense situation in Berlin, the Russian resumption of atmospheric nuclear testing, the emplacement of missiles in Cuba—appeared to fit neatly into Kennedy's theory of the Soviet world offensive. But the foregoing analysis, and the analysis of Kennedy's two great crises to follow, suggest a different explanation for these events. They suggest that these Russian actions are to be explained in part by long-standing and limited Russian aims, and in part by the offensive that the Russians perceived Kennedy as having launched *against them*. As the Soviets began to react aggressively to that perceived attack, events fell into line with the theory of the Soviet offensive.[37] Kennedy now had the enemy that his theory had always depicted. And he was faced with a series of American-Russian conflicts which followed closely his original scenario. Having done a great deal, intentionally or not, to precipitate the historical crisis he had long predicted, it remained for Kennedy to play out his part in that crisis.

The next chapter will examine Kennedy's actions in these dangerous months. But it is instructive to get a bit ahead of the story at this point and see how Kennedy was, in retrospect, to judge them. For Kennedy, the sequence of events that climaxed in the Cuban missile crisis both confirmed the theory of the post-Sputnik offensive and brought that offensive to its close. His conception of world politics, and the determined action which followed from that conception, had both been conclusively validated, in his mind, by the missile crisis. As he wrote in the Foreword to the volume containing his public papers for 1962:

> Future historians, looking back at 1962, may well mark this year as the time when the tide of international politics began at last to flow strongly toward the world of diversity and freedom. Following the

launching of Sputnik in 1957, the Soviet Union began
to intensify its pressures against the non-communist
world—especially in Southeast Asia, in Central Africa,
in Latin America, and around Berlin. The notable
Soviet successes in space were taken as evidence that
communism held the key to the scientific and
technological future. People in many countries began
to accept the notion that communism was mankind's
inevitable destiny.

1962 stopped this process—and nothing was more
important in deflating the notion of communist
invincibility than the American response to Soviet
provocations in Cuba. The combination of firmness
and restraint in face of the gravest challenge to world
peace since 1939 did much to reassure the rest of the
world both about the strength of our national will and
the prudence of our national judgment. Menacing
problems remained at the end of the year. . . . Yet it
was increasingly obvious that the momentum of the
post-Sputnik offensive had been halted.[38]

Kennedy had brought his historical theory—or something
akin to it—to reality. And now he had won a decisive victory *in
its terms*. Having created his own history, he naturally became
its hero.

It would not be fair to John Kennedy to portray his conception of international politics solely in terms of preoccupation with a worldwide communist offensive. As he remarked in
1961 about his foreign aid program, his aim was not merely
"negatively to fight Communism"; [39] he had, he stated many
times, a far more positive vision, of a world beyond the Cold
War. The keynote of Kennedy's conception of a new world
community was the idea of "diversity."

One of the clearest expressions of the theme of diversity
can be found in Kennedy's 1962 State of the Union message. He
stated that whatever the vicissitudes of American foreign
policy,

> our basic goal remains the same: a peaceful world
> community of free and independent states—free to
> choose their own future and their own system, so
> long as it does not threaten the freedom of others. . . .
> Some may choose forms and ways that we would not
> choose for ourselves—but it is not for us that they are
> choosing. We can welcome diversity—the
> Communists cannot. For we offer a world of
> choice—they offer a world of coercion. And the way
> of the past shows clearly that freedom, not coercion,
> is the wave of the future.[40]

This praise for diversity—this promise that America would
accept and even welcome diverse social, political, and economic
forms around the globe—cannot be dismissed simply as airy
rhetoric. For under Kennedy American foreign policy did begin
to move away from the rigid conception of a bipolar world
which Harry Truman had first enunciated (in the Truman
Doctrine) and which John Foster Dulles had turned into dogma. For example, Kennedy discarded Dulles' famous principle
that neutralism was immoral. He declared that a policy of
neutrality might sometimes make good sense for underdeveloped nations who were rightfully preoccupied with questions of internal development. And foreign aid or friendly gestures now flowed toward neutralist states which had only recently felt the American wrath.

Even more notable than Kennedy's acceptance of
neutralism was his appreciation of the spirit of national independence manifest throughout the formerly colonized areas of
the world. He declared America to be firmly on the side of those
seeking independence and social progress in Asia, Africa, the
Middle East, and Latin America. "Their revolution is the
greatest in human history. They seek an end to injustice, tyr-
anny, and exploitation." [41] While there were serious problems,
as will be shown, in Kennedy's understanding of that revolution, his sympathy for nationalist aspirations was genuine and
deep. It could be seen in numerous details of his foreign policy,
such as his respectful and gracious welcoming to the White
House of political leaders from the brand-new nations of Africa.

Kennedy's adoption of diversity as one of his central themes thus represented a real advance over the foreign policy of the Eisenhower-Dulles era—an advance in prudence, in flexibility, in humane sympathy. But did it also, as Kennedy's admirers have argued, represent a search for a conception of international life outside the familiar boundaries of the Cold War? Perhaps. But if the theme of diversity sometimes pointed beyond the Cold War, it more often slid right back into it. In the realm of worldwide struggle that Kennedy inhabited, it was probably inevitable that the ideal of diversity, however authentic its origins, would be turned into an ideological weapon.

The passage quoted above from the 1962 State of the Union Address indicates the kind of Cold War uses to which the theme could easily be put. Tolerance of diversity could be made into a new dimension of Cold War competition, a dimension in which America, with its pluralist tradition, fared far better than the communists. Even history—the communists' favorite justification—could be invoked against them. "No one who examines the modern world can doubt that the great currents of history are carrying the world away from the monolithic idea towards the pluralistic idea—away from communism and towards national independence and freedom." [42] Finally, the theme of diversity offered yet another opportunity to brand the communists as proponents of a "world of coercion," implacable foes of the American ideal of freedom of choice.

As an ideological weapon, there was an important element of mystification in Kennedy's conception of diversity. It distorted developments in the communist world, maintaining the image of a monolithic communism at a time when the fragmentation of the communist bloc was becoming increasingly apparent. (Even Kennedy sometimes commented upon that fragmentation.) Far more important, it presented a false picture of America's role in the world. Proclaiming that the United States would respect whatever form of society a nation independently fashioned, it helped to hide from view the enormous role played by U.S. aid, investments, and military ties in molding other societies to a shape Americans found desirable. It promised a new and tolerant noninterventionism even as the theoreticians of nation-building and counterinsurgency in the Kennedy Administration were constructing ever more sophisticated tools of intervention.

Respect for diversity not only disguised interventionism; somewhat paradoxically, it could also be used to justify interventionism. If the United States respected and welcomed diversity, it might have to send money, arms, even troops to other countries to protect diversity from its enemies. The idea that America would have to be the guardian of the "world of diversity" is evident in the words of W. W. Rostow:

> We look forward to the emergence of strong, assertive nations which, out of their own traditions and aspirations, create their own forms of modern society. We take it as our duty—and our interest—to help maintain the integrity and the independence of this vast modernization process. . . .[43]

In practice, too, the idea of diversity did not carry the Kennedy Administration very far from its Cold War posture. A case in point was its unrelenting hostility to Castro's Cuba; that hostility suggested some of the limits to the diversity Kennedy would accept. He would not, he made it clear, tolerate any new emergence of communism in the world. As Richard J. Walton has observed, "It did not seem to occur to Kennedy or his advisers that there might be circumstances when a people, through revolution, might validly choose communism as offering the best path to economic and social development." [44] Nor would Kennedy, as he told Khrushchev at Vienna, accept any revolution that was not peaceful, or adversely affected American prestige or the balance of power. So Kennedy consistently set himself, despite his expressed sympathies for the process of revolutionary change in the Third World, against the actual revolutions of the time.

The limits were further revealed by Kennedy's attitude toward the Goulart government in Brazil. The moderate Goulart was not a particularly effective President; he enacted no real social reforms, while the Brazilian economy deteriorated through unchecked inflation. Yet this was not his greatest sin in American eyes. Where Goulart particularly alienated the Kennedy Administration was in his "independent" foreign policy, which involved a bid for greater Brazilian leadership in Latin America, and a measure of resistance to America's efforts at isolating Cuba in the Western Hemisphere. (American disfavor was also stimulated by the nationalization of an ITT subsidiary carried out by Leonel Brizola, Governor of Rio Grande do Sul and the brother-in-law of Goulart, and by exaggerated reports of leftist infiltration into the Goulart government.) Goulart transgressed against the conditions of acceptable diversity; Brazil's punishment was a massive cut in American foreign aid. AID (Agency for International Development) expenditures in Brazil were reduced from $81.8 million in fiscal 1962 to $38.7 million in fiscal 1963 and $15.1 million in fiscal 1964. In contrast, when a coup by right-wing generals overthrew Goulart in the spring of 1964, U.S. aid jumped back up to $122.1 million.[45]

What can be concluded about Kennedy's conception of a world of diversity? That conception may well have represented Kennedy's best understanding of the forces of change at work in the modern world. And it suggested that his fundamental impulses toward the aspirations of other nations (particularly the "emerging" ones) were good. But it was too eloquent—and too convenient—a conception for Kennedy to resist using it as Cold War propaganda and ideological rationalization. And so the ideal of a world of diversity became another weapon in that "relentless struggle in every corner of the globe" which Kennedy was waging. Ultimately it was of a piece with the theory of the Soviet offensive, in John F. Kennedy's comprehensive new version of the Cold War.

3

"The Hour of Maximum Danger"

In the summer of 1961, and again in the fall of 1962, the United States and the Soviet Union confronted one another dangerously near the nuclear abyss. Twice in these eighteen months the two governments deliberated military measures, up to and including nuclear warfare, while their populations looked on with apprehension. The first two years of John F. Kennedy's presidential term were, in this respect, a chilling period—and a curious one, if they are contrasted to the preceding eight years. For despite all the talk of "brinkmanship" in the Eisenhower-Dulles era of foreign policy, there was really nothing in that era comparable to the Berlin crisis of 1961 and the Cuban missile crisis of 1962. John Foster Dulles had theorized about the "brink"; John Kennedy twice stood there.

The situation becomes even more curious when Kennedy's presidential rhetoric is reexamined. Clearly visible in that rhetoric is a penchant for the apocalyptic. We have already looked at Kennedy's first State of the Union message, with its prophecy of the "hour of maximum danger." A similar apocalyptic note—of imminent disaster or triumph—appeared often in Kennedy's speeches. He concluded his address to the United

Nations in September of 1961, for example, with the following words: "The events and decisions of the next ten months may well decide the fate of man for the next ten thousand years. There will be no avoiding those events." [1]

Kennedy spoke frequently of the need to avoid situations that might lead toward nuclear confrontation between the superpowers. Yet his apocalyptic utterances hinted that he was prepared for, indeed expected, such confrontations. Much of the scenario for his Presidency seemed to be already sketched out when he told the National Association of Broadcasters on May 8, 1961:

> There can be no doubt . . . that this determined and powerful system [i.e., communism] will subject us to many tests of nerve and will in the coming years—in Berlin, in Asia, in the Middle East, in this hemisphere. We will face challenge after challenge, as the communists, armed with all the resources and advantages of the police state, attempt to shift the balance of power in their direction.[2]

The apocalyptic tone, the sense of universal challenge, the recurrent atmosphere of crisis in which the Kennedy Administration lived—these were rooted, in part, in Kennedy's view of world politics. In this sense the present chapter continues the story begun in the preceding one. Yet it was not this view alone that created what could be termed a "crisis mentality" in the Kennedy Administration. Before turning to a consideration of Kennedy's two great crises—over Berlin in 1961 and Cuba in 1962—it is important to see how several features of the man came together to produce this "crisis mentality," in which the cautious pragmatist seemingly found his fulfillment in the frightening moments of global crisis.

The notion of crisis was, as indicated, inherent in Kennedy's theory of contemporary history. That theory consistently magnified the import of events, transforming localized affairs into critical battles in a global struggle between America and

Russia. Berlin, Cuba, and Vietnam all became challenges to the United States, to American nerve, determination, courage. Each brought into being a crisis of will, a decisive moment where the United States either proved its resolve or else the space of freedom in the world inexorably began to vanish. Crisis was, for Kennedy, the inescapable mark of his times.

His theory of the Presidency also highlighted the notion of crisis. Kennedy was inclined to regard presidential power as a relatively fixed quantity. Hence it could be spread out and spent on assorted ventures, such as acts of legislation, or it could be banked for use in a moment of crisis. The latter course generally appealed to Kennedy; he preferred to avoid bruising and divisive domestic fights in order to have his power and authority intact when the inevitable communist challenge came. Kennedy's caution in domestic affairs was not incongruent with his romantic and risky approach to foreign affairs; it was precisely that caution which, he thought, made it possible for him to take the risks.

If theory oriented Kennedy toward moments of crisis, so too did temperament. While he devoted energy and skill to ongoing political life, he seemed, at least to some observers, really to be at his best in periods of crisis. I can only speculate here, but from the testimony of a number of those who watched him, it seems likely that crises stimulated and excited something in Kennedy. Hugh Sidey, for instance, noticed that as the Berlin crisis deepened in the summer of 1961,

> Kennedy's own sense seemed sharper. He was brusque, more to the point. He enjoyed finding solutions to the problems as they came along, and he showed more confidence in himself and in his conclusions.[3]

The final reason that I bring forward for Kennedy's "crisis mentality" is perhaps the most important. I want to argue here that Kennedy's orientation toward crises—amounting almost to a sub rosa yearning for them—reflected the poverty of his pragmatic liberalism. Kennedy clearly wanted greatness, wanted the accolades of both present and future. Yet he was devoid of vision, empty of any substantial ideas about bettering American society or reshaping the fabric of American political life. Neither dramatic encounter with the ills of American social life nor the slow and patient enterprise of educating the American public appealed to Kennedy, because his domestic goals were conventionally framed and shallowly held.

Greatness, for Kennedy, could not lie in the task of changing society. Still, an alternate path to greatness existed, a path sanctified by American history: heroic action in moments of crisis. Lincoln in the Civil War, Wilson in World War I, Roosevelt in the Great Depression—it had become almost a formula for American historians and political scientists that Presidents established their greatness in those moments which posed the gravest dangers to the nation. In those moments, when the stakes were highest, institutional mechanisms gave way to personalized deeds, and an American political leader could reach for glory. Kennedy apparently accepted this formula. Thus, it would not matter that he stood for no great ideas or principles; his performance in crises would determine his historical stature. It is not surprising that Kennedy's admirers have been preoccupied with the Cuban missile crisis as the towering event of his Presidency. He too wished it to be his monument.

As we watch Kennedy in action in the Berlin and Cuban crises, his "crisis mentality" should be kept in mind. For that inclination to approach events in apocalyptic terms—to invest them with decisive global significance and consider them critical enough for the supreme risk of nuclear war to be accepted—shaped his response in each case. Kennedy's "crisis mentality" did not invent the tense situations in Berlin or Cuba, but it had a profound influence upon the manner in which he handled those situations. The previous chapter argued that John Kennedy's early presidential statements and actions played a key role in initiating the tense and dangerous period that began in the summer of 1961. Now, without seeking to absolve the Soviet Union for its part in these eighteen months, I wish to make perhaps an even more damaging charge against Kennedy: he was primarily responsible for the gravity of the crises that this period witnessed.

The Berlin crisis of 1961 was, in the view of the Kennedy Administration, a relatively simple matter. The Soviet Union was once again probing Western resolve; America (and its allies) would either withstand the test or else watch global influence and prestige slip away. But a genuine understanding of what was at stake in Berlin in 1961 must begin with a recognition of how complex the situation was, of how many tangled questions of history, geography, diplomacy, military strategy it featured.[4]

At the end of the Second World War the victorious Allies had divided Germany into four zones; the city of Berlin, in the midst of the Soviet zone, was similarly divided. This division was expected to be temporary, with final determination of the German question to be made at a subsequent peace conference. But the plans for a conference faded as the Cold War spread over Europe in the years 1945–48. Whether the Soviet Union hoped in these years for a reunited Germany under communist control is still a subject of historical debate; it seems obvious from their blockade of the Western zones of Berlin in 1948 that the Soviets at least hoped to drive their former allies out of the German capital. But the determined Western airlift frustrated Soviet ambitions. The blockade was ended in 1949, with somewhat ironic consequences; for as Soviet aggressiveness in Berlin and Germany started to recede, Western commitments—emotional as well as political—deepened.

In the following years the Western zones were consolidated into the German Federal Republic, while the Soviet zone in the east became the German Democratic Republic. Western policy now looked toward rearming the new West German state and incorporating it into the NATO alliance. This clearly triggered Russian fears; beginning with the Stalin notes of 1952, the Soviet Union adopted a conciliatory position on the German question. In their effort to head off West German rearmament, the Soviets were even prepared to accept the liquidation of their East German satellite. Their proposals in these years called for the reunification of Germany with, however, a stipulation that the new German state remain neutral between East and West.

Now it was the turn of the Western powers to reveal their ambitions. They insisted repeatedly that any German peace treaty must be based upon free all-German elections and a guarantee that a reunited Germany would be able to choose its own alliances (namely, NATO). As the latter condition was obviously unacceptable to the Soviets, the Western position, in this era dominated by John Foster Dulles and Konrad Adenauer, in actuality reflected a lack of interest in serious negotiations. Rather, a rearmed West Germany was made the heart of a new Western alliance, providing its architects with the dream of a structure of power so formidable that it would force a Russian withdrawal from the eastern sector.[5]

In the mid-1950s, the Soviet position shifted once more. As West Germany was rearmed, and as the Western powers continued to reject any idea of a reunified but neutral Germany, the Soviets dropped that idea and attempted instead to stabilize their shaky hold over East Germany and Eastern Europe. Having themselves recognized West Germany in 1955, the Soviets now sought Western recognition for East Germany, hoping thereby to make definitive the division of the country. It was this objective that most observers saw as underlying Khrushchev's Berlin ultimatum of 1958—an ultimatum threatening the signing of a separate peace treaty between Russia and East Germany unless Allied occupation of West Berlin was terminated within six months.

The response of the Eisenhower Administration to this ultimatum is interesting in light of the response the Kennedy Administration was to make to a similar ultimatum a few years later. For the earlier response was diplomatic, and relatively low keyed. The Eisenhower Administration refused to negotiate under the terms of an ultimatum, but coupled that refusal with a willingness promptly to resume talks on the German question. Khrushchev eventually dropped his deadline and agreed to these talks.[6]

Not surprisingly, given the respective positions of the Western allies and the Soviet Union, the talks that followed did not even approach a resolution of the Berlin and German problems. As John Kennedy took office in January 1961, those problems remained as complex, as difficult, and as potentially explosive as ever.

Kennedy came to the Presidency well versed in these past events. He possessed, in addition, a sophisticated understanding of the Soviet Union's political and economic stake in East Germany. Yet when, before becoming President, he talked of Berlin, any recognition he might have had of the intransigence and ambition on *both* sides invariably gave way to the orthodox Cold War view in which the fate of Europe, and perhaps the entire outcome of the Cold War itself, hinged upon Western resistance to Soviet designs on Berlin. Kennedy predicted, in a 1959 interview, a further Soviet threat to the city and defined that threat in terms to which he would return in 1961: "It's going to be a test of nerve and will." [7] In that same interview he made clear what his response to such a threat would be: "You must demonstrate your determination to fight." [8]

During his first few months as President, Kennedy again indicated that he was expecting trouble over Berlin. Dean Acheson, Democratic dean of the Cold War, was asked in March 1961 to undertake a study of the German situation. Acheson was given the chance to set the initial terms for the

Administration's debate on the American position toward Berlin, and he responded with an apocalyptic vision that exceeded even Kennedy's. Imperiously sweeping away the tangle of historical and political factors, his report to Kennedy proclaimed, according to Schlesinger, that

> West Berlin was not a problem but a pretext. Khrushchev's *démarche* had nothing to do with Berlin, Germany or Europe. His object . . . was not to rectify a local situation but to test the general American will to resist; his hope was that, by making us back down on a sacred commitment, he could shatter our world power and influence. This was a simple conflict of wills, and, until it was resolved, any efforts to negotiate the Berlin issue per se would be fatal. Since there was nothing to negotiate, willingness on our part to go to the conference table would be taken in Moscow as evidence of weakness and make the crisis so much the worse.[9]

Since Acheson's thesis postulated a test of will, much of his analysis centered upon the military countermeasures the West could take in the event of a Soviet move against Berlin. His preference was for a probe by a NATO division down the autobahn to West Berlin. "There was a substantial chance, Acheson said, that the necessary military preparations would by themselves cause Khrushchev to alter his purpose; but he added frankly that there was also a substantial possibility that nuclear war might result." [10]

When Harold Macmillan and his Foreign Secretary, Lord Home, came to Washington in April, Kennedy invited Acheson to the discussions on Berlin. The British (as well as a few of the Americans present) were understandably disturbed by Acheson's harsh logic. They complained further that while Khrushchev was talking about a peace conference and a treaty, the Western allies were left without any negotiating position at all. The allies were in West Berlin by the right of conquest, but after sixteen years the right of conquest was wearing thin. As Kennedy looked on, "poker-faced" (Schlesinger), Acheson then sarcastically replied to the British that "perhaps it was western power which was wearing thin."[11]

Armed with Acheson's conclusions (though not yet with his final report), convinced that Berlin was the "touchstone" of American integrity and that Khrushchev would utilize it to probe Western unity and resolve,[12] Kennedy journeyed to Vienna for his meeting with the Soviet Premier in June of 1961. When Khrushchev returned to his 1958 threat of signing a separate peace treaty with East Germany, Kennedy thus had a ready-made interpretation for Soviet motives. But other motives could easily have been adduced for Khrushchev's move. Obtaining Western recognition for the German Democratic Republic remained a vital goal for Khrushchev in 1961. It had become particularly pressing in recent months, as the swelling flow of refugees through East Berlin to the West drained East Germany of trained manpower and brought it to the verge of economic disaster. Khrushchev had to act swiftly to protect the Soviet position in Eastern Europe.[13] And, given the bellicosity of American statements and actions in the preceding months, it was not surprising that when he did act, it was in an aggressive manner. Kennedy had ignored gestures of conciliation (such as the Soviets' release of the RB-47 fliers) and adopted the rhetoric of global struggle; in moving to deal with the long-festering German problem, Khrushchev apparently decided that it was now his turn to start sounding tough.

The exchange on this subject at Vienna was sharp on both sides. Khrushchev began by describing the German situation as intolerable. After sixteen years there was still no peace treaty; meanwhile, the continued rearming of a West German state openly dissatisfied with present boundaries (the Oder-Neisse line) endangered European security. The Soviet Union desired a peace conference and a treaty; if the Western allies would not take part, Russia would sign the treaty alone. Western occupation rights in Berlin would then be at an end. Khrushchev promised that afterward there would be no interference with the internal affairs of West Berlin, though agreement on Western access would have to be worked out with the East German regime.

Kennedy replied that Berlin presented a matter of supreme national security to the United States. If America meekly accepted the loss of rights won by conquest and guaranteed by contract, its commitments around the world would be dismissed as mere scraps of paper. The abandonment of Berlin would, Kennedy declared, entail the isolation of the United States—and "he had not become President of the United States to acquiesce in the isolation of his country. . . ." [14]

The two leaders next traded accusations about endangering the peace. Kennedy acknowledged that the situation in Berlin was not satisfactory, but "conditions were unsatisfactory all over, and this was not the time to upset the world balance of power." [15] Khrushchev insisted that it was Western intransigence that kept alive Berlin tensions; his aim was not to shift the balance of power, but only to pacify the most explosive trouble spot in the world. The conversation grew harsher, as each side invoked the threat of war as the likely consequence of the other's proposed course of action. It ended ominously; Khrushchev reaffirmed his intention of concluding a peace treaty with East Germany in December, and Kennedy retorted, in parting, " 'It will be a cold winter.' " [16]

In the weeks following the Vienna meeting the atmosphere of confrontation persisted. On June 21, Khrushchev, wearing his Soviet army uniform, announced to the Russian people that a German peace treaty would be signed by the end of the year. On June 28, Kennedy told a news conference that the peace was now threatened by a new Berlin crisis that was "Soviet-manufactured." [17] Yet a few signs began to surface that the Russians might want to avoid a collision course, and that the impending Berlin confrontation might be averted. On July 5, for example, Arthur Schlesinger, Jr., was visited by a friend from the Soviet embassy. The Russian tried to reassure Schlesinger that his government had absolutely no designs whatsoever on West Berlin. When Schlesinger protested that Russian guarantees regarding Berlin guaranteed nothing, the Russian replied, " 'Well, if you do not consider these guarantees adequate, why don't you propose your own guarantees? All we want to do is to have a chance to discuss these things.' " [18]

The Russian desire to talk over the Berlin and German situations was certainly not unreasonable. After all, "it *was* 1961, sixteen years after the end of World War II, long past time for a German peace treaty." [19] Besides, the Soviets had serious problems in Germany, and a Western refusal to discuss those problems could only force them to more drastic measures. Nor was Western recognition of East Germany such a farfetched demand; it would simply have legalized a status quo that could be changed by the West only at an unacceptable cost. But the West did not even have to go this far. All that was required at the moment was an agreement to talk about German affairs. Such an agreement by the Eisenhower Administration had eased Berlin tensions in 1958; a similar agreement would, in fact, bring this Berlin crisis to a close later in 1961.

Considerations similar to these appealed to some in the Kennedy Administration. A group composed of Arthur Schlesinger, Jr., Abram Chayes, Carl Kaysen, and part-time adviser Henry Kissinger wrote several memoranda for Kennedy suggesting that too much attention was being paid to military planning and too little attention to the possibilities for negotiation. These men also were inclined to evaluate the Berlin problem as more limited and localized than the Acheson thesis would have it. Others, too, chimed in with criticisms of the hard-line Achesonian position: Ambassador to the Soviet Union Thompson, Senators Mansfield, Fulbright, Humphrey, and Pell. Yet that position, or some variant of it, remained the dominant one in Washington in the summer of 1961.

As Kennedy pondered possible American moves through

June and July, he listened to all sides of the continuing Berlin debate within his administration. He expressed interest in the Schlesinger group's memoranda. He also gave his attention to the traditional State Department view—that the Soviet objective in Berlin was to force Western abandonment of the city, thereby alienating West Germany from its allies, detaching it from NATO, and beginning the neutralization of Western Europe. But of all the explanations for Berlin, Kennedy still seemed most attracted to Acheson's test-of-will hypothesis. Indeed, he interpreted that test in very personal terms. He told James Wechsler of the *New York Post* that

> what worried him was that Khrushchev might interpret his reluctance to wage nuclear war as a symptom of an American loss of nerve. Some day, he said, the time might come when he would have to run the supreme risk to convince Khrushchev that conciliation did not mean humiliation. "If Khrushchev wants to rub my nose in the dirt," he told Wechsler, "it's all over." [20]

Kennedy ultimately rejected the course of action favored by Acheson and his backers: proclamation of a national emergency. This would have entailed immediate expansion of the military and $5 billion added to the defense budget, standby price and wage controls, and new taxation. But when the President did reveal to the nation his plans regarding Berlin, in a television address on July 25, they hardly seemed much of a defeat for the Acheson line either in tone or in specifics. Kennedy's speech on this occasion was crucial, for it sent Berlin tensions soaring to a new height. As Hugh Sidey observed: "It brought back memories of other voices from the early 1940's. The talk was war talk." [21]

Berlin, Kennedy told the American public, was not a limited problem; rather it had to be seen in the context of a communist offensive unlimited in its global ambitions.

The immediate threat to free men is in West Berlin.
But that isolated outpost is not an isolated problem.
The threat is worldwide. Our effort must be equally
wide and strong, and not be obsessed by any single
manufactured crisis. We face a challenge in Berlin, but
there is also a challenge in Southeast Asia. . . . We face
a challenge in our own hemisphere, and indeed
wherever else the freedom of human beings is at
stake.[22]

That challenge, Kennedy made clear in a restatement of
the Acheson thesis, was primarily a challenge to American
resolve. West Berlin, he declared, "has now become—as never
before—the great testing place of Western courage and will." [23]
And Kennedy was ready to take up the gauntlet.

I hear it said that West Berlin is militarily untenable.
And so was Bastogne. And so, in fact, was Stalingrad.
Any dangerous spot is tenable if men—brave
men—will make it so. . . . We do not want to fight—but
we have fought before.[24]

To match his rhetoric, Kennedy detailed an immediate
American military buildup (the third in his first six months in
office). Additional defense appropriations of $3.25 billion were
requested from the Congress. The size of each of the military
services was to be expanded, draft calls for the coming months
were doubled and tripled, and 150,000 reservists were called to
active duty immediately. If it was not a proclamation of national emergency in form, it certainly seemed so in fact. The
sense of emergency took on its most frightening aspect in a
section of the speech on civil defense. Requesting $207 million
for an expanded civil defense program, Kennedy—whether intentionally or not—evoked the prospect of nuclear war. "In the
coming months, I hope to let every citizen know what steps he
can take without delay to protect his family in case of
attack." [25]

After all these ominous words, Kennedy did hold out some

prospect for a peaceful solution to the Berlin question. Toward the end of the speech there were several paragraphs that reflected the thinking of the Schlesinger group. Expressing a willingness to consider arrangements that would guarantee the Soviet Union's legitimate security interests, Kennedy stated in these paragraphs that the United States was "ready to search for peace—in quiet exploratory talks—in formal or informal meetings." [26] It was a hopeful note but a faint one, in light of the far more numerous and dramatic military passages. And by the close of the speech, the dominant motif of bravery in confrontation had been restored. "To sum it all up: we seek peace—but we shall not surrender." [27]

The Berlin speech was a prime specimen of Kennedy's "crisis mentality." In the face of a complex political problem, he chose a dangerously simplistic and grandiose scheme of interpretation. In the face of a potentially explosive conflict between the superpowers, he chose a course of action that served greatly to magnify existing tensions. Kennedy, to his credit, did not rule out the possibility of negotiations; but he moved to mark out the lines of confrontation before diplomatic approaches were ever tried. Prior to July 25, the nature of the struggle over Berlin had still been somewhat uncertain. After Kennedy's belligerent rhetoric and announcement of a partial military mobilization on that date, the Berlin crisis of 1961 was on in earnest.

One of the most disturbing features of the "crisis mentality"—its tendency to personalize political events involving millions of people—was also exhibited in the July 25 speech. By adopting the Acheson thesis, Kennedy had reduced the Berlin question to a test of America's—and, in essence, his—courage and will. His inclination to personalize the crisis was perhaps responsible for the oddly ahistorical view of Berlin that the speech at times presented. When Kennedy proclaimed that Western courage and will were being tested at Berlin "as never before," the words seemed strange in light of the far more severe trial that the Western Allies had undergone in the 1948 block-ade. But this time it was a test of *his* will; history had been replaced here by a personal drama. Still seemingly troubled by his failure at the Bay of Pigs, and by a sense that Khrushchev thought he could be bullied, Kennedy now appeared deter-mined to prove his own political manhood, even at the cost of intensifying the crisis.

His apocalyptic tone was not lost on the American people. Public-opinion polls in the following months revealed that Americans were more worried about war breaking out than they had been at any other time in recent years. Kennedy's remarks on civil defense in particular aroused fearful fantasies in the public imagination. They helped spark a national fallout shelter craze, as business entrepreneurs raced to cater to the desperate desire for family—though not communal—survival. Ugly debate proliferated in this period about whether a man had a right to shoot a neighbor seeking entry to the limited space of his family shelter. Significantly, amid all these fears there was little opposition to Kennedy's actions; the American people accepted the President's definition of the crisis even as they were terrified by its implications.

If the speech was designed to impress Khrushchev with American determination, its visible result was only to anger him. As Arthur Schlesinger, Jr., relates, Khrushchev was then conferring with John J. McCloy at Sochi on the subject of disarmament. The day before the speech Khrushchev had been jovial and optimistic. "The next day he told McCloy emotion-ally that the United States had declared preliminary war on the Soviet Union. It had presented an ultimatum and clearly in-tended hostilities." [28] Khrushchev did add, despite his indig-nation, an assurance to McCloy that he still had faith in Kennedy's ultimate good sense.

Soviet response to the new American "hard line" was not long in coming. On August 7, Khrushchev went on television to affirm Russian determination in the Berlin affair, to discuss mobilization of reserve troops, and to muse about the prospects of nuclear war. And on August 13, just as the United States slowly and belatedly began to work out with its allies a negotiating position on Berlin, the Soviet Union moved decisively to deal with its German problem. To choke off the growing flood of refugees, East German troops and police began that day to construct roadblocks and barricades between the two sectors of Berlin, temporary barriers that were in a few days to be replaced by an ugly concrete wall. In the face of Kennedy's military preparations, Khrushchev had thus undertaken to change the Berlin situation by force—through a ruthless action against which the West was totally powerless.

The erection of the Berlin Wall caught the Kennedy Administration by surprise. None of its scenarios had anticipated such a move; they had all centered on a threat to West Berlin, not a Soviet action within the eastern zone. As Schlesinger admitted, "evidently the test-of-will thesis had diverted attention too long from the local problems of East Germany." [29] The United States and its allies could, as the Wall went up, only transmit feeble protests to Moscow. No serious consideration was given to military action against it, for it stood, after all, on East German territory.

But as morale in West Berlin plummeted, and angry criticism filled the Western press, Kennedy quickly concluded that some kind of military gesture was necessary. Accordingly, a battle group of 1500 American troops drove across the autobahn from West Germany to West Berlin, both to probe communist intentions and to raise the spirits of the West Berliners. Reaching their destination without incident, the troops were greeted by Vice-President Johnson, who had flown there as Kennedy's emissary to reaffirm American commitments.

On that August weekend when the troops were dispatched down the autobahn, the anxiety level in Washington reached new heights. Kennedy and his associates feared that the Russians might attempt to halt the American column, and that the mission might rapidly escalate into a shooting affair. From there it was not far to full-scale military conflict. As Robert Kennedy later described these days to Hugh Sidey, "We felt war was very possible then." [30]

Interestingly, the heightened atmosphere of crisis that engulfed Washington in those days was apparent nowhere else. Absorbed in their crisis planning and scenarios, Kennedy and his men seemed to inhabit a far more foreboding realm than either their allies or their adversaries. Even Americans on the potential battlefront in Germany did not share Kennedy's sense that this might be an apocalyptic moment. Witness to this was given by General Bruce C. Clarke, American army commander in Europe in 1961:

> Writing after his retirement, General Clarke even refused to call these hours a time of "crisis." "What we have had in the Berlin situation have been various forms of harassment," he said. "They have not come to the crisis state as I would define a crisis." The further away from Berlin a person got and the nearer he came to Washington, the graver the situation seemed, he declared.[31]

Khrushchev, having achieved his immediate objective by building the Berlin Wall, had no intention of pushing the crisis any further, and the American army probe was uneventful. Kennedy too seemed to draw back after his military gesture; he now began to show much greater interest than before in negotiations. Perhaps he had been sobered by the dangerous military maneuvers, which proved to be of such little consequence. Or perhaps, as Richard J. Walton has suggested, Kennedy "began to be aware that history could hardly justify nuclear catastrophe on the basis that an agreement to talk things over constituted a fatal weakness of American resolve." [32] Whatever his reasons, Kennedy now heeded those in his administration who had for weeks been pressing for America to take the diplomatic initiative. He instructed Secretary of State Rusk, on August 21, to notify the allies that the United States planned to issue an invitation to negotiations before the first of September.

Exploratory talks on Berlin began in September, as Rusk and Andrei Gromyko met at the United Nations. Little was accomplished in these and subsequent talks. Nevertheless, the Berlin crisis of the summer of 1961 had faded by mid-fall. When Khrushchev told a Party Congress in October that the West was now interested in seeking a solution to the German problem and that he was therefore dropping his December deadline for a peace treaty, it was essentially over. The two sides were still far apart on Berlin, but, as Schlesinger noted, "in the end the substance of negotiations turned out to matter a good deal less than the willingness to negotiate." [33]

The Berlin crisis faded away, but its burdens remained with the Kennedy Administration. Some of these were minor; for months afterward, to cite one example, complaints poured in from reservists, stuck for a year in active military duty that was no longer needed. But there were much more serious consequences to flow from Kennedy's handling of the Berlin situation. The American public had been alarmed and frightened, made fearful of nuclear disaster yet conditioned to hope for personal survival in the event of such disaster. American military spending had once again taken a jump, and the Soviets were responding in similar fashion, in a deadly new spiral of the arms race. And American-Soviet relations had been further impaired.

Above all, Berlin in the summer of 1961 provided the Kennedy Administration with its first major experience in nuclear crisis management. All the elements of Kennedy's "crisis mentality" had come into play in these months: the habit of investing events with decisive global significance, the choice of measures of confrontation to precede a diplomatic approach,

the sense of historical drama as a lonely political leader grappled with the terrors of nuclear war. These features of the Berlin
crisis remained vivid for Kennedy, obscuring what should have
been the lesson of these events—that the same restrained language and willingness to negotiate that finally calmed tensions
in the fall (as they previously had in 1958) could, if adopted at
the outset, have prevented the Berlin situation from ever
reaching the anguishing depths it did. Berlin in 1961 was, in
this sense, the prelude to Cuba in 1962. It was to be merely the
first act in the apocalyptic drama of the Kennedy Presidency.

The Cuban missile crisis has been, for most commentators,
the central event of the Kennedy years. Certainly it has been
the most exhaustively studied. Admirers and critics both have
picked over nearly every detail of those days in October 1962
when the world seemed closer to nuclear devastation than at
any other time before or since.[34] I have no desire to go over all
this ground again. So, while the analysis that follows devotes
considerable attention to the Cuban missile crisis, it focuses that
attention on certain features of the crisis which bear on the
themes already laid down in this chapter and the preceding
one. In essence, it treats the missile crisis as an episode—indeed
the key episode—in Kennedy's struggle against a worldwide
communist offensive, and as the supreme example of his crisis
approach to international affairs.

Again, as for the Berlin crisis, we must begin by filling in
some historical background. And again it is historical background that the Kennedy Administration tended to ignore.
This time, however, it was not sixteen years of Cold War history
that was slighted; it was the history of Kennedy's own prior
actions as President.

The last chapter recounted the massive buildup of strategic weaponry which Kennedy initiated in the spring of 1961,
despite knowledge of the substantial lead that the United States

already held over the Soviet Union in this area. The Soviet Union began to respond with increased arms expenditures of its own in the summer of 1961, only to be followed by a further increase in American defense spending at the height of the Berlin crisis. Even as that crisis began to recede, the Soviets once again picked up the pace in this new phase of the arms race. On August 30, they announced their decision to break the informal two-and-a-half-year moratorium on atmospheric nuclear testing. In the next two months approximately thirty major tests were carried out, including some in which fifty megaton "monster" bombs were detonated.

While the Kennedy Administration debated whether American testing should be resumed, it moved at the same time to impress upon the Russians its knowledge of their strategic inferiority, an inferiority not seriously reduced by the current round of tests. New intelligence estimates had, by this time, put Soviet ICBM strength at only 3.5 percent of what had been estimated in 1959.[35] Further, overflights of the USSR had pinpointed the location of the relatively few Soviet ICBMs. Now, in order to stop Khrushchev's boasting and restrain his inclination for adventuresome moves, Kennedy decided to inform the Soviets that he knew exactly how weak and vulnerable they were.

This information was leaked to the Soviets through several channels. Roswell Gilpatric, Deputy Secretary of Defense, delivered a speech on October 21, 1961, whose message was designed to be picked up by the Russians. Gilpatric disclosed that America had tens of thousands of nuclear-delivery vehicles, amounting to a second strike capability as extensive as that which the Russians could deliver by striking first. He announced, in effect, a "missile-gap-in-reverse" and broadcast the confidence that the United States now felt in its nuclear superiority. As a follow-up to the Gilpatric speech, the allies were briefed on relative American-Russian might—deliberately including some who were penetrated by Soviet intelligence, so that the information would reach Moscow by this channel as well.[36]

The impact of this signal has been described by Roger Hilsman.

> For the Soviets, the implications of the message were horrendous. It was not so much the fact that the Americans had military superiority—that was not news to the Soviets. What was bound to frighten them most was that the Americans *knew* that they had military superiority. For the Soviets quickly realized that to have reached this conclusion the Americans must have made an intelligence break-through and found a way to pinpoint the location of the Soviet missiles that had been deployed as well as to calculate the total numbers. . . . The whole Soviet ICBM system was suddenly obsolescent.[37]

Perhaps the Soviets would have been less alarmed if they had been assured that the United States would never launch a first strike against their now-vulnerable missile sites. But in the following months public discussion of American nuclear strategy served only to add to Soviet anxiety. In June of 1962, Secretary of Defense McNamara announced that future American nuclear planning would be based upon a counter-force rather than a counter-city strategy. American delivery vehicles would be targeted at Soviet missile sites instead of population centers. This may have sounded more humane—but to Soviet leaders it raised fears of an American first strike, obliterating Soviet retaliatory power and then holding Soviet cities as hostages while terms of surrender were dictated.

American actions in this period did nothing, in the eyes of the Soviets, to relieve the ominousness of American statements. Kennedy's 1962 budget, submitted to Congress in January, continued the expansion of missile production begun the previous year. And on March 2, 1962, Kennedy announced in a televised address that the United States was resuming atmospheric nuclear testing. The military rationale for the new series of tests was dubious, since the Kennedy Administration was aware that Soviet tests still left them well behind the United States in nuclear might. Kennedy had even been informed by one of his scientific advisers, Hans Bethe, that the Soviet tests were basically defensive in nature, aimed at developing solid-fuel missiles which could be placed in hardened sites as protection against a counter-force attack.[38] Nevertheless, Kennedy could not resist the pressures (from military men, hard-line scientists led by Edward Teller, and sectors of the public) to respond to the Soviet action with yet another escalation of the arms race. Nor, perhaps, was he too eager to resist; for if military factors did not require a resumption of testing, political and psychological factors appeared, in Kennedy's eyes, to do so. His television speech did, it is true, deny the importance of these factors, only to return to them later on: "Should we fail to follow the dictates of our own security, they [the Russians] will chalk it up, not to goodwill, but to a failure of will. . . ." [39]

The Soviet Union thus found itself in a dangerous position in 1962. Its adversary had a vast profusion of strategic weapons, plus accurate information as to where the greatly inferior Soviet forces were situated; further, leading American military figures seemed intent upon reorienting national strategy toward the notion of a potential first strike. As might be expected, the Soviet leadership became increasingly concerned about rectifying the strategic imbalance. But this was no easy task. For ICBMs took time to develop and produce; besides, they were extremely expensive, especially for a nation with a population weary of sacrificing consumer goods to defense needs.

The Soviet response to this dilemma was to place some of its cheaper and more plentiful IRBMs in Cuba. Five years before, faced with the prospect of Russian superiority in ICBMs, the United States had prevailed upon several of its European allies to accept American intermediate-range missiles on their soil. Now the Soviets adopted the same tactic, shipping intermediate-range missiles to their ally in the Western Hemisphere, Cuba.[40] There may have been other, subsidiary motives for the move, such as defending Cuba against threats of an American invasion (the "official" Soviet explanation). But it seems clear in retrospect—and it is becoming the explanation accepted by most students of the matter [41]—that the Cuban missile crisis had its origin in this reckless, but understandable, Soviet military move to restore at least some measure of strategic equilibrium.

It was a reckless move because it was carried out clandestinely and covered over with a fabric of deception; it was even more reckless because, in putting missiles in Cuba, the Soviets were touching upon John Kennedy's most sensitive spot. In the 1960 campaign Kennedy had blasted the Republicans for their failure to prevent the spread of communism to the Western Hemisphere. But the Cuban issue had boomeranged on him after the Bay of Pigs. This time it was he who had failed to halt Castro; this time it was he who bore the stigma of "losing" Cuba. He was thus extremely vulnerable to criticism on the subject of Cuba, and as reports began to reach Washington in the summer of 1962 that Soviet arms and troops were being introduced onto the island, such criticism began to mount. With an eye on the forthcoming congressional elections, Republican Senators (especially Kenneth Keating of New York and Homer Capehart of Indiana) scored Kennedy for his passivity in the face of this new Russian threat and demanded that some form of drastic action be taken.

Kennedy and his advisers were concerned about the Soviet military presence in Cuba, but they realized that it did not yet represent enough of a change to justify American military action.[42] Still, a close watch was kept on the island, and the Kennedy Administration decided to make it plain to the Russians that while "defensive" weapons in Cuba would be tolerated, "offensive" weapons were another matter. The warning

—aimed, it would appear, as much to quiet Republican critics as to restrain the Soviets—came in Kennedy's press conference of September 13:

> If at any time the Communist build-up in Cuba were to endanger or interfere with our security in any way . . . or if Cuba should ever attempt to export its aggressive purposes by force or threat of force against any nation in this hemisphere, or become an offensive military base of significant capacity for the Soviet Union, then this country will do whatever must be done to protect its own security and that of its allies. . . .[43]

The Kennedy Administration had implicitly committed itself, in advance, to drastic action if "offensive" weapons were placed in Cuba. Yet this was not judged likely. The Soviets themselves had repeatedly denied such an intention. Further, the United States Intelligence Board had reasoned, in mid-September, that since the Russians had never before positioned their missiles outside their own borders, they would probably not do so now, especially in an area so completely dominated by American power.[44]

Intelligence estimates, however, proved faulty. On October 15, photographs taken from a high-flying U-2 definitely established the presence of a missile site in the western part of Cuba. Kennedy was informed of the intelligence findings the next morning; angered by Soviet deception, his first impulse reportedly was to destroy the missiles with an air strike.[45] But he quickly concluded that discussion was needed, and summoned together his top foreign policy advisers. This group of between fifteen and twenty members, which was to meet daily throughout the crisis, became known as the Executive Committee (later dubbed "ExCom" by the press). In a perfect reflection of their self-image, they received the code name ELITE.[46] Fortunately, Kennedy "insiders" have given us a fairly full account of the deliberations of these men. For in these deliberations the historical misconceptions and crisis mentality of Kennedy and his associates are vividly revealed.

One problem that preoccupied the members of the Executive Committee was the rationale behind the Soviet move. According to Theodore Sorensen,[47] five major theories were advanced in their meetings:

1. *Cold War Politics*. The deployment of missiles in Cuba was another Soviet probe of America's will to resist. Khrushchev expected nothing stronger than an American protest to result. The United States would, consequently, look impotent in the eyes of other nations; its allies would lose faith in American commitments and move toward accommodations with the Soviet Union.
2. *Diverting Trap*. If the United States responded to the missiles with an attack on Cuba, its attention would be diverted from Khrushchev's real target: Berlin.
3. *Cuban Defense*. A Soviet satellite in the Western Hemisphere was so valuable to the Russians that they intended to defend it at any cost, whether against American invasion or impending internal collapse.
4. *Bargaining Barter*. Khrushchev hoped to use the Cuban missile sites as bargaining chips for a Berlin deal or an American withdrawal from some of its overseas bases.
5. *Missile Power*. Aware that they now faced a serious "missile gap," the Soviets had seized upon Cuban bases as the swiftest and cheapest means of increasing the number of missiles that they could direct against the United States. In addition, Cuban-based missiles had the advantage of bypassing much of the American early-warning system.

We do not know how each participant in the discussions

evaluated Soviet motives, but, thanks to Sorensen, we do know what Kennedy's judgment was. "His own analysis regarded the third and fifth theories as offering likely but insufficient motives and he leaned most strongly to the first." [48] Kennedy's choice of motives should hardly come as a surprise. For if he had recognized the Soviet move as an attempt to defend Cuba or to correct the strategic imbalance, it would have been tantamount to an admission that his own prior actions were at least partially responsible for driving the Russians on to such a desperate course. But such an admission would not square with his image of an aggressive communist movement intent upon world domination. By holding to the familiar test-of-will hypothesis, Kennedy was able to maintain that image. The placing of missiles in Cuba thus became, in his eyes, a new and vastly ambitious Soviet advance in their five-year-old global offensive. It was not a limited or strategically defensive move in the Cold War; it was a Soviet gamble for victory.

This interpretation colored debate over the central question which the Executive Committee discussed—the character of the American response. Restrained and low-key modes of action were rejected almost from the outset because they were deemed suggestive of weakness in the face of this extraordinary Soviet challenge. Since this was *the* decisive crisis, it demanded a show of strength. The deliberations of the Executive Committee reflected the "crisis mentality" at its peak, as Kennedy and his advisers, with scarcely a second thought, plunged into planning for nuclear confrontation with the Soviet Union.

A few voices in these meetings urged alternatives to confrontation. Initially, though he soon changed his position, Secretary of Defense McNamara proposed that the United States simply "sit tight." He argued that this deployment of Soviet missiles did not erase the American lead in strategic weapons or pose any new military threat to American security. As McNamara explained it, the United States had long been within range of Russia's missiles, and expected the Russians to put up with American missiles close by. Reacting calmly to Khrushchev's Cuban venture could prevent him from exaggerating the significance of the move. [49]

A more constant foe of confrontation was Ambassador to the United Nations Adlai Stevenson. Stevenson's role in these proceedings—later much maligned—was to press for a political solution to the growing military impasse. He wanted the United States government to start up the traditional machinery of diplomacy, either through discussions in the UN or through a high-level, secret approach to the Soviets. Stevenson recommended that the United States develop a negotiating position based upon the idea of neutralizing Cuba. In his proposal the Soviet missiles would be removed under UN supervision, and in turn the American naval base at Guantanamo would be closed down. In addition, he suggested that the United States might consider giving up its obsolete Turkish and Italian missile bases—though later, as his position became even more isolated, he dropped this suggestion.

To the majority of the Executive Committee, and to the President, these voices were not persuasive. As Schlesinger noted, Kennedy "regarded any political program as premature. He wanted to concentrate on a single issue—the enormity of the introduction of the missiles and the absolute necessity for their removal." [50] Posed in these terms, the situation demanded not talk but action. And so the deliberations of the Executive Committee were dominated, not by a consideration of *whether* America should take military action, but by a debate over *what kind* of military action it should take. As in the Berlin crisis, confrontation would precede any negotiations.

The time for selecting a military strategy was, these men felt, quite short. "They had, it was estimated, about ten days before the missiles would be on pads ready for firing. The deadline defined the strategy." [51] Why there should have been this deadline, since it was not expected that the missiles would be fired at the instant they became operational, is a question we shall take up later on. For the moment let us concentrate on the military alternatives contemplated in this atmosphere of grim urgency.

Three possible options were established: a blockade, an air strike, and an invasion. Debate soon centered on the first two, with the advocates of an air strike initially having the upper hand. An air strike was depicted at first as "surgical"; American planes could remove the Soviet growth quickly and cleanly with a few conventional bombs. But doubts then began to emerge. Bombing the missiles sites would, it was realized, directly assault Soviet military power and kill Soviet personnel; even then there was no guarantee that it would be completely effective in obliterating all the launching pads. The argument was seemingly clinched when Robert Kennedy declaimed against surprise attacks, warning that a sudden air strike against Cuba would be a "Pearl Harbor in reverse and . . . would blacken the name of the United States in the pages of history." [52]

As the air-strike plan lost ground, the notion of a naval blockade came to dominate the discussions. There were serious drawbacks to a blockade; it might involve a lengthy and uncertain confrontation, and if it succeeded in halting the shipment of further missiles to Cuba, it would not remove those already there. Further, it might serve as an invitation for the Soviets to retort by blockading Berlin. Still, it appeared preferable to an air strike for a number of reasons.

The argument for a blockade, Sorensen relates, emphasized its virtues as a "limited, low-level action." Institution of a blockade would provide the President with greater control over the pace of escalation. It would serve as a clear warning to Khrushchev of American seriousness, without humiliating the Soviet leader. Because it avoided casualties and did not involve an incursion into Cuban territory, it would be received more favorably in other countries than an air strike; this would facilitate OAS and Allied backing if an air strike or other drastic military move was subsequently required. [53]

These considerations ultimately prevailed, both for a majority of the Executive Committee and for Kennedy. The initial American answer to the Soviet missiles was to be the imposition of a blockade around Cuba (labeled a "quarantine" for legal and psychological reasons). In the orthodox treatments of the missile crisis this choice of a blockade has been accounted one of Kennedy's most brilliant moves.[54] His selection of a limited military measure that allowed step-by-step escalation has come in for bountiful praise. So, too, has his determination to follow a course of action that would not confront Khrushchev with sudden humiliation but would give him time to reappraise his blunder and space to make his retreat.

I do not mean to question the ingenuity of the blockade strategy or its desirability when compared with the idea of an air strike. Indeed, as several critics have observed, Kennedy handled the planning for the crisis quite skillfully—once he decided to treat it as a crisis. But all the extended and admiring discussions of Kennedy's "limited, low-level action" threaten to make us forget that the blockade was still a military move, and a dangerous one. It was, in the first place, an act of war against Cuba according to international law, despite the sanction hurriedly obtained from the Organization of American States. Second, it set up a direct naval confrontation between Soviet and American vessels, with terrifying consequences if the Soviets failed to back down. Finally, it did not at all preclude a rapid movement to more drastic measures; as we shall see later on in this chapter, there was to be a moment in the crisis when such measures were very close at hand.

With everything in readiness, Kennedy went on television on the evening of October 22, to inform the American people —and the Soviet leadership—that his administration knew of the presence of "offensive" Russian missiles on the island of

Cuba and was taking immediate steps to compel their removal. At the heart of his speech was a charge of Soviet duplicity, and a proclamation of Soviet challenge.

> This secret, swift and extraordinary build-up of
> Communist missiles, in an area well-known to have a
> special and historical relationship to the United States
> and the nations of the Western Hemisphere, in
> violation of Soviet assurances and in defiance of
> American and hemispheric policy—this sudden,
> clandestine decision to station strategic weapons for
> the first time outside of Soviet soil is a deliberately
> provocative and unjustified change in the status quo
> which cannot be accepted by this country, if our
> courage and our commitments are ever to be trusted
> again by either friend or foe.[55]

America, Kennedy declared, would undo this unjustified change at whatever price. "We will not prematurely or unnecessarily risk the costs of worldwide nuclear war in which even the fruits of victory would be ashes in our mouth, but neither will we shrink from that risk at any time it must be faced." [56]

Thus began a week of incredible tension. As people around the world were gripped by a nightmare of annihilation, Kennedy himself calculated the fearful possibilities. "The odds that the Soviets would go all the way to war, he later said, seemed to him then 'somewhere between one out of three and even.' " [57] He was going to the nuclear "brink"; yet, more than a decade later, his motives are still not altogether clear. I have already touched upon Kennedy's analysis of the Soviet move; now I want to probe a bit further into his interpretation of these events. What was at stake for John Kennedy in the Cuban missile crisis?

Kennedy certainly did not view the Russian deployment of missiles in Cuba as posing a new military hazard to American security. Rather, he regarded it as a political challenge, as he made clear in a television interview in December of 1962:

> They were planning in November to open to the
> world the fact that they had these missiles so close to
> the United States; not that they were intending to fire
> them, because if they were going to get into a nuclear
> struggle, they have their own missiles in the Soviet
> Union. But it would have politically changed the
> balance of power. It would have appeared to, and
> appearances contribute to reality.[58]

It was, in short, a question of prestige. The emplacement of missiles in Cuba was fitted, like most events in Kennedy's Presidency, into the theory of the Soviet world offensive; it became the latest, and most dramatic, Soviet attempt to shift the global balance of power in their own direction by humbling American pride. If America failed to force a Russian withdrawal in this case, if it had to make bargaining concessions in the UN or at a summit meeting to get rid of the missiles, its international prestige and influence would wither, and its allies would drift away toward the communist camp. The same test-of-will hypothesis that had governed Kennedy's response to the Berlin situation in 1961 was again in operation. But this time he saw it as the supreme test. With a grossly exaggerated scenario of Russian triumph and American decay seemingly running through his mind, he thus prepared to risk everything.

Kennedy accepted a nuclear showdown with the Soviet Union for the sake of political appearance—this much is clear. It is less clear, but still quite possible from what we know, that he may have *wanted* that showdown. As a number of writers (some of them favorable to Kennedy) have suggested, he may have found in Khrushchev's Cuban gamble a convenient opportunity for a confrontation he had long been seeking.

Psychological reasons may have led him to desire a test of will with Khrushchev. As we have seen, Kennedy's concern with demonstrating his toughness amounted almost to an obsession, particularly after the Bay of Pigs disaster and Vienna meeting led him to believe that Khrushchev considered him weak. He had talked tough over Berlin, but the results had been inconclusive. So in the fall of 1962, Kennedy, as Henry Pachter

concluded in his early study of the missile crisis, was still waiting for a test to present itself. "He needed an opportunity to
show his mettle. That this opportunity came in Cuba may have
given him additional satisfaction. Here was a chance to cancel
out last year's humiliation." [59]

Political reasons, too, may have motivated Kennedy actively to seek a showdown. For if he envisioned a series of
disasters ensuing from American irresolution in the face of
Cuban missiles, he also appears to have believed that forcing
the removal of the missiles would be a great Cold War triumph.
Here was a chance decisively to turn the tide, to arrest the
Soviet advance and send Russian forces scurrying back to their
own territory. The field of battle was favorable—American military preponderance in the Caribbean (as compared, say, to
Berlin) was overwhelming. So too was the propaganda field,
thanks to Soviet deceptions. Since he had taken office, Kennedy
had been trying to mount a major counteroffensive against
what he believed was a Soviet drive for world domination; in
October 1962 that counteroffensive reached its peak, as Kennedy sought to defeat the Soviet drive once and for all.[60]

If Kennedy seemingly wanted a showdown, Khrushchev
plainly did not. For a man supposedly bent upon a test of will
with his American adversary, Khrushchev was remarkably
quick to flinch. His first, angry response to the blockade was to
denounce it as an act of "piracy." But soon, though he did not
back down from his position, the fear of nuclear war came to
dominate everything he said. That fear was exhibited in his
letters to Bertrand Russell, who had appealed to his forbear-
ance, and to U Thant, who had requested both sides to suspend
their converging courses of action for the sake of negotiations.
And it was exhibited in his crucial letters to Kennedy; thus, Elie
Abel says of Khrushchev's letter of October 26: "Even in
paraphrase it reads like the nightmare outcry of a frightened
man.[61]

In accordance with the Soviet desire to pull back from a
fatal confrontation, their ships en route to Cuba did not at-

tempt to run the American blockade. At first they stopped in place; on Thursday and Friday, October 25 and 26, they turned around. Tensions momentarily abated—yet the crisis was far from over. Soviet missiles were still in Cuba. And the American position remained unchanged.

> Clearly, the President was keeping the pressure on. The missiles in Cuba would simply have to be removed. Nothing else would do. And until that happened, the blockade must remain in force.[62]

A path out of the impasse seemed to open up, however, on Friday, October 26, when a new Soviet proposal was received in Washington. First in an informal contact, and later in the day in a letter to Kennedy, Khrushchev offered to withdraw the missiles from Cuba under United Nations supervision in exchange for an American pledge not to invade the island. His desire for a peaceful settlement was underlined by his impassioned appeal to Kennedy: "Mr. President, we and you ought not now to pull on the ends of the rope in which you have tied the knot of war, because the more we pull, the tighter the knot will be tied." [63]

The majority of Kennedy's Executive Committee were cheered by the unexpected Soviet offer, and they assembled at the White House on the morning of October 27 to begin drafting a favorable reply. But as they met, a new message from Khrushchev arrived. The Russian Premier had appended an additional clause: if the Americans wanted Soviet missile bases in Cuba dismantled, they must dismantle their own bases along the Soviet border in Turkey. Walter Lippmann had publicly recommended (as had Adlai Stevenson in private) such a swap of bases earlier in the week; now the Soviets, citing the equality of rights between great powers, demanded it as a quid pro quo.

Kennedy and his advisers could have gone along with this new Soviet condition. The missiles in Turkey were obsolete and useless; the President, in fact, had earlier ordered their removal, only to be frustrated by Turkish touchiness. Further, the new Soviet proposal was, as Robert Kennedy later acknowledged, "not unreasonable." [64] Outside the United States few people could see the difference between "defensive" missiles in Turkey and "offensive" missiles in Cuba. But President Kennedy immediately rejected the proposal; such a swap was completely unacceptable to him. If it would not have resulted in any military loss to the United States, it would still have meant, in his view, a loss in prestige. American commitments, particularly to the NATO allies, would be called into question by a relinquishment of the Turkish bases in the face of Soviet pressure. Kennedy would withdraw the missiles later, when the crisis had been resolved; for now he would stand firm.

October 27 was, at least for Kennedy's inner circle, the most ominous day of the whole missile crisis. For despite the fact that the Soviets were showing an interest in a settlement, and that the positions of the two sides were really not that far apart, Kennedy decided to bring the crisis to a head. He made it clear to the Russians that unless they immediately dropped the idea of a trade of bases and returned to their original proposal, major American military action would be initiated in a matter of days.

Robert Kennedy was selected at this juncture to approach the Russians. At a meeting with Soviet Ambassador Dobrynin the President's brother rejected the idea of a quid pro quo—though he implicitly promised that the missiles in Turkey would be withdrawn once the crisis ended. His chief task, however, was to present the Soviets with a thinly veiled ultimatum. He told Dobrynin that

> time was running out. We had only a few more
> hours—we needed an answer immediately from the
> Soviet Union. I said we must have it the next day.[65]

Nor was this a bluff. Preparations for military action were rapidly completed; according to Robert McNamara, "the air strike was ready to go in forty-eight hours." [66] And an invasion of Cuba was set to follow. Talk of gradual, step-by-step escalation was abandoned; Kennedy was within two days of plunging into the most dangerous conflict the world would ever witness.

This extraordinary haste has never been satisfactorily explained. In the accounts of the missile crisis by Kennedy associates the rationale usually put forward is the "deadline"—the missiles had to be taken out, by American bombs if not by Soviet agreement, before the date upon which they became operational. But, as noted earlier, no one expected that the Soviet missiles would be fired as soon as they became operational. The deadline they posed was scarcely a military one, for they could have been removed through negotiations at a later date. An explanation hence must be sought along other lines.

The actual deadline seemed to be compounded of both domestic and foreign pressures. With the congressional elections only a few days away, the completion of work on the missile sites would presumably have spelled political trouble for the Democrats; the Republicans would maul them for permitting IRBMs to be targeted on the United States from only ninety miles away.[67] Nor would the consequences be any better in terms of America's, and Kennedy's, image and position abroad. The missiles, once operational, would be a fait accompli which Kennedy had failed to prevent. Khrushchev might even decide to raise his bargaining sights. The same considerations of prestige and appearance that had led Kennedy into confrontation with the Soviet Union thus compelled him to carry the confrontation to its climax. Having decided to force, rather than negotiate, the withdrawal of the Soviet missiles, the logic of the situation now required him to begin a major escalation of force. There is no more telling commentary on Kennedy's "crisis mentality" than this preparation for apocalypse on the eve of the crisis' resolution. This time, as Robert Kennedy makes chillingly clear in *Thirteen Days,* what John Kennedy had started only Nikita Khrushchev could stop:

> What hope there was now rested with Khrushchev's
> revising his course within the next few hours. It was a
> hope, not an expectation. The expectation was a
> military confrontation by Tuesday and possibly
> tomorrow. . . .[68]

To the relief of everyone, Khrushchev did stop it. On the morning of October 28, he transmitted another message to Kennedy, agreeing to remove the Cuban bases in exchange for the no-invasion pledge. Kennedy, wisely choosing not to gloat in this hour over his adversary's retreat, accepted the offer in diplomatic language: "I welcome Chairman Khrushchev's statesmanlike decision to stop building bases in Cuba, dismantling offensive weapons and returning them to the Soviet Union under United Nations verification. This is an important and constructive contribution to peace." [69] The Cuban missile crisis, seemingly about to enter its most dangerous phase, was suddenly over.

It would quickly be entered into history and legend as John F. Kennedy's supreme political triumph. But some, at least, remained haunted by the fears of those days. I. F. Stone put them succinctly: "The essential, the terrifying question about the missile crisis is what would have happened if Khrushchev had not backed down?" [70] After his initial reckless error, Khrushchev had acted with prudence and moderation. If he had not, Kennedy's triumph would have turned into catastrophe. Eschewing a diplomatic approach, insisting upon the use of force to compel a Russian retreat, Kennedy had brought the world to the brink of nuclear war for the sake of American prestige and influence. At the height of the crisis, he abdicated control over the outbreak of hostilities to Khrushchev's sense of restraint. This was hardly the stuff of political greatness; in the final analysis, Kennedy's conduct in the missile crisis was neither responsible nor justifiable.

The conclusion of the orthodox histories of the missile crisis is that it paved the way for a subsequent Soviet-American détente. Certainly it sobered both Khrushchev and Kennedy, and exerted a strong influence upon their further relations. Yet whether it led to a tranformation of the Cold War is a question that I shall take up briefly in the final section of this chapter. Before doing so, however, I wish to note two more long-range consequences of Kennedy's action.

For those members of the Kennedy Administration who participated in the deliberations of the Executive Committee, the successful outcome of their endeavors brought a great boost to self-confidence. Rusk, McNamara, Bundy, et al. shared in Kennedy's triumphant facing-down of the Russians. They delighted in recalling its "combination of toughness and restraint" [71]—the institution of a limited blockade and plotting from there of a careful step-by-step escalation of pressure. It was no accident that the same men, a few years later, were attracted to a similar tactic in Vietnam. With an arrogance that was in part a legacy of the missile crisis, they set out in Vietnam to reproduce their earlier victory through the "politics of escalation."

The Cuban missile crisis served, in this sense, as a precedent for Vietnam. In addition, it came to serve as a general precedent for how American Presidents should act in analogous situations. When Richard Nixon announced the blockading and mining of North Vietnamese ports in May 1972, there was little doubt that Kennedy's handling of the Cuban crisis was an important model for his action. Nixon expected the Russians to back down once again—as they did.[72] But surely there is something frightening in predicating world peace on the assumption that America's foes must and will back down first. This idea—that when the United States stands tough, employing part of its immense power and threatening to employ far more, it always gets its way—is perhaps the most important, and most tragic, legacy of the Cuban missile crisis.

Part of the conventional wisdom about Kennedy's Presidency is that his last year in office represented a hopeful, though aborted, entrance into a new era of American foreign policy. Kennedy, his chroniclers have told us, was profoundly affected by the missile crisis. He determined in its aftermath that there must be no more of such nuclear confrontations. So he embarked on the difficult path toward peace, seeking concrete agreements with the Soviet Union as the first step in building a lasting détente. The landmarks of his final search for peace were his American University speech and the Limited Test Ban Treaty; here, in Sorensen's words, Kennedy became the first President in eighteen years "to succeed in reaching beyond the cold war." [73]

Kennedy's accomplishments in his final year were, however, far more ambiguous than his chroniclers have led us to believe. They reflected a shift of focus in his approach to international affairs, but they scarcely amounted to a change in the basic structure of his Cold War theory. The record of Kennedy's last year does not provide sufficient reason to alter the picture of his foreign policy that has already been drawn. The course he had set in his first two years was not canceled by his deeds in 1963; indeed, 1963 marked, in several important respects, the continuation of that course.

After the near-catastrophe of the missile crisis, both the United States and the Soviet Union revived their dormant interest in a treaty prohibiting nuclear tests. Khrushchev wrote Kennedy on December 19, 1962, that this was the moment to put an end to all testing. Kennedy responded with enthusiasm, and discussions between the two countries began in New York the following month. But the talks snarled over the old question of on-site inspections. America and its allies feared that without inspections, the Soviets could conduct massive underground tests in secret. The Soviets, on the other hand, regarded inspections as a pretext for NATO espionage. The Western powers insisted upon at least seven inspections per year; the Russians would concede only two or three. By late spring the impasse appeared total. Kennedy told a press conference on

May 8 that present prospects for a test-ban treaty were dim.

 ˙ Rather than giving up, Kennedy decided to break the impasse. Prudently realizing the need for a new initiative, he took the opportunity of a scheduled address at American University on June 10 to set the test-ban issue in a broader context. In what has generally (and correctly) been hailed as his finest speech, Kennedy called at American University for a thaw in the Cold War. With language that was as new for him as for his audience, he asked the American people to reexamine their attitudes toward the Soviet Union. He warned them

> not to see only a distorted and desperate view of the other side, not to see conflict as inevitable, accommodation as impossible, and communication as nothing more than an exchange of threats. No government or social system is so evil that its people must be considered as lacking in virtue. As Americans we find Communism profoundly repugnant as a negation of personal freedom and dignity. But we can still hail the Russian people for their many achievements—in science and space, in economic and industrial growth, in culture and in acts of courage.[74]

Agreement with such an adversary to limit the competition in strategic weapons was certainly possible. Indeed, it had become imperative, as the burdens and perils of the arms race mounted on both sides. "Both the United States and its allies, and the Soviet Union and its allies," Kennedy thus declared, "have a mutually deep interest in a just and genuine peace and in halting the arms race." [75]

He concluded these remarks with two announcements: that he and Prime Minister Harold Macmillan were dispatching a high-level mission to Moscow to discuss a test-ban treaty; and that he was, for the present, halting further American testing as a sign of good faith. The success of the mission— headed for the Americans by Averell Harriman—was augured by the overwhelmingly favorable Russian reaction to Kennedy's speech. Khrushchev pronounced himself pleased with its call for a thaw; the Soviet press approvingly printed its text in full. The negotiations that ensued were intensive but brief. Once the difficult question of on-site inspections was set aside, by excluding underground tests from the ban, it took only ten days to reach final agreement on a treaty. The treaty was initialed in Moscow on July 25, six weeks after the American University speech.

The occasion was marked by hopeful words on both sides. Kennedy went on television on the night of July 26, to tell the American people about the successful conclusion of the test-ban negotiations. He was careful to note that the treaty did not resolve the numerous points of conflict between the United States and the USSR. "But it is an important first step—a step towards peace—a step towards reason—a step away from war." [76] And he held out the promise of further steps. "Let us make the most of this opportunity, and every opportunity, to reduce tension, to slow down the perilous nuclear arms race, and to check the world's slide toward final annihilation." [77]

For a moment it genuinely seemed as if a new era of East-West relations was opening. But there were several disquieting notes. Two weeks after his American University speech, Kennedy had embarked on a tour of America's European allies. A major stop on the tour was West Berlin, and in some remarks to a huge crowd in the Rudolph Wilde Platz he appeared explicitly to undermine the message of his recent speech:

> There are many people in the world who really don't understand, or say they don't, what is the great issue between the free world and the Communist world. Let them come to Berlin. There are some who say that Communism is the wave of the future. Let them come to Berlin. And there are some who say in Europe and elsewhere we can work with the Communists. Let them come to Berlin.[78]

contradictory

These words have sometimes been discounted as the product of an emotion-charged setting. Yet this was not the only time in these months that Kennedy's new emphasis on peace was to be swiftly followed by a resumption of his familiar Cold War stance.

Another development that cast doubt on the extent of Kennedy's change of heart was his negative response to Khrushchev's flurry of proposals for extending the détente. In statements on July 19 and July 26, Khrushchev outlined a number of potential subjects for further East-West accords: a nonaggression pact between the NATO and Warsaw Pact countries, the freezing or cutting of defense budgets, reciprocal observation posts in West and East Germany to forestall surprise attacks, a reduction of foreign troops in both German states. [79] Kennedy, however, showed little interest in pursuing these subjects. There were legitimate grounds for the American President to postpone considering them, for they would have seriously complicated the upcoming struggle in the Senate over ratification of the test-ban treaty. But Kennedy's indifference to the Soviet proposals seemed, from the available evidence, to stem from more than just this tactical consideration. It reflected a deep sense of caution about the détente itself. As Sorensen notes, "while he hoped for further agreement, he remained to the end extremely cautious in his expressions of optimism and extremely anxious not to lower our guard, even though tensions were, hopefully, lessened." [80]

The most important sign that Kennedy had not advanced very far beyond his earlier Cold War position came in the effort to secure the Senate's consent to the test-ban treaty. For in that effort the Kennedy Administration—due to a combination of external pressures and internal impulses—transformed the meaning of the treaty. What had ostensibly been an agreement to limit the arms race became, by the date of ratification, a device making possible its intensification.[81]

Kennedy had presented the treaty to the American public

as a triumph for mankind over the terrors of nuclear war. But as I. F. Stone has demonstrated, in urging the Senate and the military to approve it he depicted the triumph in rather different terms. "When the treaty had to be sold to the U.S. military bureaucracy and the U.S. Senate, it was sold not as a victory against the arms race, but as a victory in it, *an acknowledgment by Moscow of American superiority and a new way to maintain it.*" [82] By agreeing to a ban on further testing, the Russians had acquiesced in the existing American nuclear lead; ratification of the treaty, the Kennedy Administration told its doubters, would ensure continuance of that lead.

But the Kennedy Administration was not content merely with maintaining a strategic advantage; it was determined in 1963, as it had been in 1961, to extend that advantage. As Secretary McNamara informed the Senate Foreign Relations Committee on August 13, the test-ban treaty had not disrupted the Administration's plans for a long-term strategic buildup. McNamara testified that the United States already possessed over 500 ICBMs, compared to only a fraction as many on the Soviet side (estimates then ran to about 75). Yet the Administration still intended to increase American missile strength to over 1700 by 1966.[83] When it came to their schedule for missile production at least, Kennedy and his Defense Secretary gave no indication that they thought the Cold War was winding down.

These assurances of a continued arms buildup were, however, not sufficient to placate the Joint Chiefs of Staff. The Chiefs "attached 'safeguards' to their support: vigorous continuation of underground testing; readiness to resume atmospheric testing on short notice; strengthening of detection capabilities; and the maintenance of nuclear laboratories." [84] Afraid that opposition from the Joint Chiefs might sabotage his treaty in the Senate, the President accepted all their conditions. He was willing, Schlesinger explains, to make these concessions in order to move the United States one step nearer to an end of the arms race.

The treaty was ratified on September 24, by a vote of 80 to 19, but it hardly resulted in even a pause in the arms race. Haggling over the question of inspection had led to an exclusion of underground explosions from the ban; pressure from the Joint Chiefs ensured that the United States would make full use of that exclusion. More experienced than the Soviet Union in underground testing, more capable of supporting its heavy costs, the United States now launched an expanded program underground. As I. F. Stone discovered, from 1945 to August 1963 there had been, according to the Atomic Energy Commission, 98 American nuclear tests. Between that date and the spring of 1970, there were 210 tests.[85] Warheads for awesome weapons systems were developed underground: the MIRV (Multiple Independently Targeted Re-Entry Vehicle) and the ABM (Anti-Ballistic Missile). The Soviets, too, accelerated their arms development. And so the "balance of terror" was raised to a whole new level.

The hopes that the Limited Test Ban Treaty generated in 1963 were mocked by the new stage of nuclear competition which followed. By his own plans for increasing American missile strength, and by his bowing to Pentagon pressure for increasing American underground testing, Kennedy must bear his share of responsibility for that new stage.

In the fall of 1963, a further step toward a thaw was taken. Kennedy announced, on October 9, that the United States would sell a portion of its surplus wheat to the Soviet Union. But despite the growing spirit of détente, he seemed hesitant about abandoning former postures. There was an interesting parallel that fall to his contradictory statements in June. On September 20, he appeared before the United Nations to discuss the quest for peace and, in some of his most eloquent prose ever, set an exacting standard for both the United States and the Soviet Union. "If we fail to make the most of this moment and this momentum, if we convert our newfound hopes and understandings into new walls and weapons of hostility, if this pause in the Cold War merely leads to its renewal and not to its end, then the indictment of posterity will rightly point its finger at us all." [86]

Four days later he left on a tour of several western states. Although the subject of the tour was conservation, Kennedy could not resist talking about world events. And though he continued to discuss the test-ban treaty and the prospects for peace (before a public that seemed to welcome peace sentiments far more eagerly than the President had anticipated), he nonetheless spiced his remarks with bits of the old Cold War vocabulary. He told a Duluth audience on September 24 that the United States must "maintain the freedom of dozens of countries . . . maintain the balance of power against a monolithic Communist apparatus." [87] To a Great Falls, Montana, audience on September 26, he repeated his familiar line that "we are the keystone in the arch of freedom." Neatly characterizing American global interventionism, he declared, "in a dangerous and changing world it is essential that the 180 million people of the United States throw their weight into the balance in every struggle, in every country, on the side of freedom." [88]

Was Kennedy, as his admirers have claimed, changing his view of international politics in the final months of his life; was he beginning to look beyond the boundaries of the Cold War? Certainly some of his perspectives were shifting. A growing revulsion against nuclear war, and an attendant desire to bring the behemoth of nuclear technology under control, were apparent in his statements and actions during this period. So too was the intention of relaxing the strained relationship between the United States and the USSR, reducing the mutual state of tension by finding areas of common interest. But the recurrent Cold War language, the caution in pursuing a détente, the sub rosa commitment to a continuing arms race—these indicated how little his fundamental conceptions had been altered. If Kennedy helped to bring about the beginnings of a détente in

1963, it was not really because he thought the Cold War was ending. Rather, he tended to view the détente as the product of his triumph in the missile crisis, *a temporary admission* by the Soviets of American superiority in both the military and the political sphere.

That Kennedy believed the Cold War, though now less dangerous, was far from over was plain in his words to a University of Maine audience on October 19, 1963:

> The United States and the Soviet Union still have wholly different concepts of the world, its freedom, its future. We still have wholly different views on the so-called wars of liberation and the use of subversion. And so long as these basic differences continue, they cannot and should not be concealed. They set limits to the possibilities of agreements; and they will give rise to further crises, large and small, in the months and years ahead. . . .[89]

While the thaw in American-Russian relations made direct confrontation between the superpowers unlikely in the immediate future, it did not, in Kennedy's view, alter the nature of the conflict in the Third World. The next chapter will describe Kennedy's approach to the Third World. He had often proclaimed it the decisive battlefield in the global struggle. Now, in his final months, it came even more to be the focus of his attention and concern. To the Inter-American Press Association, in an address at Miami on November 18, he renewed his pledge to combat Castroism in Latin America: "We in this hemisphere must . . . use every resource at our command to prevent the establishment of another Cuba in this hemisphere." [90] In this same period American involvement in the war in Vietnam was, with the overthrow of Diem, seriously deepened. The détente had not curbed Kennedy's foreign policy activism; it served only to redirect that activism toward the Third World.

Kennedy's intention to go on with the struggle, especially in the Third World, was reaffirmed in the speech he was to have delivered to the Dallas Citizens Council on the afternoon of November 22, 1963. Whatever had been his new departures in his last year, his rhetoric at the end echoed the rhetoric at the beginning. "We in this country, in this generation, are, by destiny rather than choice, the watchmen on the walls of world freedom." [91]

4

Global Liberalism

John F. Kennedy's record in the Third World was, on the surface, a puzzling blend of the generous and the ignoble. Among Kennedy and his fellow New Frontiersmen, a sophisticated yet compassionate understanding of Third World problems seemed to exist. Marking that understanding were fresh departures in American foreign policy: the idealistic Peace Corps, a solicitous concern for the new nations of Africa, and, most notably, the Alliance for Progress campaign for economic development and social justice in Latin America. Yet, parallel to these undertakings was a history of repressive military intervention in the affairs of the Third World. Here, too, there were landmarks: the invasion of Cuba and the increasingly bitter struggle against the Viet Cong guerrillas in South Vietnam.

Doubtless there was genuine ambivalence in Kennedy's approach to the Third World, ambivalence fostered by a liberal's simultaneous desire for, and fear of, change. But ambivalence should not, in this case, be equated with inconsistency. For one consistent theme ran through almost all of Kennedy's ventures in the Third World—counterrevolution. Whatever other sympathies he professed, John Kennedy was a determined counterrevolutionary. His overriding aim was to banish

the specter of radical revolution from the underdeveloped nations by channeling the forces of change into a "democratic
revolution." The "democratic revolution" promised evolution-
ary change within a democratic framework, free from the dis-
ruption and violence of a radical social upheaval. It turned out
to mean only the status quo in an elaborate new guise.

This chapter focuses on the two most important examples
of Kennedy's Third World policy: the Alliance for Progress and
the war in Vietnam. At first glance they may seem the polar
opposites of that policy, its positive and negative sides. But
closer examination discloses that they are not so very far apart.
I begin with a consideration of the Alliance, where Kennedy's
rhetoric of "democratic revolution" reached its crescendo. Before doing so, however, it may be useful to recall that he had
long before previewed that rhetoric in reference, not to Latin
America, but to Vietnam.

On June 1, 1956, then-Senator Kennedy delivered an address before a conference of the American Friends of Vietnam.
He offered lavish praise on this occasion for President Diem's
accomplishments, for his "amazing success ... in meeting
firmly and with determination the major political and economic crises which had heretofore continually plagued Vietnam." [1] Still, he declared, far more needed to be done—by
America as well as by the Diem regime.

> We should not attempt to buy the friendship of the
> Vietnamese. Nor can we win their hearts by making
> them dependent upon our handouts. What we must
> offer them is a revolution—a political, economic, and
> social revolution far superior to anything the
> Communists can offer—far more peaceful, far more
> democratic, and far more locally controlled.[2]

The history of the Alliance for Progress can be recited
relatively quickly; it takes only a few pages to describe its major
events and achievements. What requires fuller consideration is

the story of what didn't happen—the Alliance's glaring failure to fulfill its own goals or, indeed, to make even a dent in the stagnant economic and social order of the Latin American countries. That failure reveals much about the nature of present-day Latin America; it reveals far more about the political understanding of John Kennedy and his circle of advisers.

The Alliance for Progress was hailed, when it was announced in March 1961, as the start of a new era in United States–Latin American relations. But reassessment of America's hemispheric policy had already begun in the Eisenhower Administration. After Vice-President Nixon's ill-starred trip to South America in 1958, and the triumph of the Cuban revolution in 1959, Washington policy makers had observed with alarm the rising tide of discontent in an area long taken for granted. By 1960, they were agreed on the need to pour more energy and money into Latin America. At the Bogotá Conference the Eisenhower Administration thus pledged $500 million as an American "social progress fund" for Latin American development.

Despite Eisenhower's initiative, Kennedy as a presidential candidate considered the Republicans vulnerable on the subject of Latin America. He made it one of his key campaign issues, adopting the slogan "Alliance for Progress" (coined by Richard Goodwin) to describe his own prospective program. After his election, plans for this Alliance rapidly took form; by March 13, 1961, Kennedy was ready to unveil them to a White House assemblage of the Latin American diplomatic corps.

He painted his program in glowing terms. "I have called on all people of the hemisphere to join in a new Alliance for Progress—Alianza para Progreso—a vast cooperative effort, unparalleled in magnitude and nobility of purpose, to satisfy the basic needs of the American people for homes, work and land, health and schools. . . ." [3] The new partnership of North and South would encompass both economic development and social restructuring—national planning and technical aid, agrarian reform and tax reform, public housing, education, and health care. And it would operate within the framework of democratic institutions, proving definitively the compatibility of representative government with material progress. Kennedy did not hesitate to call his Alliance a new hemispheric "revolution": "Let us once again transform the American continent into a vast crucible of revolutionary ideas and efforts. . . ." [4]

The Alliance for Progress was born in hope, but also in fear. Little was said about it at the time, yet it was apparent to everyone concerned that the Alliance was America's response to the Cuban revolution, its contrivance for heading off the eruption of Castro-style revolutions throughout the hemisphere. The rapid promulgation of this new Latin American policy betrayed the nightmare of Fidelismo at its base. "It was," Ronald Steel observed, "neither charity nor a guilty conscience but Fidel Castro who provided the inspiration for the Alliance for Progress. . . . The Alliance for Progress might never have seen the light of day, let alone grown into childhood, had Fidel not injected the fear of communism into official Washington." [5]

Barely more than a month after the announcement of this program for forestalling copies of the Cuban revolution, Kennedy struck at the original. On April 17, a brigade of 1400 Cuban exiles under the direction of the CIA were set ashore at Cuba's Bay of Pigs. Their hope was to spark a general uprising against the Castro regime; if this did not occur in a few days the invaders could melt away into the mountains and commence guerrilla warfare. The CIA was highly optimistic about the scheme; Kennedy, while expressing some doubts, went along in the faith that the Cuban populace would rise up against what he himself had characterized as a government "seized by aliens." [6] But in a matter of days the Cuban militia crushed the invasion force and took most of its members prisoner.

We already possess numerous accounts of the self-deluded planning for the invasion, and the disastrous bungling once it took place. It is more important for our purposes to consider what the Bay of Pigs augured for Kennedy's Latin American policy. For in the abortive invasion of Cuba, several key features of the Alliance for Progress were foreshadowed.

First, however, we must dispose of the argument that Kennedy and his associates learned their lesson with the Bay of Pigs. It is true that they learned something useful—not to trust so completely in the CIA and its vaunted expertise. But this hardly constituted an admission that unrelenting hostility to the Cuban revolution and an attempt to undo it by force were wrong in themselves. Kennedy and his men were quick to acknowledge that their plans had been mistaken; for their intentions, they never apologized.[7]

Kennedy's Cuban invasion plan, like his Alliance, promoted liberal reform elements as the alternative to Castroite revolutionaries. While the invasion force was being readied, a White Paper on Cuba was simultaneously prepared by the Kennedy Administration. This White Paper accused Castro of betraying the Cuban revolution by his turn toward communism; it placed the United States in the position of endorsing the original goals of the revolution. And representing these original goals was the Cuban Revolutionary Council, the American-backed group that was to form the nucleus of a provisional government once the invasion had succeeded. The head of the Council was Dr. Miró Cardona, who had been the first prime minister of Castro's revolutionary regime; an important faction of the Council was led by Manuel Ray, a leftist underground leader before 1959, and later Castro's Minister of Public Works.

The Revolutionary Council turned out to be neither very effective nor very liberal. Factional disputes and personal squabbling rendered the Council ineffectual throughout the planning stage of the invasion. When the invasion finally began, its leaders were helplessly cut off from events in their "hiding place," an isolated Florida air base. As to its liberal credentials, Schlesinger's account is humorously revealing. At one point he and several colleagues had to persuade Miró Cardona that the Council's proposed manifesto to the Cuban people was not what the Kennedy Administration wanted.

> We pointed out that the Council draft was filled with impassioned appeals to the foreign investor, the private banker, the dispossessed property owner, but had very little to say to the worker, the farmer or the Negro. I remarked at one point, "It would be foolish if the Cuban Revolutionary Council turns out to be to the right of the New Frontier." We suggested that the Council must reassure the Cubans that it had no intention of destroying the social and economic gains of the last two years.[8]

If reluctant liberals made up the political arm of Kennedy's Cuban invasion force, the military arm was even worse. At the beginning, former henchmen of the Batista dictatorship had been specifically excluded from the invasion brigade; other exiles, whatever their political stripe, were welcomed. But the political composition of the brigade eventually shifted to the right, in accordance with CIA preferences. Manuel Ray's supporters in particular were cut out of the venture. The Kennedy Administration went along with this shift, out of a mixture of deference to the CIA and outright ignorance of its maneuvers. When these "freedom fighters" finally hit the beaches of the Bay of Pigs, their claim to be the heirs of the authentic Cuban revolution was dubious indeed. Schlesinger, despite the apologetics, is again revealing:

> Apart from professionals who had served in Batista's army, few real Batistianos had slipped in, but some notorious Batista criminals somehow showed up on the boats on the way to Cuba (to be subsequently displayed by Castro as representative members of the Brigade). The officers, though not active Batistianos, stood considerably to the right of the Revolutionary Council. The rank and file were politically

heterogeneous. The only common purpose was to
return home and get rid of Castro.[9]

The selection of such men to play the role of Cuban revolutionaries provided a strong hint of what was coming in the
"democratic revolution" that the Alliance for Progress had
promised. Reliance on ineffectual, half-hearted liberals and
temporizing with corrupt rightists were to prove recurrent features of the Alliance. The Bay of Pigs also set a more ominous
pattern for the Alliance—the readiness to resort to force to
suppress radical revolution. Kennedy made it clear, with the
invasion of Cuba, that the principle of nonintervention would
not restrain the United States from striking at any revolutionary movement or regime in the Western Hemisphere in which
communists were a factor. The threat of force which accompanied the Alliance would be partially hidden from view, both
by its rhetoric of peaceful change, and by the absence of any
further situation during Kennedy's Presidency in which force
had to employed. Still that threat was always present, as will be
made plain when we examine Kennedy's military program for
Latin America.

In the immediate aftermath of the Bay of Pigs, however,
Kennedy was too irate to hide the threat.

> Let the record show that our restraint is not
> inexhaustible. Should it ever appear that the
> inter-American doctrine of non-interference merely
> conceals or excuses a policy of nonaction—if the
> nations of this Hemisphere should fail to meet their
> commitments against outside Communist
> penetration—then I want it clearly understood that
> this Government will not hesitate in meeting its
> primary obligations which are to the security of our
> Nation![10]

The Kennedy Administration was soon eager to forget its
blundering Cuban invasion. But for Latin Americans the in-

vasion was not so easily forgotten; it remained a powerful object lesson in the U.S. response to social revolution in the hemisphere.

While Kennedy's popularity in Latin America sagged temporarily after the Bay of Pigs, hopes for the Alliance for Progress remained high. The Alliance was formally organized at a conference of the Inter-American Economic and Social Council held in Punta del Este, Uruguay, in August 1961. In his written message to this conference Kennedy returned to the generous purposes of his March speech. Profound changes in the social and economic structure of Latin America were again foretold: "For there is no place in democratic life for institutions which benefit the few while denying the needs of the many, even though the elimination of such institutions may require far-reaching and difficult changes such as land reform and tax reform and a vastly increased emphasis on education and health and housing." [11] And a vast infusion of American care, as well as American money, was pledged: "Only an effort of towering dimensions—an effort similar to that which was needed to rebuild the economies of Western Europe—can ensure fulfillment of our Alliance for Progress." [12]

Although some of the Latin American delegates to the conference were skeptical in private, publicly all (except Cuba's Che Guevara) endorsed the plans of Kennedy and his chief representative, Treasury Secretary Douglas Dillon. When the conference ended on August 17, those plans had been incorporated into an official Charter of Punta del Este. The ambitions of the Alliance can be seen in the social goals which the Charter set forth: comprehensive agrarian reform, tax reform, accelerated urban and rural housing development, accelerated programs of health and sanitation, elmination of illiteracy. The economic goals were equally ambitious: a national development plan for each country, fair wages, stable prices, Latin American economic integration, and a per capita growth rate of 2.5 percent a year. There was also a clear political goal: to protect and strengthen the institutions of representative democracy in the hemisphere. Toward all these ends the United States pledged $20 billion over the next ten years, slightly more than half in public assistance, the rest in private funds.

The history of the Alliance during the remainder of Kennedy's Presidency presents a dreary picture of inaction or failure. A year or two after Punta del Este the bright hopes of its founding had all but dissolved. Growth rates for the Latin American economies as a whole lagged far below the 2.5 percent figure. Land and tax reforms were, in most cases, hopelessly bottled up in conservative legislatures. As for the Alliance's commitment to democracy, the years 1962–63 witnessed repeated setbacks for democratic institutions in Latin America in the face of a resurgent militarism. In 1962 the governments of both Argentina and Peru were toppled by military coups; in 1963 four more governments—Guatemala, Ecuador, the Dominican Republic, and Honduras—fell under military control. These developments could not, of course, all be attributed to the Alliance. Still, it had rapidly become apparent that the Alliance could not live up to its name—and would not disturb Latin America's stagnation.

Confronted persistently with criticisms of the Alliance, Kennedy found it hard to disguise his gloom. All that he could do was to cite the difficulties that the Alliance faced—the complexity of Latin America's problems, its shortage of trained personnel to develop and administer reform programs, the opposition of vested interests to such programs—and to counsel patience. Sometimes even he found it difficult to follow that counsel. On the second anniversary of the Punta del Este conference, for example, he responded to a press conference query on Latin America with obvious frustration: "The problems are almost insuperable. . . ." [13] Yet the grandiloquent rhetoric was never abandoned completely; four days before his death Kennedy declared: "The task we have set ourselves and the Alliance for Progress, the development of an entire continent, is a far greater task than any we have ever undertaken in our history." [14]

At the time of Kennedy's death, supporters of the Alliance still could claim that its reforms would take hold in a few more years. By the end of the decade, those supporters had to admit that the critics had been right all along—by almost any standard imaginable the Alliance was a failure. None of the goals fixed at Punta del Este had been achieved. As Susanne Bodenheimer notes, figures compiled by the United Nations Economic Commission for Latin America actually show that "Latin America's problems of urban poverty, unemployment (particularly in rural areas), slow industrialization, inequalities of income and living standards, dependence upon foreign capital, foreign indebtedness, and slow expansion of foreign markets have become more critical during the last ten years . . . the annual average growth rate during the 1960's was lower than that of the previous decade and fell far short of targets established in 1961." [15] Progress in land and tax reform was pathetically slow. Housing, sanitation, health care were no better for the great majority of Latin America's poor in 1970 than they had been in 1960. The fate of the Alliance could be summed up by its campaign against adult illiteracy; after ten years, statistics showed no appreciable increases in adult literacy in Latin America. [16]

Why was the Alliance for Progress such a failure? Before this question can be answered, a prior question must be asked: what was the real intention of those who created the Alliance? What purposes, and whose interests, was the Alliance designed to serve? On this question opinion has, for the most part, been divided into two camps. Liberal supporters have regarded the Alliance as a sincere effort to bring material progress and social justice to Latin America. Radical critics, on the other hand, have viewed it as simply a new tool for preventing revolution and protecting America's economic stake in Latin America. A noble experiment which foundered on the rock of Latin American realities, or an ideological fraud which in good measure succeeded in forestalling social change for yet another decade—these have been the terms in which most discussions of the Alliance have been couched.

While there is greater substance, in my opinion, in the argument of the critics, both sides have a hold on part of the truth about the Alliance for Progress. The Alliance goal of social change was genuine—as was its calculation of American self-interest. I shall treat the Alliance in each of these aspects—first as a failed "democratic revolution," then as a successful strategy for preserving the American economic empire in Latin America.

If we turn to writers who supported the Alliance, we find an interesting explanation proposed for the failure of Kennedy's "democratic revolution." Beyond the festering problems, bureaucratic inertia, and conservative resistance that hamstrung the Alliance, these writers stressed its incapacity to create a political "mystique" in Latin America. Despite the grand purposes and elevated language at its founding, the Alliance had come to seem just another aid program. As Tad Szulc, a *New York Times* journalist, put it,

> . . . the concept of the Alliance somehow failed to electrify Latin America, contrary to what optimists in Washington had hoped and notwithstanding the early Latin American enthusiasm for the new Administration. Despite the noble and inspiring words of President Kennedy, the Alliance quickly proved to be virtually empty of the desperately needed political and psychological content. It was unable to project a mystique that would captivate the attention and the imagination of Latin Americans—as the Castro revolution had done in Cuba and in the rest of the Hemisphere.[17]

That the Alliance for Progress failed to develop a mystique that inspired and involved the people of Latin America was true enough. But that failure could not, as these writers imagined, be attributed to an inattention to ideology or a paucity of public-relations efforts on the part of Washington. Though its backers did not realize it, the weakness of its political appeal was inherent in the basic theory of the Alliance itself.

If we examine the major premises of that theory closely, we can begin to see why it was bound to fail in Latin America. I shall consider four of these premises: (1) elitism and the fear of mass action (revolution from the top); (2) social change as manipulation by outside agencies (revolution from the outside); (3) maintenance of existing economic arrangements while "expanding the pie" for all (nondisruptive revolution); and (4) violence as the prerogative of the established order (nonviolent revolution). Each premise was essential to Kennedy's global liberalism. Each had its counterpart, too, in his domestic liberalism. The Alliance was to be an elaborate projection of the Kennedy Administration's pragmatic liberal faith—and a telling commentary on the illusions sustaining that faith.

The first (and most important) premise in the theory of the Alliance for Progress was that the Latin American revolution must be led by established elites. On his initial presidential visit to Latin America in December 1961, Kennedy spelled this out to an audience of dignitaries at the San Carlos Palace in Bogotá, Colombia:

> The leaders of Latin America, the industrialists and landowners are, I am sure, ready to admit past mistakes and accept new responsibilities. For unless all of us are willing to contribute our resources to national development, unless all of us are prepared not merely to accept, but initiate, basic land and tax reforms, unless all of us take the lead in improving the welfare of our people; then that leadership will be taken away from us and the heritage of centuries of Western civilization will be consumed in a few months of violence.[18]

He made the same appeal—and issued the same apocalyptic warning—on the first anniversary of the Alliance:

> Those who possess wealth and power in poor nations must accept their own responsibilities. They must lead the fight for those basic reforms which alone can preserve the fabric of their societies. Those who make peaceful revolution impossible will make violent revolution inevitable.[19]

In these statements Kennedy appeared to rest the hopes of the Alliance on the large landowners and industrialists of Latin America, i.e., on its traditional ruling class. Actually, his conception of revolution from the top was more sophisticated than this. The oligarchs had to be courted with promises that their interests would be protected, and threatened with visions of a communist bloodbath; otherwise their resistance might prove fatal to the Alliance. They were to play a role in the Alliance out of enlightened self-interest, but certainly not the leading role. This was reserved, in Kennedy's theory of the "democratic revolution," for the progressive sectors of the middle class.

These middle-class elements were identified by Kennedy's theory as Latin America's "democratic left." They comprised business entrepreneurs, technical experts, lawyers, teachers, students, journalists, reformist politicians. Strongly nationalistic, passionately eager to modernize their societies, these progressive bourgeois would be the natural allies of Kennedy's program. The liberal goals of the Alliance were identical to their own. But in order for them to function effectively as a vanguard, they required leadership. Kennedy and his advisers thus envisioned dynamic political leaders bringing to fruition the "democratic revolution" in each Latin American country. They even had a model for this kind of leadership—President Rómulo Betancourt of Venezuela. Betancourt was continually held up by the Kennedy Administration as a shining example for other Latin American politicans to emulate. When he visited Washington early in 1963, Kennedy greeted him with extravagant praise: "You represent all that we admire in a political leader." [20]

Missing from this theory of the "democratic revolution" was that section of the population usually deemed the motor of revolutionary change—the masses. The Alliance for Progress did not, of course, ignore Latin America's poverty-stricken majority. It cited their needs in most of its programs; in some areas it brought them concrete benefits—houses, schools, hospitals, sanitation systems. But insofar as it invoked their actual political participation, that invocation always retained a hollow air. Calling on the workers and peasants was, for Kennedy, primarily a ritual, performed as easily before the Colombian elite in the San Carlos Palace as at a housing project in the Bogotá slums.[21] The Alliance could not really afford to mobilize Latin America's workers and peasants, could not afford to draw its strength from their mass action. For that action might get out of hand, might rapidly push beyond the Alliance's moderate goals, might turn suddenly and unpredictably into radical revolution. The masses of Latin America, already stirred by the upheavals of the Cuban revolution, had to be kept fundamentally quiescent; it was, in large part, for this end that the diffusion of services at the bottom of the social system and sharing of power at its middle and top were designed.

Both the theories of modernization then prevalent in Washington (such as that of W. W. Rostow) and the urgent need for an alternative to Castroism led Kennedy and his advisers to place their faith in Latin America's middle class. Most of the members of that class, however, failed to play the part assigned to them. The authentic nationalists or radicals, especially among the intelligentsia, generally shied away from the Alliance, suspicious that it was a new garb for "Yanqui imperialism." As for the bulk of the middle class, their goals were not, as it turned out, those proclaimed by the Alliance. They proved less interested in modernizing their society or

improving the lot of its poor than in holding on to privileges
that were, for an underdeveloped country, already substantial.
The Latin American bourgeoisie were not the progressive democrats whom modernization theorists have idealized from the
European and American experience. Rather, as the Mexican
sociologist Rodolfo Stavenhagen has observed,

> ... they are economically and socially dependent
> upon the upper strata; they are tied politically to the
> ruling class; they are conservative in their tastes and
> opinions, defenders of the status quo; and they search
> only for individual privileges. Far from being
> nationalists, they like everything foreign—from
> imported clothing to the *Reader's Digest*. They
> constitute a true reflection of the ruling class, deriving
> sizeable benefits from the internal colonial situation.
> This group constitutes the most important support for
> military dictatorships in Latin America.[22]

If Latin America's middle class refused to act in accordance with the theory of the "democratic revolution," so too
did its political leadership. Those leaders who might be
considered liberals (Quadros and Goulart in Brazil, Frondizi in
Argentina, Belaunde in Peru, Velasco and Arosemena in
Ecuador, Lleras Camargo in Colombia, Villeda Morales in
Honduras) were ineffectual when they tried to carry out reforms, which was not very often. Most of the time their rhetorical commitments to the changes the Alliance dictated were not
matched by any action. This incompetence irritated Washington—but less so perhaps than the "independent" course in foreign policy which some of them tried to pursue. When Frondizi
and Arosemena, both of whom had feebly resisted the American effort to isolate Cuba, were tossed out of office by military
coups, hardly any protest was forthcoming from the Kennedy
Administration.[23]

The most successful liberal leader was, of course, Rómulo
Betancourt of Venezuela. Betancourt gave enthusiastic support

to the entire Alliance platform. But a brief look behind the reformist façade in Venezuela discloses some interesting things about this political hero whom Kennedy admired so strongly. During Betancourt's presidential term (1959–64) the economic structure of Venezuela remained virtually unaltered. The massive, dominating power of foreign companies over Venezuela's oil resources was not challenged. Some progress was made in diversifying the economy—the reduction of Venezuela's dependence on oil production was a goal of all the political parties—but many of the new enterprises were outlets for American corporations or were jointly owned by Venezuelan and American capital. As for Betancourt's vaunted agrarian reform program, its effect upon the landowning oligarchy can be seen in the following statistics. Before the program was begun, 22 million hectares of land were occupied by large estates; when the program reached its end, the figure had fallen only to 21.5 million hectares.[24]

Betancourt's commitment to the transformation of his country's regressive economic structure could thus be questioned. The same was true of his record as a democrat. As left-wing agitation grew in the early 1960s, affecting even units of the Venezuelan military, government repression was intensified. The suspension of constitutionally guaranteed civil liberties, announced by the Betancourt regime during four days of leftist-inspired disorders in November 1960, remained in effect nearly a year and a half. Outdoor political assemblies were forbidden without government authorization, the freedom of the press was sharply curtailed, the government wielded the power to invade homes and offices without search warrants and to jail suspected revolutionaries without trial. Civil liberties were finally restored in April 1962, only to be suspended once more that fall. The Betancourt government justified such "emergency measures" in light of growing leftist violence and insurrectionary plotting. The left was indeed guilty of violence in this period. But so too were Betancourt's own supporters;

during these years scores of students and young leftists were shot down on the streets of Caracas, their killers identified in many cases as policemen or thugs from Betancourt's Acción Democrática party. Whatever the exigencies of Venezuelan politics, the repressiveness of Betancourt's regime did not accord well with Kennedy's glowing portrayal of the "democratic revolution"; it was a reality that the New Frontiersmen who dealt with Latin America struggled to excuse or, more conveniently, to ignore.[25]

To cap the frustrations of Kennedy's abortive revolution from the top, the oligarchs, who were supposed to step aside for middle-class leadership, instead clung tightly to their own power. They were not attracted by Kennedy's promises or frightened by the dangers he had conjured up. "In most countries the land-owning rich were less worried by Fidelismo than by the loss of their privileges through Alianza reforms. Washington's gory picture of imminent revolution seemed exaggerated, while its prescription for reforms horrified them."[26] Using their strategic political position, especially in national legislatures, the oligarchs managed in most Latin American states to block even moderate land or tax reforms. Despite their intransigence, they remained secure in the knowledge that the United States would not unseat them, indeed needed them as a bulwark of social stability in the face of the revolutionary threat. Kennedy had attempted to manipulate their fears; in the end it was perhaps *his* fears that had been the more cleverly manipulated.

A basically conservative bourgeoisie, half-hearted liberal politicians, an entrenched oligarchy—these were the leaders of Kennedy's "democratic revolution." But even if it had been blessed with better leadership, that revolution would have been a hopeless proposition. For, as revolutionary theorists have always understood, however important leadership may be to the success of a revolutionary movement, the real force of revolution derives from the masses, from their needs and their power.

It is only the urgency of their demand for justice that can sweep away the obstacles, intellectual as well as physical, to fundamental social transformation. The Alliance for Progress excluded the Latin American masses from a significant political role because it feared their revolutionary potential. It thereby became, not a "democratic revolution," but a farce masquerading under its name—as Arthur Schlesinger, Jr., unwittingly made clear:

> The Charter of Punta del Este was a summons to a democratic revolution—nor was revolution a word feared by the architects of the Alliance. . . . Of course most of the governments endorsing this summons were far from revolutionary.[27]

Linked to the premise of revolution from the top in Kennedy's theory was the premise of revolution from the outside. It was the President of the United States who proclaimed the Alliance for Progress. It was American leadership that pushed and prodded reluctant Latin American governments into the "democratic revolution"; it was American bureaucrats who retained, in large measure, administrative control over its workings. Latin American "self-help" programs were widely discussed; American direction of the Alliance as a whole was taken for granted. Kennedy and his associates viewed revolutions around the world as the product of outside direction. In their disastrous misperception it was not indigenous forces but Moscow and Peking masterminds who had initiated revolutionary struggles in Laos, South Vietnam, the Congo. If the communists could make revolution from afar, so too, the thinking in Washington went, could the Americans.

Latin America was, it should be remembered, regarded by Kennedy as a critical battlefield in the global struggle between the Soviet bloc and the Free World. The Soviets had already gained one hemispheric base, on the island of Cuba; they were eager, in Kennedy's view, to establish further satellites on

America's doorstep. The revolutionary threat in Latin America was thus dual: Castroite revolutions which expropriated American property and roused anti-American sentiments, and which simultaneously constituted Soviet victories in the post-Sputnik world offensive. If Kennedy did not make the Latin American revolution, Castro and Khrushchev soon would. Kennedy's "democratic revolution," by channeling the forces of change away from radical economic and social transformation, was seen as a blow to the plans of both his foes. Along with his confrontal stance in the Berlin and Cuban missile crises, and his counterinsurgency program in Vietnam, the effort to direct a democratic revolution in Latin America was part of what he considered his great historical task—a global counteroffensive to halt the relentless communist advance.

Revolution from the outside proved just as impossible as revolution from the top, and for much the same reasons. Most Latin Americans skillfully resisted American manipulation. The oligarchs and conservative bourgeois had little desire to buy the Alliance package of reforms. Those who desired fundamental change, on the other hand, understandably scorned the package because of its American label. As for the accompanying ideology, it too found few takers beyond the liberal politicians and technocrats who manned the Alliance. The Alliance's history suggested a lesson for which Kennedy and his advisers were ill prepared—that revolutionary spirit simply could not be infused in a society from the outside.

Neither of the above ideas—revolution from the top and revolution from the outside—was as odd as another notion Kennedy professed: the nondisruptive revolution. "Democratic revolution" was, of course, to necessitate changes for Latin America—in land tenure, employment, education, tax structure, and many other areas. But the social fabric was to be left intact. The many would get new social and economic opportunities; the middle and upper classes, while in some cases called upon to make sacrifices, would in general retain what they had. No one would pay too heavy a cost. Whereas Castroite revolution, Kennedy suggested in a statement quoted earlier, required the greatest of costs: "The heritage of centuries of Western civilization will be consumed in a few months of violence."

The costs of the Alliance indeed proved quite bearable for Latin America's privileged groups. Take the case of agrarian reform. Where agrarian reform was carried out at all under the aegis of the Alliance, it was generally in one of two forms: parcelation or colonization.[28] "Parcelation," a method favored by Venezuela and Colombia, involved the voluntary sale of acreage by large landowners to the government. The landowners were paid the market price for what they sold. The peasants were not given the land; they had to purchase it, in installment payments, at cost price, including a charge for the wages of the officials handling the transaction. "Colonization" involved the resettlement of peasants on virgin land owned by the government. Here, too, there was no challenge to the rural oligarchy, no attempt to redistribute the land that was the source of its excessive wealth as well as its inordinate political power. Instead, peasants were provided with titles to a piece of wilderness—often with no equipment, no credit, not even a road to get to their "farms."

Agrarian reform under the Alliance also proved scarcely any burden for American companies with extensive land holdings in Latin America. The case of Honduras provides an almost comic illustration of this. In his eagerness to join the Alliance for Progress, the President of Honduras, Villeda Morales, copied almost without change Venezuela's model agrarian reform law. But whereas oil-rich Venezuela had the foreign currency to compensate American corporations for any land it expropriated under its agrarian reform law, Honduras could offer only its own long-term bonds as compensation. These hardly appealed to American landowners—principally the United Fruit Company—who complained to the Kennedy

[handwritten marginalia: the large landowners and wealthy bourgeois retained most of their land and power, the peasants lives virtually remained unchanged. U.S. intervene just enough to insure the hold — as well as the L. Am govt hold — rhetoric]

Administration about Villeda Morales' misguided enthusiasm.

The situation was rectified when Villeda Morales visited the United States. The Honduran President and his wife were welcomed graciously at the White House by the American President and his wife. Then they traveled to United Fruit Company's corporate headquarters, where Villeda Morales was set straight about the company's requirements and desires. When he returned to Honduras the agrarian law was swiftly revised; in its new form it was deemed "livable" by American interests.[29]

Such agrarian reform programs were not very comic, however, to Latin America's impoverished peasants. "Nondisruptive revolution" meant that their lives remained essentially unchanged. Kennedy and his advisers displayed a willful ignorance about the nature of revolution. Authentic revolutions strike both widely and deeply, touching every aspect of social life, uprooting and remaking economic, political, cultural patterns. Kennedy's proposed revolution had no such intent; it was designed to preserve as much as to change. It spoke of saving "the heritage of centuries of Western civilization," a euphemism for a social order that was basically stagnant, repressive, and unjust. Of course Kennedy and his colleagues did not approve of much of that social order, and wished to reform it. Still, they were not willing to see it swept away, for, beyond all other considerations, American property and power in Latin America were grounded in that social order and would disappear along with it.

One last aspect of Kennedy's "democratic revolution" remains to be discussed: its insistence upon peaceful change. Kennedy offered to Latin America the vista of economic development and social justice free from the violence and suffering of the Cuban revolution. By working within constitutional processes to enact the programs of the Alliance, advocates of change could, he promised, fulfill their goal without bloodshed. Given the extremely powerful resistance to change by the oligarchy and military in most Latin American countries, this notion of a nonviolent revolution was a dubious one. Still, it was an idea that might be respected for its humaneness—if it had reflected a genuine commitment to oppose violence in Latin America. But the Kennedy Administration made no such commitment.

While the Administration ruled out violence as a means of achieving social reform in Latin America, it was quite ready to employ violence against its revolutionary rivals. Earlier we saw how Kennedy sought forcibly to overthrow the Castro regime in Cuba by sponsoring an exile invasion. Although he failed to unseat Castro, his determination hardened after the Bay of Pigs that no further Castros would come to power in Latin America by means of guerrilla warfare. Hence, he inaugurated a major change in America's military program for Latin America. "During 1961, the decision was made to shift the basis for military aid to Latin America from hemisphere defense to internal security, from protection of the coasts to internal defense of Latin American governments against Castro-Communist guerrilla warfare." [30] For Latin America, as for the rest of the Third World, the Kennedy Administration's tool for combating communist subversion would be its new military speciality—counterinsurgency.

Latin America's militaries now began to receive in abundance the weapons of counter-guerrilla warfare: jeeps, helicopters, small arms. Numerous of their officers were trained in the Army's Special Forces School at Fort Bragg, North Carolina. An Inter-American Police Academy was established at Fort Davis in the Canal Zone, to train Latin American policemen in various antisubversive methods. Nor was the American role restricted to these forms of assistance. As Tad Szulc reported, "A sizable unit of the Special Forces troops—the Seventh Group—was transferred to the Canal Zone, the site of the United States Caribbean Command, early in 1962 to act as a pool of antiguerrilla advisers to the Latin American armies and, if the need should ever arise, to be used in action on the request of a friendly government." [31] Green Berets stood poised in the Canal Zone to ensure that if Kennedy's peaceful democratic revolution failed, revolution led by Castro-style guerrillas would fail as well.

Fear of those guerrillas drove the Kennedy Administration (and its successors) into an increasingly intimate relationship with the Latin American military. The military was the ultimate bulwark against radical revolution; as such, it deserved whatever strengthening the United States could give it. Thus, "U.S. military aid to Latin America during the 1960's jumped 50 percent per year over that granted during the 1950's." [32] There was some embarrassment in Washington over this support by the proponents of a "democratic revolution" for an institution widely regarded as reactionary and authoritarian. But this embarrassment was smoothed over, in part by the development of "civic action" programs in which the military, by building roads and sanitation systems, supposedly demonstrated that it was an efficient modernizing agent (and also, it was hoped, won the loyalty of the rural population).[33]

The flurry of weapons and equipment, training missions, and civic-action programs descending upon Latin America's military did not exactly foster the Alliance's aim of strengthening democratic institutions in the hemisphere. Instead, it contributed to a markedly visible resurgence of militarism. In 1962–63 alone, there were six successful military coups. Ironically, the new counterinsurgency units often played a key role in these coups. As Edwin Lieuwen observed,

> In Peru, the antigüerrilla commandos spearheaded the ouster of President Manuel Prado. In the Dominican Republic, the United States-trained police joined the Army in ousting President Bosch, following which both the police and the antiguerrilla units, trained during 1963 by a forty-four-man United States Army Mission, were used to hunt down Bosch's

non-Communist partisans in the name of anti-
Communism.[34]

Throughout Latin America the military proved stronger than
the "democratic left," whose limited power crumpled swiftly.
By its vigorous support for the military, the Kennedy Administration neatly managed to sabotage the political forces upon
which it had banked so much of its own hopes.

Kennedy increased American aid to the traditionally
antidemocratic Latin American military because they were a
safeguard against Castro-style revolution. In order to eliminate
the threat of Castro himself, he was apparently prepared to
accept even more dubious tactics. Information is just now
coming to light about some of these tactics. Reports of CIA
assassination plots against Castro have been substantiated by
numerous sources. CIA training of Cuban invasion forces
through 1963 has also been revealed. While President Kennedy's personal involvement in these matters is still unclear,
such schemes can certainly be viewed as the underside of the
Kennedy Administration's extensive and obsessive campaign to
remove Fidel Castro from power.

The more public side of this campaign was the effort to
isolate Cuba, economically and politically, from the rest of the
Western Hemisphere. Under President Kennedy's direction,
measures were taken to damage the Cuban economy, to create
shortages and other hardships that would turn the people
against Castro. As Robert Hurwitch, the State Department's
Desk Officer for Cuba, noted with some satisfaction, though
"the economic program itself would not bring down the Castro
regime ... it did contribute to the confusion and virtually
chaotic economic conditions in Cuba." [35]

The heart of Kennedy's political campaign against Castro
was an effort to obtain inter-American sanctions against Cuba
or, that failing, to have Cuba banished from the Organization

of American States. At the second Punta del Este conference, held in January 1962, the larger states (such as Brazil, Argentina, and Mexico) balked at these American proposals. Desperately needing votes, Kennedy's representatives were prepared to deal with anyone. The swing vote turned out to be Haiti—under "Papa Doc" Duvalier, the most vicious dictatorship in the hemisphere. So, as Arthur Schlesinger, Jr., who was one of the American representatives, relates: "We finally yielded to blackmail and agreed to resume our aid to the airport at Port au Prince." [36]

This was only one instance of the Kennedy Administration's continued consorting with dictatorships in Latin America. Whatever the democratic pretensions of the Alliance, the pro-American votes in the OAS and anticommunist stance at home of dictators like Duvalier, Somoza of Nicaragua, or Stroessner of Paraguay were too valuable to permit a cutoff of American aid. When questioned about its financial support for such governments, the Kennedy Administration resorted to pious phrases. Typical were those of Teodoro Moscoso, chief AID administrator for the Alliance:

> Dictatorships have given me more moral suffering than any others. I came into this job with my mind made up to ignore them. But I've changed my mind somewhat. You've got to keep a flame alight in the hearts of their people.[37]

As an attempt to create a democratic ideology that could rival Castroism in its appeal to the restless populations of Latin America, the Alliance for Progress was a clear-cut failure. As a force for economic development and social justice in the hemisphere, the dimensions of its failure were also plain. But when it came to the question of protecting and extending American investments in Latin America, the pronouncement of Alliance failure was much harder to make.

Of course, the political and economic sides of the Alliance were never really separate. The specter of Castroite revolution, which Kennedy's "democratic revolution" was designed to combat, posed more than a political hazard to the United States; its deeper threat was to America's enormous property holdings in Latin America. This American economic empire shook with every new reverberation from Havana. It was a fundamental—though seldom stated—task of the Alliance to restore it to its former stability. In the pages that follow I shall review some of the ways in which the Alliance met that task.

Before doing so, however, it should be made clear that few of the New Frontiersmen conceived of their work in terms of stabilizing an economic empire. For they viewed the economic problems of Latin America through a massive ideological screen, which shut out all hints of imperialism; where others might recognize exploitation, they mainly saw beneficence. A brief look at one of the foundations of their ideology—Walt W. Rostow's *The Stages of Economic Growth: A Non-Communist Manifesto* (1960)—will bring out some of its more potent distortions.

Rostow was far more influential as a policy maker under Johnson than under Kennedy, but as a theoretician of economic development it was his conceptual vocabulary—the "takeoff" into "self-sustained growth"—which most of the New Frontiersmen employed in order to discuss the problems of the Third World. His comprehensive schema of economic change —a worthy rival, he thought, for the theory of Karl Marx—was declared to be applicable to all countries, the underdeveloped as well as the advanced.[38] It detailed how the advanced nations had gone through a "takeoff" period, driven to economic maturity and, in some cases, entered into an era of high mass-consumption; then, it indicated how the underdeveloped countries might begin the same dramatic modernization process.

The Western nations were, in Rostow's theory, a worthy model for the underdeveloped nations to emulate. He acknowledged that the Soviet Union and Communist China had also made major economic advances, but these were de-

nounced as "inhumane." Not only was the West the correct
model; it also had a far different attitude toward Third World
development than did the communist bloc. Communism was
"a disease of the transition";[39] the communists scored their
greatest victories when they seized countries on the brink of
"takeoff"—a socially unsettling stage—and diverted them from
the normal, healthy modernization process. In contrast, the
West hoped only to aid that process along. It was sometimes
negligent of the Third World—strong internal demand in particular kept Western resources at home—but Rostow hoped
that his book, and others like it, would reengage the West's
attention to the problems of underdeveloped countries.

For Rostow, Western imperialism was a thing of the past;
as for American imperialism, it simply did not exist in his
view.[40] A reader of his book would have no sense at all of the
extent to which Western (particularly American) capital dominated the economies of many underdeveloped countries. By
ignoring the facts of Western economic penetration into the
Third World, Rostow was able to avoid some serious problems
in his economic growth model. He did not have to explain, for
example, how an underdeveloped country could begin its
takeoff when its key industries or resources were owned by
foreign corporations. He did not have to show how decisive
economic growth could be initiated by a nation when foreign
corporations determined the rate of investment in its major
sectors in terms of their own interests and needs, and trans-
ported the bulk of profits from those sectors back to the advanced nations. Just as his portrait of the historical process of
economic growth in America and Europe had made no mention of the role of accumulated capital available from the de-
spoliation of other continents, so too did his analysis of the
contemporary process of economic growth in the Third World
ignore the continuing force of Western exploitation. Rostow's
book was overblown and inaccurate as economic theory and
economic history—but for a liberal administration intent upon

economic interventionism in the Third World it made superb ideology.

The economic reality of Latin America bears little relationship to Rostow's theory. Latin America has long been one of the principal arenas for American economic expansion. United States control over large portions of its agricultural and mineral wealth extends back into the nineteenth century. Since the 1930s American investors have also established a powerful position in its belated process of industrialization. As the Brazilian economist Teotonio Dos Santos notes, "American investments (and foreign capital in general) not only have tended to penetrate more deeply into Latin America, but also have become more and more thoroughly integrated in the industrial sectors." [41] Looking at the years immediately preceding the inauguration of the Alliance for Progress, American economic penetration of Latin America continued to be both extensive and highly profitable. From 1951 to 1961, the net flow of capital from Latin America to the United States (profits in excess of direct investments) totaled approximately $4 billion.[42]

The example of the Cuban revolution, with its expropriation of American corporate property as well as the property of domestic landowners and industrialists, opened up for American capitalism the fearful prospect of a loss of all Latin America. To counter this threat, the Alliance for Progress chiefly relied, as we have seen, on a mixture of democratic reforms and military repression. Yet it also had available other tools to safeguard American property in the hemisphere. Two of these tools might be mentioned here: the Investment Guaranty Program and the Hickenlooper Amendment.

The Investment Guaranty Program insured American citizens and corporations investing abroad against losses due to nationalization or inability to convert local currency into U.S. dollars. The 1963 Foreign Assistance Act provided that any underdeveloped country which failed to sign an investment guaranty treaty with the United States would cease, after De-

cember 31, 1965, to receive American aid. Similarly, the Hickenlooper Amendment (which President Kennedy opposed but
did not publicly fight [43]) to the Foreign Assistance Act of 1962
provided that foreign aid would be cut off from any country
which either nationalized or placed excessive tax burdens upon
corporations owned by Americans; aid might be continued
only if "equitable and speedy" compensation was offered or the
taxes rescinded. Both these provisions were designed largely
with Latin America in mind; they sought to forestall Latin
American governments from following the Cubans' example in
terminating the privileged American position in their economies. Despite the Alliance claim to promote the economic
development of Latin American nations, any development
measure that infringed upon American property interests was
expressly denied to them.

U.S. aid to Latin America under the Alliance also reflected
the interests of American investors. That aid was primarily in
the form of loans rather than grants (which had been given to
European nations under the Marshall Plan and which continued to be given in large amounts to American dependencies like
South Vietnam, South Korea, and Taiwan). In order to qualify
for loans, either from the United States government or from the
international banking institutions which participated in the
Alliance, it was usually necessary for Latin American governments to show that they were pursuing a policy of monetary
and fiscal stabilization, i.e., credit restraint and balanced budgets. This ruled out deficit financing for measures like agrarian
reform, or public works to alleviate unemployment; it severely
limited Latin America's developmental alternatives. But it was
good conservative banking for the World Bank or the International Monetary Fund. And even more important to those
banks and to the American officials with whom they closely
cooperated, it ensured a stable—and thus "healthy"—climate
for private investment.[44]

As for the aid that was given to Latin American nations

under the Alliance, the bulk of the money never left the United
States. Much of American assistance was "tied"—it could only
be used for the purchase of commodities in the United States, at
American prices (thus creating a substantial subsidy for American businesses). From these loans the Latin Americans at least
received goods; from other loans they received nothing save a
release from past debts. The figures on debt servicing, reported
by Levinson and de Onis, are a remarkable comment on the
Alliance. From 1961 to 1969, American assistance to Latin
America totaled $10.28 billion. Net disbursements (gross dis-
bursements less repayment and interest), however, were only
$4.8 billion. More than half the funds allocated for the Alliance
stayed in the United States to service Latin American debts.[45]

We have seen how little Latin America benefited from the
Alliance. How did American businesses fare under it? In the
first years of the Alliance American investment in Latin America declined, amid fears of imminent revolution and even of
Alliance reforms. But the nightmare of Castroism receded after
the Cuban missile crisis, and when Brazil was "stabilized" in
1964, American corporations once again began to look to the
south. By the late 1960s expansion was brisk. As a market for
U.S. goods and services, Latin America ranked second only to
Canada. American private investment in Latin America was
also on the upsurge; in 1969, the Department of Commerce
detected "a gradual shift in investment from Canada and
western Europe to Latin America and other countries." [46] The
ideal of the "democratic revolution" had long since died, but
American imperialism in Latin America was still vigorous.

The Alliance for Progress, despite its noble pretensions,
furthered American imperialism in Latin America. While most
of its reforms failed to take hold, its efforts to maintain and
increase American investments in the hemisphere were substantially successful. To some backers of the Alliance this outcome was no doubt satisfactory; their commitments had always
been to the American corporate order in Latin America. In

Kennedy's case, however, the Alliance was a profound disappointment. Kennedy was not a self-conscious or cynical imperialist. His motives were more complex; indeed, they were a prime source of the sort of contradictions that beset the Alliance from the outset.

Kennedy's relationship to the business community with regard to Latin America illustrated some of these contradictions. During the early days of the Alliance he spoke of putting the national interest of the United States (in Latin American development) above the interests of American corporations; further, he criticized the traditional idea that private investment was the panacea for Latin America's problems. In the Charter of Punta del Este encouragement of private enterprise was only one of the numerous goals—and it was overshadowed by the more dramatic reforms. But American business was not happy about being relegated to this secondary place in U.S. policy toward Latin America. Hence, Schlesinger reports, the Alliance came under "growing pressure from United States companies doing Latin American business to talk less about social reform and more about private investment." [47]

As investment in Latin America lagged, Kennedy eventually succumbed to the pressure. References to the virtue of foreign investments now became more frequent in his speeches. By the time of his 1963 message to Congress on foreign aid, this had become a dominant theme: "The primary initiative in this year's program relates to our increased efforts to encourage the investment of private capital in the underdeveloped countries." [48] Such capital was, he told the Inter-American Press Association on November 18, 1963, a key to the Alliance's eventual success: "If encouraged, private investment, responsive to the needs, the laws, and the interests of the nation, can cooperate with public activity to provide the vital margin of success as it did in the development of all the nations of the West. . . ." [49]

Kennedy also began, in this period, to work more closely

with the top executives of American corporations that had substantial investments in Latin America. On November 19, 1963, he wrote to David Rockefeller to express his interest in the Business Group for Latin America, which Rockefeller headed. Kennedy welcomed the formation of this new group, whose membership list read like a Who's Who of the American corporate elite; it would, he said, "provide an exceptional opportunity for improved consultations between the United States Government and the business community on certain aspects of U.S.–Latin American affairs." David Bell, director of the Agency for International Development, was designated as the coordinator for relationships between the Administration and corporate leaders; he was to facilitate contacts between various federal agencies and members of the Business Group.[50]

It was not business pressure, however, or business connections that ultimately made John Kennedy the servant of American imperialism in Latin America. A more crucial factor was his own ideological conviction. Kennedy saw himself, not as a tool of American corporations, but as a proponent of Latin American modernization. In the theory of modernization he had adopted, American investment was an aid to Latin American development; the profits flowing back to the United States were matched by the Latin Americans' profit in obtaining a modern industrial base. The protection and extension of the American economic stake in the hemisphere benefited all concerned. Kennedy thus was ill equipped to notice the contradictions: capital flowing out of Latin America faster than it flowed in, American corporations "developing" Latin America by exploiting its resources and subordinating its economic needs to their own, "nationalistic" and "progressive" bourgeoisie who collaborated with American corporate allies in maintaining a stagnant status quo. For all his analysis of Latin America's problems, Kennedy never grasped what was the single greatest roadblock to its progress—American imperialism.

Kennedy's goals in Latin America—material progress

linked with reform, military suppression of revolutionary activity, protection of American property holdings—were, in his mind, fully consistent and congruent. But the first did not materialize; the record for the second was mixed; only the last was effectively accomplished. Reform and growth could not coexist in Latin America with repression and imperialist exploitation. Whatever generous and liberating impulses Kennedy's mode of global liberalism possessed were, therefore, inevitably subordinated in Latin America to its more selfish and repressive aims.

Until the early 1970s, John Kennedy's part in the Vietnam War had been underestimated, even by most critics of American policy. The agony of "Johnson's war" made Kennedy's mistakes in Vietnam seem mild in comparison. But such a view is no longer tenable. The revelations of the Pentagon Papers, and the well-documented analyses of the Institute for Policy Studies, have made clear a continuity in Vietnam planning between the Kennedy and Johnson Administrations. Beyond this, they have located in the Kennedy Administration the origin of most of the assumptions that later governed Johnson's conduct in the war. Richard J. Walton sums up concisely the new historical appreciation of Kennedy in Vietnam: "Vietnam is Kennedy's most lasting legacy. . . ." [51]

In my narrative of Kennedy's actions in Vietnam, I unavoidably cover some of the same ground as other recent studies. My principal concern, however, is somewhat different from theirs. It is to place the Vietnam experience in the context of Kennedy's global policy, in particular his approach to the Third World. To do this, I return briefly to a discussion of Kennedy's conception of world politics and the military strategy devised in light of that conception. Also, I draw upon the foregoing analysis of the Alliance for Progress for comparisons with New Frontier thinking in Vietnam. My aim is not to provide a comprehensive history of Kennedy's involvement in

Vietnam; rather, it is to investigate what Vietnam meant for Kennedy, and what American involvement there reflected about the politics of his Administration.

In an earlier chapter we examined Kennedy's conception of a world haunted by ceaseless conflict. According to that conception, the relentless advance of the Soviet Union and its communist allies after the launching of Sputnik in 1957 had turned every corner of the globe into an East-West battlefield. The communists' tactics in this intensified phase of the Cold War were chiefly two: nuclear "blackmail" by the Soviet Union, and "nibbling away" by its allies and agents at the periphery of the Free World through subversion and guerrilla warfare. Both were designed to achieve the same end: a shift in the international balance of power, an erosion of Free World security, and, eventually, world domination by a communist order. Together, they constituted the supreme crisis of the era —in Kennedy's words, "the hour of maximum danger."

It was America's unique "burden" and "glory" to defend freedom against this communist challenge. A series of Kennedy metaphors—"keystone in the arch of freedom," "sentinel at the gate," "watchman on the walls of world freedom" [52] —continually reasserted U.S. global responsibility. But the concomitant of this responsibility was involvement. Global interventionism was sanctioned for America by its historical destiny; Americans sent to foreign nations became, by definition, the safeguards of freedom.

> There are 1 million Americans serving outside the
> frontiers of the United States. I don't know of any
> country in history that has had such a high percentage
> of its population serving outside its borders for such a
> long time on a mission of freedom.[53]

The Kennedy Administration devised a response to each aspect of the communist challenge. Soviet nuclear blackmail (as the Administration interpreted it) was to be frustrated by displays of American resolve, in the showdowns over Berlin and the Cuban missiles. Against communist nibbling in the Third World the American answer was dual. Modernization and nation-building theories were employed in an attempt to overcome the poverty and social instability upon which communist agitation fed. And to protect the process of modernization from those who would seek to wreck it, a new military strategy—counterinsurgency—was developed. We have seen how modernization theories worked out in the case of Latin America; in the case of Vietnam we shall witness counterinsurgency too in its heyday.[54]

The subject of counterinsurgency seemed to hold a special fascination for John Kennedy. Believing that the military had not paid it sufficient attention, he made the development of an American antiguerrilla force his personal project. He read up on guerrilla warfare in the texts of Mao Tse-tung and Che Guevara, expanded the Special Forces and bestowed on them the elite green beret over Pentagon objections, even supervised the selection of new equipment for American jungle fighters. He also sought to pass his enthusiasm on to the rest of his administration; the State Department, for example, was instructed to establish a counterinsurgency course which would be mandatory for all personnel assigned to Third World countries. The American counterinsurgency establishment which burgeoned throughout the 1960s was fundamentally Kennedy's creation, as Maxwell Taylor pointed out in a 1965 speech: "I think we should look to President Kennedy as the architect in large measure of the programs and policies of my government and eventually of many other governments directed at facing the challenge of what was originally called subversive insurgency." [55]

There was a strong element of romanticism in all this concern with counterinsurgency. The talk was of grim and almost invisible struggle; the names ("Seals" for the Navy commandos, "Jungle Jims" for the Air Force antiguerrilla teams) and insignias (Army Green Berets), on the other hand, were laden with highly visible glamour. The appetite for heroics that marked the New Frontier clearly had its military counterpart in the new counterinsurgency units. Kennedy himself was not immune to the Green Beret image. Its aura of toughness was, we have seen, something he continually attempted to cultivate. Even his celebrated reading of Mao and Che, in order to learn how they might be defeated, suggested the kind of self-image which his counterinsurgency project fed; military strategy had been transformed here, at least psychologically, into a mode of personal combat.

As both a key element in the global counteroffensive against communism, and a favorite pet project, the counterinsurgency apparatus was rapidly expanded by Kennedy. During his administration American forces trained to fight what were then known as "unconventional wars" were increased by 500 percent. Strategic (i.e., nuclear) and conventional forces were substantially increased at the same time, in accordance with the theory of flexible response.[56] Some of the conventional weaponry, indeed even some of the new strategic arsenal, was recognized by Kennedy to be potentially of use in an "unconventional war." Questioned at a press conference early in 1963 about why the United States continued to build manned bombers in an age of missiles, he gave a prophetic answer: "There may be a good many struggles in the globe in the late sixties and early seventies which are not subject to solution by missiles; [there] may be more limited wars[s], . . . where manned bombers may be very useful." [57]

The fruit of this fascination with counterinsurgency was Vietnam. The deepening American involvement in the Vietnamese civil war during the Kennedy Administration could be traced back to a host of rationales, but most of these had something to do with counterinsurgency. In the first place, Vietnam was seen as a fertile proving ground for the new antiguerrilla apparatus. Maxwell Taylor, testifying before a congressional committee in 1963, certified its virtues as America's prime counterinsurgency "laboratory":

> Here we have a going laboratory where we see
> subversive insurgency, the Ho Chi Minh doctrine,
> being applied in all its forms. This has been a
> challenge not just for the armed services, but for
> several of the agencies of Government, as many of them
> are involved in one way or another in South Vietnam.
> On the military side, however, we have recognized
> the importance of the area as a laboratory. We have
> had teams out there looking at equipment
> requirements of this kind of guerrilla warfare. We
> have rotated senior officers through there, spending
> several weeks just to talk to people and get the feel of
> the operation, so even though not regularly assigned
> to Vietnam, they are carrying their experience back to
> their own organization.[58]

Even more important than the idea of a proving ground was the notion of Vietnam as a test case for the communist doctrine of "wars of liberation." Kennedy had fixed on Khrushchev's speech of January 6, 1961—proclaiming "wars of liberation" to be the means to a socialist future—as the new communist gospel. Insurgency in Vietnam thus took on a new dimension. It now became Moscow's (or alternately Peking's) effort to test the utility of its theory in a vulnerable sector of the Free World. If America failed to meet the test, and victory went to the insurgents, the theory would be verified in communist eyes; guerrilla warfare would soon proliferate everywhere. America had, in Robert McNamara's words, "to prove in the Vietnamese test case that the free world can cope with Communist 'wars of liberation' as we have coped successfully with Communist aggression at other levels." [59] In order to discourage peasant revolutionaries throughout the Third World —and the communist masterminds who presumably manipulated them—Kennedy and his advisers set out to crush the insurgency in Vietnam.

This interpretation does not, of course, accord with what Kennedy's chroniclers have told us. They portray him as expanding the American role in Vietnam only with great reluctance. Schlesinger, for instance, argues that Kennedy, "who had watched western policy in Vietnam in the early fifties with the greatest skepticism and who as President used to mutter from time to time about our 'overcommitment' in Southeast Asia, had no choice now but to work within the situation he had inherited." [60] No doubt Schlesinger is correct in recalling Kennedy's skepticism and doubt—but left out of his picture is that passion for counterinsurgency which overmastered such doubts. Kennedy, the designer of a new apparatus of counter-revolution, was not trapped into the war in Vietnam. As the following narrative shows, he chose that war.

In the early months of Kennedy's Presidency the subject of Vietnam was overshadowed by events in neighboring Laos. But the dramatic growth of the Viet Cong-led insurgency could not be ignored for long. On April 12, 1961, White House adviser W. W. Rostow presented Kennedy with a memorandum asserting that it was now time for "gearing up the whole Vietnam operation." [61] Responding to this memorandum, Kennedy on April 20 established a task force on Vietnam, headed by Deputy Defense Secretary Roswell Gilpatric. Its job, as Kennedy defined it, was "to appraise . . . the Communist drive to dominate South Vietnam" and "to recommend a series of actions (military, political and/or economic, overt and/or covert) which, in your opinion, will prevent Communist domination of that country." [62]

The Gilpatric task force report recommended that Kennedy immediately dispatch 400 Special Forces troops to Vietnam, and that he instruct the Pentagon to study a further buildup. It also proposed consultations with President Diem on the possibility of a bilateral military alliance between the United States and South Vietnam. It was recognized that both the deployment of the Special Forces troops and the proposed alliance were violations of the Geneva accords of 1954, yet this was not considered a major obstacle. The troop movement would not be publicized; the alliance, if it was contracted, would be legitimized "on the grounds that the Geneva accords have placed inhibitions upon Free World action while at the same time placing no restrictions upon the Communists." [63]

On May 11, Kennedy adopted these recommendations in the form of National Security Action Memorandum 52. The dispatch of 400 Special Forces troops was approved, as were negotiations for a bilateral alliance. Kennedy also approved plans for initiating a campaign of covert warfare against North Vietnam. Undercover teams were to be infiltrated into the north for purposes of "sabotage and light harassment." [64] Overflights of North Vietnam were to be conducted as well; their mission (specified in language which disclosed Washington's incredible misunderstanding of who its foe was) was "to harass the Communists and to *maintain morale of North Vietnamese population.*" [65]

National Security Action Memorandum 52 marked Kennedy's first major escalation of American involvement in the war in Vietnam. His decisions on this occasion disclosed a great deal, both about how the war was to be fought and about how it was to be interpreted. The sending of Green Berets and the program for covert warfare pointed to the conception of a "subterranean" war, largely hidden from public view. The rationalization for violating the conditions of the Geneva accords foreshadowed a series of mystifications designed to keep the war hidden. That undercover operations were directed against North Vietnam was particularly revealing. It indicated that, despite a scarcity of evidence, the Kennedy Administration had already fixed on North Vietnam as the real aggressor in the south.

In the following months the President sent a series of representatives to South Vietnam. Lyndon Johnson's mission, on a visit to Saigon in May, was to bolster Diem's confidence in the United States by inviting him to "request" American troops. To Washington's surprise Diem, fearful of appearing a colonial puppet, declined the invitation. Johnson nonetheless came away impressed; publicly lionizing Diem as the "Churchill of Asia," in private he urged Kennedy to commit the United States to a major effort in South Vietnam. Professor Eugene Staley's mission was more successful. With the enthusiastic collaboration of Ngo Dinh Nhu, Diem's brother and "eminence grise," Staley devised a war plan for Vietnam centered around the idea of "strategic hamlets." [66] I shall discuss the strategic hamlet system in some detail later in this chapter; it was to be the pivot for the entire counterinsurgency undertaking.

By October, Diem had reversed his previous stand; in the face of mounting Viet Cong pressure he now wanted American ground troops. So Kennedy announced yet another mission to Vietnam, this time headed by Maxwell Taylor and W. W. Rostow. The purpose of the Taylor-Rostow mission, Ralph Stavins notes, "was to examine the feasibility of dispatching U.S. troops; Kennedy specifically recommended that the mission look into the question of troop requirements." [67] Arriving in Saigon in mid-October, Taylor and Rostow were greeted by Diem's declaration of a state of emergency. In this tense atmosphere Taylor twice conferred with Diem; afterward he sent a series of messages back to Washington, containing his proposals for further American action. These proposals ignited fervent discussion in Washington; they served, ultimately, to inaugurate the next phase in America's participation in the war.

Taylor argued in favor of introducing a sizable American military force into South Vietnam. He recognized that there were several potential disadvantages to such a course of action: weakening of the American strategic reserve, engagement of American prestige, future pressures for reinforcement, the risk of escalation into a major Asian war. Yet once having noted

these disadvantages, he promptly dismissed them. With reasoning that was to typify the Kennedy Administration's (and its
successors') understanding of the war, Taylor cabled to Kennedy the following assessment of North Vietnamese weakness
and American power:

> The risks of backing into a major Asian war by way of
> SVN are present but are not impressive. NVN is
> extremely vulnerable to conventional bombing, a
> weakness which should be exploited diplomatically in
> convincing Hanoi to lay off SVN. Both the D.R.V. and
> the Chicoms would face severe logistical difficulties in
> trying to maintain strong forces in the field in SEA,
> difficulties which we share but by no means to the
> same degree.[68]

The military task force Taylor recommended was to be
composed of about 8000 men. It was to conduct logistical
operations in support of the South Vietnamese army, and
combat operations when required by self-defense; further, it
was to serve as an emergency reserve for the Diem government
in the event of a military crisis. More important than its military functions, however, were its symbolic functions. It would,
in Taylor's words, "provide a U.S. military presence capable of
raising national morale and of showing to Southeast Asia the
seriousness of the U.S. intent to resist a Communist takeover." [69] The perception of international politics as a test of
will, which has cropped up so often in this account of Kennedy's foreign policy, was again evident in Taylor's war scenario. A path to victory was thereby defined—encourage
Saigon and discourage Hanoi by demonstrating American will
and determination.

Taylor also urged a major administrative change, defined
as the establishment of a "limited partnership" between the
United States and the government of South Vietnam. The
Kennedy Administration was dissatisfied with Diem's bureau-

cracy as an instrument for prosecuting the war; it had shown itself to be both inefficient and resistant to carrying out even a modicum of social reform. So Taylor proposed that the United States "provide individual administrators for insertion into the governmental machinery of South Vietnam in types and numbers to be worked out with President Diem." [70] He had in mind a shadow bureaucracy of dedicated Americans, whose know-how, drive, and commitment to reform would, in the jargon of the day, "win the hearts and minds of the people" for the Saigon government.

As in the Alliance for Progress, the Kennedy Administration conceived of social reform as the key in Vietnam to weaning the peasants away from the guerrilla movement. But Diem refused to bend to the periodic American clamoring for reform. Taylor's "limited partnership" would have circumvented this roadblock to American plans. It would have placed American personnel in a position to do what Diem and his underlings resisted doing—eliminate corruption, weed out incompetence, provide social services (land, schools, health care) to the people. In Latin America the Kennedy Administration thought it could inspire and direct a "democratic revolution" from the outside. In Vietnam the limitations of America's tools were more obvious; hence, it became essential for Americans to move in and actively run the campaign for social change themselves.

U.S. troops and U.S. administrators were both seen, in Taylor's report to Kennedy, as supplying South Vietnam with the vital spark which the Diem regime could not provide. Underlying all his proposals was the assumption that the influx of Americans would demonstrate to the dispirited South Vietnamese "the élan and style needed to win." [71] Whatever understanding Taylor had of Vietnamese realities, it was subordinate here to the bloated mystique of the New Frontier. He —and his colleagues—hoped to cure the Diem regime's corruption and authoritarianism with American dedication, and also to combat the Viet Cong revolutionaries with American pragmatism. If all this failed, there was, of course, a safety factor—American power.

Receipt of Taylor's report inspired other Kennedy Administration officials to offer their own Vietnam proposals. Those of Dean Rusk and Robert McNamara were especially noteworthy. As Ralph Stavins has observed, "what is striking about the recommendations by the Secretary of State and the Secretary of Defense is that each, within his particular domain, went beyond the suggestions made by General Taylor." [72] Where Taylor had spoken of a "limited partnership" in administration between the United States and the Diem regime, Rusk cast aside the euphemism of cooperation to speak frankly about American control. He wanted to determine what might be expected from Diem "if our assistance forces us to assume de facto direction of South Vietnamese affairs." [73] McNamara similarly outdid Taylor's proposals on the matter of troop requirements. Endorsing the request for an initial 8000 combat troops, he envisioned a possible North Vietnamese and Chinese response in force. But, he assured the President, "in view of the logistic difficulties faced by the other side, I believe we can assume that the maximum U.S. forces required on the ground in Southeast Asia will not exceed 6 divisions, or about 205,000 men." [74] The highest-ranking civilian officials in the Kennedy Administration were, it would seem, even more ready than Kennedy's chief military adviser to immerse the United States in the Vietnamese conflict.

Despite agreement among his senior advisers, despite Diem's appeals, Kennedy decided in November 1961 against the immediate dispatch of American combat troops to Vietnam. He stated, in National Security Action Memorandum 111, that the "objective of our policy is to do all possible to accomplish our purpose without use of U.S. combat forces." [75] Noting widespread public criticism of the Diem regime, Kennedy further expressed the intention of calling on Diem to introduce the kind of reforms that could win the support of both his own population and foreign opinion. Toward this end he requested of Diem, along the lines of the Taylor report, an American "share in the decision-making process in the political, economic and military fields as they affect the security situation." [76]

Kennedy's decision was *not* a rejection of the Taylor report. While the President vetoed combat troops, he agreed with Taylor's contention that an expansion of the American war effort was needed. In place of the immediate deployment of 8000 troops, he ordered a protracted buildup of American military manpower and matériel in Vietnam. United States "support troops" and "advisers," helicopters and heavy weapons, thus began to flow into South Vietnam in growing numbers at the end of 1961. Whatever their nomenclature, American troops were to perform a major combat role in the next two years. By the time of Kennedy's death there would be over 16,000 of them—double the number in Taylor's proposal.

The decision against combat troops has been one of the most disputed aspects of Kennedy's handling of the war. For some of his admirers, plainly anxious to dissociate Kennedy from Lyndon Johnson's subsequent employment of troops, his choice reflects a healthy suspicion of a purely military approach toward Vietnam. Sorensen, for example, argues that Kennedy perceived more clearly than the majority of his associates that military force was insufficient to defeat the insurgents.[77] In Sorensen's view Kennedy understood the limitations of American military intervention in Vietnam; he saw that the primary effort had to be political as well as military, and it had to be made by the South Vietnamese themselves.

Critics have viewed Kennedy's decision in a different light. Ralph Stavins has argued that what Kennedy chose at this juncture was to increase American involvement in the fighting, yet disguise that fact by conducting Vietnam as a "private war." More concerned than his advisers about adverse public sentiment toward the Diem regime, both in the United States

Stavins! Why he kept Assert the mili. actions

and abroad, Kennedy wanted to keep secret the growing
American military commitment to the regime. The elaborate
set of guises for American military personnel, as well as the
misleading of the press and other tactics, were designed to
protect this secret, to ensure that the extent of American participation in Vietnam remained the private knowledge of the
Kennedy circle. In Stavins' analysis only this dimension of
secrecy separates Kennedy from Taylor, Rusk, or McNamara
—"he disregarded the counsel of his advisers only to the extent
that they preferred a public war." [78]

Stavins' argument is intriguing, yet it seems to me somewhat miscast. Certainly there were factors militating against a
visible American military escalation in Vietnam. The possible
unsettling of the shaky compromise in Laos and the chance of a
confrontation with the Soviet Union elsewhere in the world
disturbed Kennedy in this regard, as did congressional and
public opposition to the use of American troops.[79] But beyond
these factors was a more fundamental question: what sort of
war was the United States fighting in Vietnam? Taylor's
proposed 8000 troops, and McNamara's projection of a further
six divisions, pointed to the conception of Vietnam as a basically conventional war. Kennedy was not yet ready, I believe,
to accept this conception. He still viewed Vietnam primarily
within the context of the communist doctrine of "wars of liberation"; Vietnam was to be the testing ground for American
ability to discredit that doctrine. Application of conventional
power at the insurgency stage of a "war of liberation" would
have been, in his eyes, both premature and ineffectual. What
Kennedy chose in November of 1961 was, then, not so much a
"private war" as an "unconventional war." He was committing
the United States, as Sorensen observed, to its first major
counterinsurgency venture.[80]

Sorensen is, in a sense, correct in characterizing Kennedy's
stance as "political" rather than "military." Contrary to most
of his senior advisers, Kennedy believed that meeting the chal-

Kenn. saw in "pol. terms" more than military

?? objectives (caution) rationals involved

lenge of Vietnamese insurgency required "an emphasis on political, economic and social action into which very carefully
calibrated military measures were interwoven." [81] He sympathized with the views of junior advisers like Roger Hilsman
and Michael Forrestal, who thought the key to victory in Vietnam was "winning the hearts and minds" of the peasants by
offering both reform and security inside the strategic hamlets.
In *this* sense Kennedy did favor a "political" approach to Vietnam. Yet the debate between the "military" and "political"
approaches was really over tactics only; both sides were equally
intent on prosecuting the war more vigorously. The horrors of
an increasingly brutal war would be wreaked upon Vietnam by
the advocates of the new "political approach" just as by the
proponents of traditional military methods.

By mid-November of 1961, Kennedy had decided to increase military aid to Diem, with the hope that this move would
"encourage" the South Vietnamese President to welcome
Americans into his bureaucracy and begin the process of social
reform. But Diem, unhappy that the combat troops he had
requested were not forthcoming, spurned the American con-
cepts of "limited partnership" and social reform. He complained that the United States was asking him to relinquish a
substantial portion of South Vietnamese sovereignty in exchange for little extra in the way of support. Anxious not to
upset further the brooding Diem, Washington quickly backed
down on the demands for reform and participation in decision
making. Diem would be supplied with a host of new American
"advisers" and weapons, regardless of the political course he
followed.

The ensuing American buildup was swift. According to the
Pentagon Papers, "the number of American servicemen in
Vietnam jumped from 948 at the end of November to 2,646 by
January 9 and would reach 5,576 by June 30." [82] The addi-
tional advisers and equipment seemed to improve Saigon's
military position through the first half of 1962. American-

piloted helicopters in particular plagued the Viet Cong, who were forced to retreat from some of the territory they had taken over in previous fighting. But this change in the momentum of the war did not last long. "During the course of the year the Vietcong learned to cope better with the helicopters and compensated for the superior firepower of the other American equipment by capturing a considerable part of it for their own use. The tide of battle once more began to turn against Saigon." [83]

Accompanying the broadening of the war's scope in this period was an intensification of its terror. The Viet Cong struck back at the newly strengthened Diem regime with a mounting campaign of terrorism. Their deeds were more than matched, however, by technological horrors devised in America. Entire Vietnamese villages were scorched by American-made napalm, dropped from planes sometimes piloted by Americans. Crops and livestock were destroyed by chemical bombardment, lest they serve the needs of the guerrillas; the technique of defoliation was, by 1962, being used over extensive areas of rural Vietnam.

The sanctioning of defoliation by President Kennedy's Special Group for Counter-Insurgency (co-chaired by Maxwell Taylor and Robert Kennedy) indicated something of the manner in which the New Frontiersmen regarded Vietnam. Ralph Stavins, who had access to notes from the meetings of the Special Group, has written that

> as early as 1961, the defoliation program, originally designated Operation Hades and subsequently accorded the euphemism Operation Ranchhand, was granted Presidential approval. Limited at first as an experimental measure, it soon became an exercise in wholesale crop destruction. The expanded program received strong financial and political support. Discussions of Operation Ranchhand in Washington were instructive, especially as they illuminated the

amount of bureaucratic concern for the consequences
of their own decisions. There was none. Indeed, what
was most striking about the discussions of the
defoliation program at the Special Group meetings
was the total absence of inquiry into the nature of the
program. No limits were ever established, no results
examined, no damage surveyed. Concern about the
program focused on the single question of whether
the South Vietnamese military had given their
consent.[84]

The actual techniques employed in the Vietnamese "laboratory" apparently did not much interest most top officials in the
Kennedy Administration. They acted like scientific administrators, glad to facilitate whatever projects experimenters in the
field cooked up. Unconcerned about the consequences of those
projects, they initiated a decade of destruction in Vietnam. The
barbarism of American conduct in Vietnam, which fired an
antiwar movement into protest against the Johnson Administration, began with these little-noticed programs of the Kennedy Administration.

The Kennedy Administration was also responsible for setting another pattern in Vietnam—the resort to mystification
and deception to hide the reality of American actions from the
press and public. Washington's judgment was that the public
was too unsophisticated to understand the necessity of Americans fighting and dying for the aloof, dictatorial Diem. So an
attempt was made to conceal the expanding U.S. involvement.
Troop deployments were not publicized; participation by
American units in combat operations was played down. The
attempt was frustrated, however, by an aggressive, dedicated
band of American reporters determined to expose what they
saw rather than repeat what they had been officially told. To
the consternation of the Kennedy Administration, these reporters portrayed a war that was, with American help, rapidly
widening—and yet still going poorly for the Diem regime.

As newspaper articles about U.S. soldiers killed or heli-copters shot down became more frequent, Kennedy personally took a hand in the war between the American press and the American mission in Vietnam. His Press Secretary, Pierre Salinger, relates that "President Kennedy was particularly sensitive about some of these articles. It was my view at that time that we should be prepared to take the good stories with the bad in Vietnam, but the President pushed hard for us to tighten the rules there under which correspondents could observe field operations in person." [85] Keeping reporters stuck in Saigon was one tactic to curtail unfavorable stories; on occasion, Kennedy was prepared to adopt even stronger tactics. Thus, he tried to terminate the Vietnam assignment of David Halberstam, one of the most critical of American journalists, through an unusual display of presidential "persuasion." Salinger has acknowledged that the President "suggested to Arthur Hays Sulzberger, the new publisher of the *New York Times*, that he might give Halberstam a vacation and remove him from Vietnam." [86] This venture at press management in Vietnam, like most others during the Kennedy Administration, did not succeed. Halberstam stayed.

During 1962, the pivotal program in the counterinsurgency effort was launched. This was the strategic-hamlet system, designed by Eugene Staley and Ngo Dinh Nhu and enthusiastically promoted by the British antiguerrilla expert, Sir Robert K.G. Thompson. The story of the strategic hamlets in 1962–63 deserves particular attention, for it typifies the fate of the Kennedy Administration in Vietnam.

The concept of strategic hamlets recognized that the source of a guerrilla army's manpower and supplies was not an external power but the indigenous population itself. To defeat that army, military measures alone were insufficient; the fundamental task was to separate the guerrillas from their base of support—the people. Strategic hamlets were conceived of as enforcing this separation, by physically removing the rural population from the clutches of the Viet Cong.[87]

Since Viet Cong success with the peasantry was believed to derive from a mixture of coercion and political promises, the strategic hamlets too were to have a dual nature. First, they were to be fortresses. By enclosing them with moats and barbed wire and supplying the villagers with arms, the sway of Viet Cong terror was to be broken. The peasants could then feel secure in yielding their allegiance to the government in Saigon. Second, the hamlets were to serve as loci for social reform. To best the Viet Cong political appeal, the government would send civic-action teams into them as the bearers of social change. These teams would gain the peasants' allegiance by providing varied services: extending agricultural loans, constructing schools, digging wells, establishing village administrative and police systems. This was the heart of the "political approach" to Vietnam.

It was an essential feature of the strategic hamlets that they form a tightly knit and highly controlled system. As Roger Hilsman, one of the leading exponents of the hamlets in the Kennedy Administration, put it:

> There had to be hedgehogs of strategic hamlets, slowly spreading out like an oil blot from the sea toward the mountains and jungle. Plastic identity cards had to be issued, curfews established, and provincial forces trained to set up checkpoints and ambushes during curfew hours. An iron grid of security had to be established to control the movement of both goods and people, of rice and recruits. A solid bloc of these hamlets, firmly established and consolidated, had to be extended outward to make a zone of security.[88]

There were several parallels between the strategic-hamlet program and the "democratic revolution" which the Kennedy Administration was simultaneously conducting in Latin America. Reform was, in each case, perceived to be the best means of undercutting the appeal of guerrilla revolutionaries. But in Vietnam, as in Latin America, the Kennedy Administration banked on an improbable agent of social reform. The Diem regime, staffed by ex-colonial bureaucrats and beholden to large absentee landowners, was not about to "revolutionize" the Vietnamese countryside. Its officials understood the reform aspects of the strategic-hamlet program more as an opportunity to enrich themselves than as a chance to woo the peasants. "Widespread corruption attended the enterprise, so most of the peasants could not discover the promised social services and usually were not even adequately compensated for the land they had been forced to abandon." [89] In Vietnam, as in Latin America, revolution from the top simply meant no revolution at all.

Another similarity was in the strengthening of the apparatus of repression. The Kennedy Administration, it will be recalled, developed training academies for Latin America's military and police, and supplied them with brand-new equipment in order to prepare them for the task of suppressing domestic discontent. The strategic-hamlet program in Vietnam was even more ambitious in its vision of repression. It proposed to extend a government presence into every village, to police —through curfews, checkpoints, identity cards—the entire countryside. Its objective was, in Hilsman's phrase, "an iron grid of security," where all movement was under control and all activity under surveillance. In this setting the government could, without competition, presumably go about "winning the hearts and minds of the people." [90]

The most obvious parallel between the strategic hamlets and the Alliance for Progress was that both were failures. Vietnamese peasants resented being forced from their ancestral homes into what were often little better than concentration camps. Their resentment grew as the promised social reforms evaporated amid governmental corruption. Worse, the hamlets could not even protect peasants from the fighting. Military security was lax, especially since Ngo Dinh Nhu rushed to construct hamlets haphazardly throughout the country; the Viet Cong were continually overrunning vulnerable sites. Despite all these problems, the Kennedy Administration remained optimistic about its strategic-hamlet program until the fall of Diem. "When Diem was assassinated in 1963," Ralph Stavins notes, "thousands of strategic hamlets collapsed overnight." [91] The wreckage could no longer be ignored.

It is instructive to observe how the adherents of the strategic-hamlet program accounted for that failure. For Roger Hilsman, the blame rested, not with the concept, but with its implementation. A valuable tool for counterinsurgency had been wrecked in Vietnam by the ambitious Nhu, who ignored the "oil blot" principle in his haste for personal control over the countryside, and by the American military, whose large-scale ground operations and interdiction bombing alienated the same peasants whom the hamlets were seeking to win over. Hilsman never questioned the worth of his favorite scheme; he only bemoaned the fact that it had not been applied properly or vigorously enough. One of his suggestions, for example, was the improvement of police work inside the hamlets; tighter surveillance over the peasants' movements was needed, he argued, to weed out Viet Cong agents.[92] The liberal Hilsman was, in the end, reduced to advocating a stronger, more totalitarian mode of control over the people of South Vietnam.

Such was the fate of the "political approach" to Vietnam. As an alternative to the military's favored course, it offered only paper reforms and extensive if clumsy repression. Understanding that the problems of the Vietnamese people were the key to the outcome of the war, the only solution it could provide was to pen up those people. An exercise in counterrevolution, the strategic-hamlet program failed to grasp both the hopeless corruption of America's ally and the enduring strength of its foe. When it collapsed, Vietnam was essentially lost to the practitioners of counterinsurgency. The advocates of conventional methods, of ground troops in the south and bombing in the north, now took over completely the planning of the war.

Through the last half of 1962, and the early part of 1963, there was widespread optimism within the Kennedy Administration concerning the war. Although Kennedy intimates would later claim that the President did not share that optimism, in public he expressed the prevailing view. He remarked in his 1963 State of the Union message that "the spearpoint of aggression has been blunted in Vietnam." [93] But in May, the unpopular and unstable Diem regime began to come apart. South Vietnamese troops fired into a Buddhist crowd in Hue on May 8, killing eight and setting off widespread demonstrations. Bloody clashes between Diem's forces and the Buddhists, and the horrifying self-immolation of Buddhist priests, continued through the summer, exposing vividly the bankruptcy and brutality of the government to which the United States had tied its fortunes in Vietnam. The American public at last started to glimpse the fact that something was amiss in Vietnam—and Kennedy, despite all his work at press management, suddenly found himself burdened with a major political liability, in the person of Diem.

In August, after Diem and his brother Nhu dispatched their own Special Forces troops to raid Buddhist pagodas throughout the country, the Kennedy Administration began to consider ridding itself of this liability. The tortuous history of subsequent American complicity in the plot to overthrow Diem has been related in detail in the Pentagon Papers, and need not occupy us here. Parallel to this history, however, are a series of public statements Kennedy made on Vietnam, and these do merit our attention. For they reveal what stakes the President, despite his disillusionment with Diem, perceived in a continuing American involvement in Vietnam.

Kennedy's most oft-quoted remark from this period seems to restrict the American commitment; certainly it has been brought forward as such by his defenders. He told Walter Cronkite in a television interview on September 2:

> I don't think that unless a greater effort is made by the Government to win popular support that the war can

> be won out there. In the final analysis, it is their war.
> They are the ones who have to win it or lose it. We
> can help them, we can give them equipment, we can
> send our men out there as advisers, but they have to
> win it, the people of Vietnam, against the
> Communists.[94]

Later in the same broadcast, however, Kennedy spoke out firmly in opposition to a possible American withdrawal from Vietnam. "I don't agree with those who say we should withdraw. That would be a great mistake. . . . This is a very important struggle even though it is far away." [95]

The case against withdrawal was couched in more dramatic terms a week later (September 9), when Kennedy was interviewed by David Brinkley. Brinkley inquired whether Kennedy had any doubts about the "domino theory." His answer disclosed how conventional—and how sweeping—Kennedy's Cold War thinking still was:

> No, I believe it. I believe it. I think that the struggle is
> close enough. China is so large, looms so high just
> beyond the frontiers, that if South Vietnam went, it
> would not only give them an improved geographic
> position for a guerrilla assault on Malaya, but would
> also give the impression that the wave of the future in
> southeast Asia was China and the Communists. So I
> believe it.[96]

In light of this danger America had no choice but to remain in Vietnam.

> What I am concerned about is that Americans will get
> impatient and say because they don't like events in
> southeast Asia or they don't like the government in
> Saigon, that we should withdraw. That only makes it
> easy for the Communists. I think we should stay.[97]

Vietnam was, for Kennedy, a pawn in the global struggle between East and West. Which elements the United States

supported there were not important, as long as they did not
interfere with the conduct of the struggle. It was only when
Diem's heavy-handed repression threatened to destroy the
anticommunist cause that Kennedy and his advisers began to
search for a more pliant agent in Vietnam. The criterion of
their search was purely instrumental, as Kennedy made clear in
a press conference statement on September 12: "What helps to
win the war, we support; what interferes with the war effort we
oppose. . . . We are not there to see a war lost. . . ." [98] That
statement could be construed as a sanction for napalm, defoliation, population relocation; certainly the only change it envisioned in Vietnam policy, in the last months of Kennedy's
life, was the end of his long sponsorship of Ngo Dinh Diem.

Kennedy was shaken when the coup which his administration backed resulted in the murder of Diem. Yet there was no
hesitation in American support for the new South Vietnamese
government. Nor was there any pause in American planning for
the war. If Kennedy was privately musing about a withdrawal
after the 1964 presidential election, as Kenneth O'Donnell was
to claim a number of years later, his thoughts were apparently
unknown to those actually entrusted with Vietnam planning.
On November 20, just two days before Kennedy was assassinated, Ambassador Lodge and General Harkins met with Dean
Rusk, Robert McNamara, McGeorge Bundy, and Maxwell
Taylor in Honolulu to consider "possible increased activity" in
Vietnam. [99] Their consensus, arrived at in that meeting, was to
establish the starting point for the war policy of the Johnson
Administration. When Johnson took over the Vietnam War from Kennedy,
much of its later shape was already discernible. The Kennedy
Administration had supplied a political rationale for American
engagement—the defense of South Vietnamese freedom against
aggression from the North. It had also supplied a psychological
rationale—demonstrating American willpower and sustaining

American prestige against the challenge of communist "wars of liberation." The Johnson Administration inherited, in addition, a willingness to employ any methods, no matter how ugly, considered necessary to win the war; its uses of napalm, defoliation, and population removal were only extensions of programs introduced in 1961–63. Finally, there was the legacy of deception. Lyndon Johnson was only carrying on what John Kennedy had begun in his persistent campaign to mystify the public about the nature of American involvement in Vietnam.

Johnson, of course, magnified America's role far beyond that established by Kennedy, dispatching hundreds of thousands of American troops to the South and scores of American bombers against the North. Here too, however, there was a link between the two administrations. Kennedy had conducted the war primarily in terms of a counterinsurgency strategy. At the time of his death that strategy was clearly failing. The strategic-hamlet program was in shambles, and Viet Cong power was unmistakably on the rise. The choice was plain: either begin a withdrawal from Vietnam, or escalate the conflict to a new level, upon which the enormous conventional warfare capacities of the United States could be utilized. Kennedy expressly opposed withdrawal. So too did Lyndon Johnson. Johnson chose—as I believe Kennedy would have, given the logic of his position—not to accept defeat in Vietnam, but rather, with the forces provided by the "flexible response" military which Kennedy had created, to expand the war.

In the early days of his Presidency Kennedy declared that the United States faced "a relentless struggle in every corner of the globe." The history of his administration became the history of that single struggle—in Germany, Cuba, Latin America, and Vietnam. Vietnam was a particularly significant arena in the struggle, an arena where the United States would, in Kennedy's view, prove its facility in the same surreptitious arts in which the communists excelled. It was the great test case for counterinsurgency—and hence for Kennedy's entire conception of American global counterrevolution. When counterinsurgency failed in Vietnam, that conception would be substantially modified. Yet by this time the stakes of American involvement were already far too high. With new strategies and new programs, Kennedy's successors carried on his counterrevolutionary campaign in Vietnam.

5

Corporate Power and the "New Economics"

Two images predominate in the public memory of John Kennedy's economic achievements. One is of Kennedy as "the first Keynesian President," [1] the first President avowedly to employ modern economic theory and method in an attempt to revivify the sluggish American economy. The other is of Kennedy as the target of enormous business hostility; the bitterness generated by the clash between the Kennedy Administration and Big Steel in April 1962 is taken as typifying the business community's rejection of the New Frontier and its longing for the more congenial environment of the Eisenhower Administration. Together, these images account for Kennedy's reputation as a progressive in economic matters, a fit inheritor of the Democratic legacy of Woodrow Wilson and Franklin Roosevelt.

The historical record provides some foundation for that reputation. Kennedy did break fresh ground in American political economy—he did so, in fact, in the face of business antipathy, congressional reluctance, and public indifference. And the substantial success of his innovative measures, which guided the most extended economic expansion in recent American history, [2] produced a new consensus in American economic life.

Yet if Kennedy can, in this sense, be termed an economic

167

progressive, in another, less obvious sense he must be considered an economic conservative. For his innovations were by no means intended to alter the existing structure of the American corporate economy. His policies posed no obstacle to the continued domination of the economy by giant oligopolies whose wealth and power permitted them, contrary to the myth of competitive capitalism, to control output, prices, employment, and investment. Instead, Kennedy's "New Economics" helped to stabilize and rationalize the corporate economy, to underwrite its risk taking and guarantee its market. Contrary to the shortsighted perspective of a majority of businessmen, Kennedy's economic policies instituted an era in which corporate profits and corporate power soared.

In describing his economic program as conservative, I do not mean to imply that President Kennedy was some sort of secret friend of business. His sympathies undeniably lay with the underdogs in American society—the poor, the unemployed, the minorities. But sympathy invariably took a back seat to the real determinants of policy: political calculation and economic doctrine. Political calculation led Kennedy to appease the corporate giants and their allies in government. Economic doctrine told him that the key to the expansion and health of the economy was the expansion and health of those same corporate giants. The architects of Kennedy's "New Economics" liked to portray it as the technically sophisticated and politically neutral management of a modern industrial economy. It is more accurately portrayed as pragmatic liberalism in the service of corporate capitalism.

Kennedy's 1960 campaign established what was to be the overarching theme of his presidential economics: economic growth. As the American economy stumbled into a recession in the last half of 1960, Kennedy blasted the Republican party not only for the mistakes of the moment, but also for the failures of nearly a decade. Gross national product (GNP) had risen slowly under the Eisenhower Administration, particularly in the late 1950s. American economic growth in this period lagged well behind the rate of the previous decade. The economy was plagued by a persistent slackness, with unemployment rates high and numerous industrial plants idle. The domestic picture was bad enough, but the international reverberations made it even worse. For the United States had fallen considerably behind in the global economic growth "race," annually outdistanced by both its Soviet adversary and its European and Japanese allies.

Senator Kennedy promised to put America back into the competition by boosting the present, sickly growth rate of approximately 3 percent per year up to a healthy 5 percent. The path he would take to renewed vigor was still somewhat unclear. But his commitment was not. Economic growth, he declared in 1960, would be his number one domestic priority.

The subject of economic growth—a favorite item of debate throughout the late 1950s and early 1960s—was inextricably bound up with the status of the Cold War during the 1960 campaign. Kennedy's pledge to get the nation moving again was a pledge to protect America's endangered superiority over the Soviets on the battlefront of production. (The Republicans, in contrast, insisted that the threat was overblown, that the United States possessed a commanding economic lead.) It was also a pledge to restore the tottering prestige of the American free enterprise system in its global contest with socialism. The former corporate executives who manned the Eisenhower Administration had clumsily, if inadvertently, damaged American business in the eyes of the world; the liberal politicians and experts in the Kennedy camp proclaimed their readiness to undo that damage.

Viewed as a Cold War issue, economic growth necessitated a unified effort from all sectors of the American economy. Group or class conflict had to be subordinated to a national consensus on turning back the Soviets' economic challenge.

Kennedy echoed the thinking of a number of economists (such as W. W. Rostow) here, calling for a shift of attention from questions of income distribution and relative power among classes to the problem of producing national abundance. He criticized his own constituency, as Sorenson notes, for raising class demands. Appearing before the Steelworkers Convention, he rejected their president's argument for a thirty-two-hour work week. To meet the challenge of the communists, Kennedy declared, America had to produce abundance; it could not afford to ration scarcity. [3]

The campaign's talk of bold economic advances was somewhat muted after the election. The narrowness of his victory and the apparent conservatism of the new Congress led Kennedy in his first months in office to proceed cautiously in economic affairs. His 1961 legislative recommendations hence produced few innovations, falling considerably short of expectations aroused during the campaign. His rhetoric too was cautious, adhering rather closely to the dictum of balanced budgets; the Keynesian vocabulary favored by his economic advisers seldom intruded into Kennedy's public discourses at this point.

While the recession of the previous fall had grown worse by the time of his inauguration, the antirecession package Kennedy presented to Congress on February 2, 1961, was economically conventional and politically safe. Its contents paralleled in most respects measures recommended by President Eisenhower to combat the 1958 recession.[4] Proposals for a thirteen-week supplement to unemployment benefits, aid to the children of the unemployed, aid to distressed areas, emergency relief to feed grain farmers, and new public housing stirred up little controversy in Congress. (There were two other measures in the February 2 package—one to increase social security payments and another to raise the minimum wage and extend its coverage—but these were not, properly speaking, antirecession measures.)

exercised conservative fiscal policies due to
pol. constraint - narrowness of victory Conserv. Congress
, bal, of payments problems

Corporate Power and the "New Economics"   **171**

Nor did Kennedy's proposals arouse much controversy
outside Congress. The business press, for example, pronounced
itself pleased with this initial display of presidential moderation. Strong criticism of Kennedy's antirecession moves came
only from the left. A number of liberal economists lamented the
continuance of the regressive fiscal approach to which Kennedy's election had supposedly signaled an end, and called for a
vigorous program of federal spending or a counter-recessionary
tax policy.[5]

Political constraint was not the only factor responsible for
the new Administration's caution. There was also the nagging
balance-of-payments problem. Starting in the late 1950s, the
American deficit in its international accounts had mounted
sharply. The dollars flowing abroad for imports, foreign investments, tourism, and military and foreign aid far exceeded
the amounts coming in from exports, foreign tourism, and
dividends on overseas investments. As a result, there was a
growing and potentially dangerous depletion of American gold
reserves. This danger pushed the new Administration's monetary policy in a restrictive direction. Short-term interest rates
were kept high, discouraging domestic borrowing, in order to
prevent the outflow of foreign short-term capital. The balance-of-payments situation was also seen as an important constraint upon fiscal policy (federal spending and taxation). The
argument was that too large a budget deficit—for example,
through a strong antirecession program—might undermine
foreign confidence in the American economy, and initiate a run
on American gold as foreign holders of dollars cashed in.

More revealing than the antirecession program as an in-
dicator of the Administration's future economic course was the
President's first appearance before a major business group. On
February 13, 1961, Kennedy addressed the National Industrial
Conference Board. Concerned to reassure business of the new
Administration's friendly attitude, he confided to the members
of the board: "I feel . . . that I can claim kinship here. . . ."[6] He

went on to prove to the assembled corporate executives that that assertion of kinship rested on something far deeper than personal goodwill, that it went to the heart of his economic plans and hopes. He told them:

> Our revenues and thus our success are dependent upon your profits and your success. Far from being natural enemies, Government and business are necessary allies. . . . We know that your success and ours are intertwined—that you have facts and knowledge that we need. Whatever past differences may have existed, we seek more than an attitude of truce, more than a treaty—we seek the spirit of a full-fledged alliance.[7]

In his speeches before business groups President Kennedy was often to pay lavish tribute to the free enterprise system—a ritual of obeisance that cost him nothing. His frequent calls for a government-business alliance, however, were far more seriously meant. Whatever hostility businessmen might bear toward the Kennedy Administration, the Administration could scarcely afford to display reciprocal feelings. For, as the words above indicate, Kennedy felt that he needed business. Upon business success rested an increase in government revenues; upon business success rested, in large part, the attainment of the Administration's economic growth objectives. The preservation of corporate confidence—and the avoidance of measures that limited corporate profits or undermined corporate strength—would be seen as an imperative by Kennedy. As we shall observe later on, the one time he did deny big business its desires (in the steel affair), he had to make up for it with compensatory gratifications. The history of the Administration's relations with business can best be understood as the history of this strange alliance, which business refused to recognize even as it reaped most of the benefits, and to which the Administration felt inescapably bound even as its members sometimes sputtered with indignation toward their "allies."

The alliance started off on a shaky footing. Kennedy's initial tax program, announced in April of 1961, aroused significant business opposition. Its central proposal, a tax credit for new investment in plant and equipment, was devised by the President's Keynesian-oriented economic advisers principally as a stimulus to production and employment. With unemployment rates high and industry hampered by idle and obsolete plants and equipment, the corporations seemed to need an incentive in order to risk new investment. In Keynesian theory, such investment would boost the entire economy. Administration economists were assuming a "trickle down" effect, whereby investment sparked by the tax credit would create a host of new jobs and ultimately spread benefits to all sectors of the economy.

Economic expansion was not, however, the sole motivation for the proposed tax credit. The measure was also designed, quite explicitly, as a gesture to the business community. It was intended as a demonstration to industry of the Administration's interest in its modernization and improved profit position—a concrete follow-up to Kennedy's pledge of cooperation in February.

But the investment credit, a greater tax plum than anything the Eisenhower Administration had offered the corporations,[8] was greeted with unexpected coolness in the business community. Businessmen—and their congressional sympathizers—objected to the Administration's "sliding-scale formula," by which the size of the credit varied with the size of the investment, offering the greatest tax break to firms that purchased more than their usual amounts of equipment. Complaining that the formula was an unworkable gimmick, they argued for an across-the-board credit benefiting all corporations equally. The Administration's proposal won it little affection from business, which wanted an even more advantageous tax break and was, besides, skeptical of favors coming from a Democratic President.

Business opposition was further aroused by Kennedy's accompanying proposals, which looked to the closing of several loopholes in the existing tax structure. These reforms would have: (1) cracked down on corporate expense accounts; (2) instituted withholding on dividends and interest (in order to prevent evasion of taxes); (3) tightened up the taxation of earnings by American firms abroad; (4) repealed the special tax privilege awarded income from dividends. Kennedy was, with these proposals, honoring the Democratic party's long-standing commitment to rectify gross inequities in the tax structure. But the business community mobilized its strength against the reform package, and the President retreated. In the final bill, approved by Congress in 1962 after endorsement by the Administration, expense accounts had been spared save for a few ineffectual restrictions, the provision for withholding on dividends and interest had been dropped, minor improvements were made in taxing overseas earnings, and the privileged status of dividend income emerged unscathed. In the view of Senator Joseph Clark of Pennsylvania, the bill was a "tax dodger's delight." [9]

Although the tax bill was bottled up in Congress throughout 1961, all of Kennedy's antirecession measures had been enacted by summer of that year. Their effect upon the recession was difficult to gauge. Economists outside the Administration generally argued that the recession was ending anyway, as private spending picked up the slack well before the impact of additional government expenditures could be felt. They did credit the Kennedy program with speeding the economy's recovery.[10] The most significant Administration contribution in these months to economic recovery was seldom discussed, however, in economic terms. This was Kennedy's rapid acceleration of American defense spending. Three separate presidential requests to Congress (in March, May, and July) hiked military appropriations in 1961 by approximately $6 billion. As we saw in an earlier chapter, the primary impetus for

*Economic priorities: economic growth
to 5% from 3%: inflation control through
wage and price controls*

this highly consequential military buildup was Kennedy's conception of an intensified Cold War, whose decisive stage coincided with his term in office. But Administration officials were not unmindful of the economic benefits to be derived from the buildup. And for a Democratic Administration leery of the opposition of business and Congress, nothing was safer as a goad to economic growth than defense spending.[11]

With recovery successfully under way, Kennedy's attention increasingly turned to the problem of inflation. Stability in prices was to become an economic priority second only to growth for his administration. Inflation would have scuttled many of its domestic plans, while simultaneously retarding American exports and intensifying the balance-of-payments problem. During the fall of 1961, the struggle against inflation centered on the impending negotiations in the steel industry. In private contacts with the involved parties the President argued for the virtues of price stability and the importance of the public interest. He strongly requested the steel industry to forgo a price increase, and the steel workers to limit their wage demands.

Kennedy's effort to hold down wages and prices was formalized and expanded in the "wage-price guideposts," first enunciated by the Council of Economic Advisers in their January 1962 annual report. A persuasive rationale for these nonbinding guideposts was developed by the chairman of the Council under Kennedy, Walter W. Heller:

> They pit the power of public opinion and Presidential persuasion against the market power of strong unions and strong businesses. They try to bring to the bargaining tables and board rooms where wage and price decisions are made a sense of the public interest in noninflationary wage and price behavior. Indeed, they try to appeal also to labor and management's broad self-interest in avoiding a self-defeating

> price-wage spiral. Their major thrust, then, has been
> through the process of informing labor, management,
> and the public of the explicit ways in which wage and
> price decisions should be geared to productivity
> advances if they are to be noninflationary. Under the
> guideposts, wage rate increases averaging no more
> than the average national increase in productivity . . .
> are seen as noninflationary.[12]

The most dramatic challenge to the Council's guideposts
was to come from business, in the steel affair. Labor, too, was
restive about the guideposts, but generally went along because
they had been promulgated by a Democratic administration.
Despite widespread opposition, the Kennedy Administration
was proud of its guideposts. They served, along with the
later tax cut, as prime examples of what the Administration
considered its neutral, nonideological management of the economy.

The neutrality of the guideposts was faulty, however. For
their stronger thrust was at labor. While business complained of
interference in its price decisions, pricing standards were vague.
The Council's discussion of prices was, in the words of economic
reporter Bernard Nossiter, "too academic and imprecise to
guide any corporate price setter." [13] The same did not hold true
for wages. Wage increases were yoked directly to current figures
on productivity; any union surpassing those figures was measurably culpable.

Nor was it only that labor was governed by more precise
standards than management. More important, those standards
precluded some traditional labor concerns. They ruled out the
possibility that wage increases might come out of corporations'
expanding profits, or that wages might claim a larger percen-
tage of corporate income. Improved productivity was the sole
legitimation for higher wages; the symbolic, if not the economic, meaning was that workers should get better pay only to the
extent that they did better work. For a union to argue on
grounds other than productivity, to question, for example, the

equity of the prevailing distribution of income between management and labor in its industry, was now illicit.[14] The guideposts, Nossiter pointed out, clearly implied that there was to be "no change in the relative shares of labor and the other claimants for the economic pie." [15]

Steel was the key testing ground for the new guideposts. The story of Kennedy's conflict with Big Steel deserves retelling, for that conflict, and its aftermath, were significantly to shape his relationship with business. The steel industry had acceded to Kennedy's pleas in the fall of 1961, and foregone a threatened price hike. In January 1962, the President and his Secretary of Labor, Arthur Goldberg, met with Roger Blough of U.S. Steel and David McDonald of the Steelworkers to discuss their upcoming contract negotiations. According to Theodore Sorensen, both Kennedy and Goldberg emphasized (in this meeting and in telephone communications) their desire for a quick steel settlement. They wanted a contract that would not necessitate any hike in steel prices; to obtain that contract they offered to use their influence with the union. The steel industry accepted this offer, although it gave no formal pledges on the subject of prices.[16]

The Administration adopted an active role in the subsequent negotiations; it played a major part in convincing McDonald to approve the most modest steel contract in decades.[17] Steelworkers' wages remained constant under this new contract; improvements in their fringe benefits amounted to only around ten cents an hour. Kennedy, warmly praising both sides, hailed the settlement as a triumph in the battle against inflation. But this triumph turned sour, as Roger Blough notified the President in a White House visit on Tuesday, April 10, that U.S. Steel was raising its prices by $6 per ton.

Blough's announcement naturally aroused the President's ire. Kennedy felt that he had been personally duped into helping the steel industry secure a beneficial contract, on the basis of a tacit agreement that it had no intention of honoring. The prestige of the Presidency had been invoked for the industry's ends throughout negotiations—and then mocked by its surprise price hike. The potential economic damage too was considerable. Big Steel's action threatened not only to shatter the price guidelines, but the wage guidelines as well. No other union, Kennedy recognized, would adopt the Steelworkers' moderate approach if the steel industry's grab for higher profits proved successful.

Kennedy possessed few statutory weapons with which he could combat the price increase. What he did have was the presidential power of persuasion—and this he wielded forcefully. A press conference was fortuitously scheduled for the day following Blough's visit to the White House. Kennedy used this convenient forum to blister the leaders of Big Steel.

> Simultaneous and identical actions of United States Steel and other leading steel corporations, increasing steel prices by some $6 a ton, constitute a wholly unjustifiable and irresponsible defiance of the public interest. In this serious hour in our Nation's history . . . the American people will find it hard, as I do, to accept a situation in which a tiny handful of steel executives whose pursuit of private power and profit exceeds their sense of public responsibility can show such utter contempt for the interests of 185 million Americans.[18]

Along with this verbal thrust, there were several Administration countermoves against the action of the steel industry. Secretary McNamara announced that the Defense Department had directed its contractors to purchase steel wherever possible from firms that had not lifted their prices. The Justice Department began an investigation into possible collusion in the steel industry, citing the series of identical price increases that followed the U.S. Steel announcement. Behind the scenes, Administration officials sought to persuade those few major companies that had not yet followed the lead of U.S. Steel to hold the line, thus forcing those who had to rescind the $6-a-ton increase. The prime target for these efforts was Inland Steel of Chicago, whose President, Joseph Block, was then serving on Kennedy's Labor-Management Advisory Committee.

Friday morning, April 13, Inland Steel announced that it would not raise its prices. Kaiser Steel, a smaller firm, followed suit. The pressure of competition was building against the giants of steel. And they buckled almost immediately. By early afternoon Bethlehem Steel, the nation's second largest steel producer, had rescinded its price raise; shortly after five P.M., U.S. Steel capitulated.

While in public the Administration was quick to conciliate Big Steel—Kennedy insisted at his next news conference that he harbored "no ill will against any individual, industry, corporation, or segment of the American economy" [19]—in private there was a good deal of self-congratulation over this "victory for the American Presidency." [20] Kennedy's vigorous response to the challenge of Roger Blough had, the New Frontiersmen felt, rallied public opinion, rescued presidential prestige, and saved the Administration's antiinflation program. An interesting criticism of this view soon appeared, in a book written shortly after the steel affair, *Steel and the Presidency, 1962,* by Grant McConnell. According to McConnell, Kennedy's performance in these April days was skillful above all in disguising the essential impotence of government in such a situation. It was not presidential jabs at Big Steel, but competitive market forces in the industry which actually compelled the price rescission. These forces, McConnell contended, "were much more important in bringing about the abandonment of the price increase than the actions of the President. Those actions showed weakness, not power." [21]

The truth of the matter, I suspect, lies closer to the view of the Administration. As McConnell rightly observed, Kennedy was limited to oblique assaults on the price increase; his direct power in this situation was not great. Yet McConnell failed to ascribe sufficient credit to Kennedy for setting market forces into motion. In mobilizing strong public sentiment against the price hike, and then appealing to Inland Steel against the background of that sentiment, Kennedy indicated how effectively presidential persuasion could influence the "free market." Nor was this the extent of Kennedy's achievement in the steel affair. For once sufficiently angry to confront corporate selfishness, he made use of a weapon the corporations dreaded: the glare of public attention, spotlighting the concentrated and irresponsible power of giant firms in a supposedly "free market." Kennedy was striking at the corporations' point of ideological vulnerability. It was, most likely, their fear of this presidential weapon, as much as the force of market competition, which accounted for Big Steel's hasty retreat.

Almost certainly Kennedy's firm response to the actions of Roger Blough saved his wage-price guidelines. Given the circumstances surrounding steel industry negotiations, and the pivotal role of steel in the American economy, Blough's gambit, if unchecked, would have unleashed new inflationary forces. Although the business community would soon assault Kennedy for his misdeeds, it would, after Blough's failure, pose no more major challenges to the President on the price front. Labor, though also unhappy with guideposts which hindered it even more than management, continued to adhere to the prescribed limits on wage increases out of political loyalty. Fragile and flawed as they were, the guideposts thus helped the Kennedy Administration maintain an excellent record on prices. Despite Republican warnings, on no subject would John Kennedy prove less assailable than price stability.

The steel "crisis" of 1962 was a significant victory for Kennedy. But succeeding months were to witness an even more significant victory for the business community. The pages that follow set out the logic of this striking turn of events.

In the immediate aftermath of the steel confrontation the Kennedy Administration made several conciliatory gestures toward business—and was conspicuously spurned. Kennedy's standing in the business world had been low even before April of 1962. Sophisticated corporate leaders—those concerned with the functioning of the corporate system as a whole—were sympathetic to most of the Kennedy Administration's economic efforts. But the majority of businessmen, traditionally more parochial and interest-bound, had been uncomfortable with the New Frontier from its inception, despite its repeated offers of cooperation and alliance. They were suspicious of Kennedy's academic advisers, and resentful that business people were not welcomed into the White House by Kennedy in the same enthusiastic fashion as Eisenhower. They were unhappy, too, about the majority of Kennedy's economic policies; they especially abhorred the price guidelines, even though the more powerful wage guidelines placed the federal government squarely behind the corporate quest for stable labor costs.

Now, unhappiness erupted into indignation over what businessmen perceived as the President's "dictatorial" intrusion into the free market. Indignation was fueled, too, by a newspaper story disclosing that Kennedy, after Blough's visit to the White House, had quoted his father as saying all businessmen were sons of bitches. (The situation was not markedly improved when Kennedy, correcting the story at his next press conference, substituted steelmen for businessmen.) It reached a fever pitch when, on May 28, the stock market suffered its largest single-day dip in prices since the 1929 crash. The decline was primarily the consequence of overvalued stocks, but business was swift to pin the blame on the President, insisting that his coercion of the steel companies had destroyed investors' confidence. Although several influential corporate leaders tried to check excessive animosity toward Kennedy, much of the business community appeared close to a declaration of war on the Administration. And the economic recovery of 1961 seemed to some Administration economic advisers, in that late spring of 1962, in danger of abortion.

Kennedy's response to this situation took two forms: an

appeal to dialogue and reason, and an offering of concrete benefits to win back business favor. Let us first consider the appeal to dialogue. In this appeal Kennedy did more than simply attempt to reason with his business critics. He laid out the fundamental economic thinking and objectives of his administration, in a concise and dramatic form that merits attention.

The central theme in Kennedy's attempted dialogue with business was first tried out at a meeting of the White House Conference on National Economic Issues in late May. Kennedy argued before this gathering that the day for impassioned partisan debates on economic issues was past. Echoing the "end of ideology" literature of the 1950s, he declared that the modern American economy could be prudently directed only by managerial expertise.

> The fact of the matter is that most of the problems, or at least many of them, that we now face are technical problems, are administrative problems. They are very sophisticated judgments which do not lend themselves to the great sort of "passionate movements" which have stirred this country so often in the past.[22]

Kennedy expanded upon this theme in what was to become his best-known speech on economics, the Yale Commencement Address of June 11, 1962. At Yale—an academic forum, yet dear to the eastern corporate elite—the President again dismissed economic partisanship. "The central domestic problems of our time . . . relate not to basic clashes of philosophy or ideology but to ways and means of reaching common goals—to research for sophisticated solutions to complex and obstinate issues."[23] The greatest impediment to sophisticated solutions, Kennedy went on, was the persistence of economic "mythology." His task at Yale was to begin dispelling that mythology.

He pinpointed three major areas of illusion about government and the economy. First was the myth of oversized government. Kennedy contended that the growth of the federal government had to be understood in relative terms; he pointed out that, leaving aside defense and space expenditures, the federal government since the Second World War had expanded less rapidly than any other sector of the economy. A second myth concerned fiscal policy and the budget. The record of the postwar years, Kennedy remarked, demolished the notion that budget surpluses kept prices stable while budget deficits produced inflation. The same record also undermined the popular myth of a skyrocketing federal debt; the federal debt was, in fact, climbing far more slowly than either private debt or the debts of state and local governments. Finally, Kennedy assaulted the claim that each and every setback to the economy derived from business's lack of confidence in the national administration. Responding to the current charges that he had sunk the stock market, he noted that "business had full confidence in the administrations in power in 1929, 1954, 1958 and 1960, but this was not enough to prevent recession when business lacked full confidence in the economy." [24]

At the end of the speech Kennedy returned to his original theme—partnership in place of partisanship, expertise instead of ideology.

> What is at stake is not some grand warfare of rival
> ideologies which will sweep the country with passion,
> but the practical management of a modern economy.
> What we need is not labels and cliches but more basic
> discussion of the sophisticated and technical
> questions involved in keeping a great economic
> machinery moving ahead.[25]

In many respects the Yale speech still reads well. Kennedy's debunking of economic myths was valuable instruction for the American public. And there was little to quarrel with in

his remarks on deficit spending or the federal debt. Still there
was something disturbing about the speech, something that
lent credence to Bernard Nossiter's comment about an
"irresistable irony in Kennedy himself, decrying economic
myths while refurbishing old ones and disseminating some new
ones." 26

Behind the façade of dialogue at Yale, Kennedy was
striking back at his critics. His thrust here was against the right,
against the dogma of business and the Republican party. The
myths Kennedy had exploded lay at the heart of business's
attack against his administration. By calling for a shift of attention away from ideology to technical concerns, he was hoping to lure business away from its misguided attack and toward
a discussion that would be conducted on *his* terms.

The logic—and perhaps the intent—of Kennedy's argument extended further, however, than an attempt to quiet
right-wing critics. It also could be turned against the left—
against either Kennedy's left-liberal critics or the disadvantaged groups (the poor, the unemployed, the minorities) who
might form, at some future time, a new "passionate movement." In Kennedy's call for "practical management" by a
centrist, nonideological elite, the views of left and right alike
were declared irrelevant to economic debate. Both stood con-
demned by their partisanship and ignorance; at best they could
only confirm the wisdom of handing economic affairs over to
the President, his professional advisers, and those responsible
statesmen in business and labor who followed the cues from
Washington. Throughout this study of the Kennedy Presidency
we have come across powerful elitist and managerial impulses.
At Yale, Kennedy was allowing those impulses free rein.

By depicting contemporary economic issues as technical,
Kennedy was asserting that the general economic course of the
United States was already fixed, that there were no more subjects still needful of vigorous public debate. The complexity
and technical difficulty of modern economics can indeed be

forbidding. Kennedy himself experienced some problems in this regard. But the rhetoric of technical expertise obscured the fact that many *basic* economic choices remained open to the American public—though they could be closed by the experts' fiat. The central economic assumptions of the Kennedy Administration were not above challenge; in fact, they were often challenged in these years, by an assortment of critics.

The priority of economic growth, for instance, was frequently called into question. It was primarily conservatives then who raised questions that many liberals and radicals would echo a decade later: "Do we, the richest nation in the world, need to be richer? What benefits could faster growth confer that we cannot have now through better use of our existing resources? Is the control of our growth a proper function of government?" [27] (The destructive impact of rapid economic growth upon the natural environment—another issue of widespread concern in the 1970s—was seldom perceived by anyone in the Kennedy years.) Similarly, the choice as to whether federal fiscal policy should aim at encouraging private consumption or orient itself toward improving the nation's stock of public goods was still unsettled. The Kennedy Administration itself was sometimes privately troubled by John Kenneth Galbraith's repeated reminders of America's public squalor, yet it never broached to the public the choice between private and public goods. Nor was it simply a technical feature of economics that the Administration decided in 1961 and 1962 to stimulate corporate investment and let benefits "trickle down" rather than providing tax breaks and other benefits directly to the middle and lower classes. Kennedy's consistent "leaning" toward business—of which more will shortly be disclosed—stemmed from a combination of economic doctrine and political calculation that was scarcely above public consideration or criticism.

Removal of the Administration's economic goals from the partisan arena, where their worth might be debated, to a rarefied atmosphere in which experts devised techniques of implementation, was one implication of Kennedy's words at Yale. Another was that it was time to close the books on those historic conflicts that had galvanized economic and political forces so often in America's past. The Democratic party had, for years, drawn much of its power from such conflicts. Ever since the political demise of William Jennings Bryan, a traditional Democratic strategy had been to capitalize on class conflict in election years and to muffle it in between. But at Yale, Kennedy rejected even the appearance of class conflict. The rhetoric of Roosevelt in 1936 or Truman in 1948 had ceased to hold any relevance for him. No longer depicting itself as the foe of the "economic royalists" and the "friend of the common man," the Democratic party was henceforth to be characterized, in Kennedy's view, as the neutral manager of the American industrial machine.

Interestingly, in the same year as Kennedy's Yale speech, Gabriel Kolko published *Wealth and Power in America,* demonstrating that "a radically unequal distribution of income has been characteristic of the American social structure since at least 1910," [28] that tax loopholes and other devices continue to protect the enormous fortunes of the rich while the concentration of stock ownership and structuring of corporate directorships preserve their inordinate power. And in the years that followed the unequal distribution of resources and power in the American economy was again to become a subject which fired at least some Americans' passions. A decade after the Yale speech, the Democratic presidential candidate, George McGovern, reversed Kennedy's position and called upon the American electorate to reopen this question. Yet the coolness with which McGovern's economic proposals were received suggests that Kennedy's mode of thinking had triumphed after all. The majority of Americans were seemingly unconcerned about the economy's contrasting sectors of wealth and poverty, power and powerlessness. They had learned to accept the "practical man-

tokens: liberation of depreciation allowances

agement" of the economy by a triad of the President, his economic experts, and his "responsible" associates in the corporate
and union hierarchies.

In the summer of 1962, however, the business community
refused to heed Kennedy's appeal for dialogue. Kennedy's
conception of "practical management" was not yet congruent
with corporate orthodoxy. So the President, "disappointed,
concluded that he would have to bide his time." [29] Unable to
patch up the rent in the government-business alliance on the
terms he desired, he decided to court business with tokens it
could not refuse. For the twelve-month period following the
steel confrontation of April 1962, the hostile business community would become, ironically, the Administration's most-
favored constituency.[30]

In July of 1962, the Treasury Department announced a
liberalization of depreciation allowances. The revised depreciation schedule permitted businesses to speed up by nearly a
third the rate at which they could write off newly purchased
machinery and equipment for tax purposes. It was hoped that
this tax break would spur them into replacing aging machines
with newer and more productive models; at a time when Administration economists feared a recession, it was considered a
useful instrument of economic expansion. But economic doctrine was secondary here to political considerations. Depreciation liberalization, the Kennedy Administration knew, was a
reform the business community very much wanted. As Theodore Sorensen observed, it had long been "the No. 1 item on
business' list of requests, but [had been] abandoned by the
previous administration as too difficult." [31] Through this act of
generosity—from which Eisenhower and his advisers had shied
away—business was to save an estimated $1.5 billion in the first
year alone.

The attractiveness of new corporate investment was bol-
stered again three months later, when Congress finally enacted
the investment tax credit. Business resistance to the Adminis-

tration's proposed sliding-scale formula for the credit had helped to tie up the 1961 tax bill in Congress. In the final version of the bill, the Administration dropped its formula in favor of a flat 7 percent credit. As the business community had insisted all along, every firm would receive the same tax break, regardless of whether its new investment was higher or lower than its customary outlay. Despite the opposition of liberal and labor groups, who favored tax relief for middle- and low-income citizens, the chief beneficiary of Kennedy's 1962 tax bill was, once again, business.

Together, liberalized depreciation and the 7 percent investment credit resulted in a reduction of business taxes by approximately $2.5 billion in 1962, an 11 percent tax cut for corporations.[32] Although the business community proved grudging with its appreciation, the twin Administration measures apparently did stimulate additional capital investment in the last half of 1962 and in 1963. Their "trickle down" effect was open to doubt, however. Unemployment figures, for instance, continued at the same distressing level throughout this period.

Probably more significant than these short-term results, though, was the long-range effect of Kennedy's tax privileges for corporate investment. His successors employed the Kennedy precedent to rewrite depreciation schedules and invent investment tax credits even more advantageous to business. Such tax breaks for investment so shrunk corporations' taxable base that corporate income tax was reduced dramatically.[33] Through Kennedy's measures (and their later extensions) the federal government increasingly underwrote capital investment in the "free market." Liberal depreciation allowances and investment credits helped to diminish the risk of corporate investment, as well as improve its profitability. As Kennedy had promised, business had much to gain from its alliance with government. The tax breaks of 1962, along with the tax cuts of 1963 (examined later in this chapter), were an important step toward the fulfillment of a long-standing business dream: a stable, secure, high-profit corporate economy.

Benefits continued to flow business's way. The Administration's 1962 bill on drug regulation, establishing new standards of effectiveness and labeling, was deemed highly satisfactory by drug manufacturers. Kennedy's communications satellite bill gratified the business community even more. The new U.S. communications satellite system, though dependent on the government's space technology, was placed in private hands. A private corporation was set up to own and manage the system, with provision for public participation and federal regulation. Within the Administration, some Kennedy advisers expressed regret over this new fillip to the business community; in the Senate, a small band of angry liberals conducted an unsuccessful filibuster against this "giveaway" to business.[34]

Kennedy also sought during this period to remind businessmen of the advantages that already accrued to them from various federal programs. In his 1963 Economic Report he noted how greatly industry had benefited from existing federal research projects and promised to propose "new means of facilitating the use by civilian industry of the results of government-financed research." [35] Though primarily couched in terms of improving productivity and contributing to economic growth, this federal absorption of the expense of developing advanced technologies represented a considerable subsidy to business. Federal aid to education, Kennedy informed businessmen, was yet another boon to the corporate economy. Speaking at a symposium of the American Bankers Association in February 1963, he described aid to education in language that suggested the educational creed of Clark Kerr: "Investment in education yields a substantial return in new research, new products, new techniques, in higher wages and purchasing power, and a greater supply of college-trained manpower." [36]

The most important Administration measure (apart from the revised depreciation schedule and investment credit) in restoring rapport with the business community had been introduced well before the steel affair. This was the Trade Expansion Act of 1962. Recent developments in international

economics—particularly the spectacular growth of the European Common Market—had, it was felt within the Administration, rendered obsolete America's reciprocal trade law. If the
United States was not to be excluded from booming foreign
markets, if it was to take advantage of exciting opportunities in
foreign trade, far more flexible tools for setting American tariffs
had to be placed by Congress in the hands of the executive
branch. The President required greater freedom than existing
law permitted to negotiate agreements with foreign trading
partners. The Administration's bill granted this discretion to
the President; it presented him with a five-year authority to
reduce all tariffs by as much as 50 percent and to cut tariffs up
to 100 percent on commodities traded predominantly by the
United States and the Common Market.

Kennedy perceived the expansion of trade as a key to
solving many of America's economic difficulties. So the Trade
Expansion Act of 1962 was made the Administration's legislative "centerpiece." [37] It far overshadowed, for example, the
struggling Medicare bill. Kennedy's most lofty rhetoric, usually
reserved for the global struggle against communism, was called
into service to dramatize the normally prosaic subject of tariffs.
In his 1962 State of the Union message he told Congress and the
public: "We need a new law—a wholly new approach—a bold
new instrument of American trade policy. Our decision could
well affect the unity of the West, the course of the Cold War,
and the economic growth of our Nation for a generation to
come." [38] A barrage of speeches throughout the first half of 1962
kept up Administration pressure on Congress for the trade bill.
Kennedy promised sweeping benefits from its passage: economic expansion; stable prices (foreign competition would
force American firms to improve their efficiency); reduction in
the balance-of-payments deficit; a strengthening of Western
unity; a blow to the communist trade offensive; a boost to
American Free World leadership; and, best of all, greater prosperity for every group in the American economy, for businessmen, workers, and farmers alike.[39]

Some of Kennedy's associates regretted the President's concentration on trade reform to the exclusion of other issues; they felt it, in Schlesinger's words, to be "a misdirection of the Administration's limited political resources." [40] But a number of corporate leaders, and their political allies, rallied to this promised stimulus for American exports. Initially there was opposition, from Congressmen leery of voting the President new discretionary authority, from businessmen fearful that their own industries might be injured. But Kennedy's speeches, an extensive lobbying campaign by the President and his aides, and special concessions to the textile and chemical industries eventually won most businessmen and their political spokesmen over to his side. By May, Kennedy had collected endorsements for his bill from former President Eisenhower and Vice-President Nixon. Even after the steel affair, business support continued to grow, particularly as the more sophisticated members of the corporate elite came to grasp the prospective benefits the bill offered. The campaign for trade reform thus helped, along with the Administration's other gestures toward the business community, to soothe the hard feelings business was nursing toward Kennedy in the spring and summer of 1962.[41]

With business backing, the trade bill cleared Congress rather easily in the fall of 1962. The vote in the House was 298 to 125; in the Senate it was 78 to 8. The results of the Trade Expansion Act, however, fell short of Kennedy's expectations. When President De Gaulle of France vetoed Britain's entry into the Common Market early in 1963, immediate hopes for Western economic unity were dashed. Nor was the reduction of tariffs accomplished in the dramatic fashion Kennedy seemingly had envisioned. European representatives proved stubborn and tough in ensuing negotiations, dubbed—to the President's discomfort—the "Kennedy Round." The flexibility on tariffs that Kennedy's bill made possible was undoubtedly useful in America's long-term trade policy. But in retrospect the bill's critics seemed justified in their insistence that this subject did not deserve to be *the* top legislative priority of the Kennedy Administration.

Perhaps the most interesting feature in this intensive campaign for trade reform was Kennedy's belief that through expanding American exports he might vanquish the nagging balance-of-payments problem. The persistent deficit in America's international accounts had been cited by Administration spokesmen at the time of its initial antirecession program (and later as well) as a powerful restraint upon fiscal and monetary policy. If increased exports eliminated, or at least materially reduced, this deficit, Kennedy would presumably gain a freer hand in economic policy making. Yet what was left out of his balance-of-payments equation was the fact that exports were hardly the central issue. The *favorable* balance of trade (exports over imports) for the United States in these years amounted to nearly $5 billion annually. The *unfavorable* balance of payments was produced by the high level of American overseas investment, and by government spending on military forces and installations abroad. And these the Kennedy Administration was not about to reduce.

Given his delicate relationship with business, Kennedy was hesitant about proposing restrictions on the continually growing corporate outlays for new foreign plants.[42] He did move finally, in 1963, to tax foreign bond issues floated in the United States; but this was offset by his encouragement to American investors, in his Foreign Aid message of that same year, to expand their activities in the Third World. As for military spending abroad, Kennedy's "flexible response" doctrine did not permit any substantial cutback. Defense Secretary McNamara was able to economize on military expenditures overseas, and several NATO allies increased their military purchases in the United States, but these gains were largely negated by the buildup of conventional forces in Europe during the Berlin crisis and the accelerating dispatch of Green Berets to Southeast Asia and Latin America. These new military expenditures were soon sacrosanct; no one advocated pruning the ranks of the Green Berets to conserve American gold. Since, as Kennedy himself stated on occasion,[43] there would have been no balance-of-payments problem if it were not for American military expenditures abroad, the requirements of "flexible response" doctrine remained an immovable barrier against his unflagging efforts to eliminate the payments problem.

Maintenance and expansion of America's overseas empire —multinational corporate enterprises and a global military establishment—doomed Kennedy to repeat Eisenhower's frustrating experience with the balance of payments. As Seymour E. Harris, a part-time economic adviser to the Kennedy Administration, ruefully admitted: "Despite the major attention given to the dollar problem and the innumerable measures taken, the over-all deficit continued at about $3 billion per year." [44]

Kennedy had stood up to Big Steel in April of 1962—and then spent the next twelve months proving that he had meant no harm, that he was really a friend of the business community. The denouement of a period in which business had been showered with benefits came, fittingly, in steel. In April 1963 the Wheeling Steel Company announced selective price increases. Tensions briefly flared in Washington, there were debates within the Administration about possible forms of retaliation—but in the end Kennedy was not prepared to tangle with the steel industry a second time. (It was also a somewhat different situation: selective rather than across-the-board increases, no personal affront to the President.) He restricted himself to a public statement indicating that selective steel-price increases in response to changing supply and demand were compatible with general price stability. After the President's conciliatory position was made clear, the giants of the steel industry followed Wheeling Steel's lead. But perhaps as fearful of another showdown as the Administration, they limited their average price increases to a little over one percent.[45]

By this time Kennedy's primary focus had shifted away from price stability anyway, back to the problem of economic expansion. He was in the midst of his campaign for a tax reduction and reform bill, the bill that was to make his reputation as a Keynesian and an economic innovator. Before turning to that campaign, it might be appropriate to interrupt the narrative at this point, in order to assess the Kennedy Administration's developing alliance with business. I hope in the next several pages to explore more deeply some of the sources, consequences, and implications of this troubled partnership.

To understand Kennedy's conception of the place of business in the American economy, we might start with the familiar metaphor of the "economic pie." According to this metaphor, the wealth of the economy can be visualized as a huge pie, from which constituent groups (business, labor, farmers, the government) receive various-size slices. The usual relationship between these groups resembles a quarrel over whose slice should be larger and whose smaller. But the doctrine of economic growth by which Kennedy was guided envisioned the prospect of a larger pie, with a bigger slice for everybody. It aimed for a shared prosperity which would end the traditional squabbling over income distribution. "Our primary challenge," Kennedy thus told the U.S. Chamber of Commerce barely two weeks after his battle with Big Steel, "is not how to divide the economic pie, but how to enlarge it." [46]

Economic growth would, in Kennedy's view, benefit all Americans. But to stimulate economic growth the federal government had to pay special attention to, be particularly solicitous of, big business. For big business held the dominant position in the American economic structure. Economic concentration was a fact that could hardly be overlooked in any realistic conception of the economy. As John Kenneth Galbraith noted,

> In 1962 the five largest industrial corporations in the
> United States, with combined assets in excess of $36
> billion, possessed over 12 percent of all assets used in
> manufacturing. The fifty leading corporations had
> over a third of all manufacturing assets. The 500
> largest had well over two-thirds.[47]

These industrial giants dwarfed in economic significance the far
more numerous small businesses, farmers, or independent pro-
fessionals. To talk about the American economy was, to a
considerable extent, to talk about such corporations. To seek its
rapid expansion was, unless one considered the possibility of
fundamental structural changes, almost inevitably to seek their
rapid expansion.

Although this logic may appear overly simple, it was the
logic that governed much of the Kennedy Administration's
economic policy. It explained, for example, the Administration's persistent efforts to underwrite new corporate investment; the investment tax credit and liberal depreciation
schedule were justified as means to economic expansion via
corporate expansion. It explained, too, the proposed reduction
of corporate income tax rates in 1963; the high level of these
rates was criticized as an irksome deterrent to corporate expansion. President Kennedy himself employed this logic on
more than one occasion: "This country cannot prosper unless
business prospers." [48]

Equally significant with the actions that such logic dictated were the actions, or even statements, it foreclosed. Although
Kennedy had, in his Yale speech, repudiated the maxim that
business confidence in the national administration was a
prerequisite to economic vigor, in his actions and remarks directed toward the business community he consistently strove to
gain that confidence. And this included studiously avoiding—
save for the exceptional circumstances of the steel affair—measures which might arouse corporate ire. When, nonetheless, the
business community raged against him in 1962, he refused

publicly to respond in kind. Treating business almost as if it were a spoiled child throwing a tantrum, Kennedy saw his task as soothing its temper with kindly paternal words. At the height of business's outpouring of spleen against him and his administration, he remarked to Arthur Schlesinger, Jr.:

> The problem is that the business community no longer has any confidence in itself. Whenever I say anything that upsets them, businessmen just die. I have to spend my time and energy trying to prop them up.[49]

The priority of economic growth, of a larger economic pie, impelled Kennedy to help the corporations on numerous occasions, and to refrain from hurting them unless their behavior became—as had that of U.S. Steel—intolerable. Yet it was not only the doctrine of economic growth which accounted for the corporations' favorable position during the Kennedy Presidency. For an administration preoccupied with computing the arithmetic of power in America, the political clout of the business community was a factor to be placed alongside its economic might. Though that community had not elected Kennedy to the Presidency, he worried that it could always make him look bad, especially with a Congress in which he already had a surfeit of troubles. So he walked gingerly in the presence of businessmen, hopeful at least to assuage their anger if he could not acquire their support. It is questionable, however, how well this tactic served Kennedy. For sophisticated corporate leaders seemed at times to play upon his political sensitivity. Instead of responding with gratitude for the benefits he had conferred upon them, they renewed their complaints in order to receive even more. As Nossiter observed, "They learned that the President tried to relieve rather than resist pressure; the less support they admitted they were getting, the more he was likely to give." [50]

Such factors led Kennedy, who had no great love for

businessmen, to pursue doggedly an alliance with the business community. But though he talked repeatedly of rational partnership, he was answered most of the time with irrational bursts of hostility. No matter what rewards he bestowed upon businessmen, Kennedy could not overcome their suspicions, could not compel their recognition of their common interests. Understandably, there was deep disappointment and frustration within the Administration over the obtuse consciousness that characterized most of the business community. Even Douglas Dillon, the Administration's foremost link to the eastern corporate establishment, commented upon this obtuseness: "I don't think that there had been a President in a long time who had basically done as much for business . . . [but] it took the business community a long time to recognize this." [51]

If business suspicion of Kennedy was largely irrational, there was nonetheless a sense in which Kennedy helped to fuel that suspicion. For the political image he had established during the 1960 campaign, and had maintained thereafter—the image of a dynamic young President determined to start America moving again—was threatening to many businessmen, particularly the less sophisticated ones. They continued to fear that Kennedy was planning an upheaval in the American economy, despite all the evidence to the contrary. It was not so much the specifics of his economic program that disturbed them as the style in which they were presented, their outward garb of novelty and change. In short, businessmen shared the same incapacity as most other Americans when it came to John Kennedy—they could not distinguish the style from the substance. Lyndon Johnson, on the other hand, pursuing the same economic programs as Kennedy, even employing the same academic advisers, had excellent relations with the business community. His prosaic rhetoric, his homilies on free enterprise, his whole style were reassuring to businessmen; they could relax in the knowledge that here was no subverter of the reign of corporate capitalism.[52]

Still, the intense opposition to Kennedy must be accounted irrational. For business had much to gain from the New
Frontier—much more than tax breaks and higher profits, more
indeed than even the sophisticated New Frontiersmen realized.
In the areas of ideology and power, where gains and losses are
subtle and intangible, the economic approach of the Kennedy-Johnson Administrations was to provide a substantial
windfall to the corporate structure.

Ideology has long been a troublesome subject for giant
corporations that dominate the American economy. As numerous writers have pointed out, these corporations wield enormous power over resources and even lives—yet no doctrine
satisfactorily legitimates that power. What justifies control over
the American economy by the handful of men who run these
corporations? By what means, if any, are they held accountable
for their exercise of power? Corporate ideologists have come up
with a host of solutions to this problem: corporations do not
really have much power; or, corporate power is checked by the
countervailing power of other large institutions (e.g., labor
unions and government); or, corporate power is employed by
industrial "statesmen" for the public good. But none of these
solutions has stood up well under close scrutiny. Corporate
power still stands essentially naked.[53]

In his clash with Big Steel, Kennedy seemed to be raising
exactly such questions. His press conference blast at "a tiny
handful of steel executives whose pursuit of private power and
profit exceeds their sense of public responsibility" threatened to
attract the glare of public attention to an ideological controversy that had so far been fought out mainly on a restricted,
intellectual level. Yet in his anxiousness to conciliate business
after the steel affair, Kennedy quickly foreswore this threat.

Instead, he returned to a doctrine of government-business
partnership that went at least part way toward clothing the
corporations with a badly needed legitimacy. Big business became, in Kennedy's doctrine, an ally of government in fostering

economic growth. And since there was no surer measure of national welfare than economic growth, business turned out, in fact, to be the servant of the public good. Also, since economic growth was a critical arena of Cold War competition, business took on the additional role of a bearer of American prestige. Contributing both to domestic prosperity and international success, corporate power could not be weakened without seriously weakening the nation. Business health and strength were, this supposedly antibusiness President repeatedly argued, inseparable from the health and strength of America. The argument might not have been original—indeed, it unconsciously echoed the celebrated corporate logic of General Motors' Charles E. Wilson—but coming from a liberal President it represented, for the corporations, a significant step toward ideological invulnerability.

A gain in power by the corporations accompanied their enhanced ideological position under Kennedy. Most businessmen perceived the Kennedy Administration only as a power threat; they interpreted its interventions in the economy (e.g., the wage-price guideposts) as a quest for federal power at business expense. There was some truth in this apprehension, but there was an equally important sense in which the Administration's interventions in the economy augmented the stability and strength of the corporate structure.

In some areas of the economy the Kennedy and Johnson Administrations greatly tightened the structural links between government and business. William D. Phelan, Jr., has outlined in detail the fruitful connection between the McNamara Defense Department and defense contractors—particularly newer firms with contacts at high levels in the Democratic party. As the McNamara-streamlined Defense Department expanded in both size and functions throughout the 1960s, defense contractors solidified their ties to the DOD (through, for example, the Defense Industrial Advisory Council established in 1962) and utilized those ties for corporate expansion which, in many cases, reached spectacular proportions. Phelan's data indicates that for the 43 fastest growing contractors, annual sales or operating revenues increased from slightly over $6 billion in 1960 to almost $11 billion in 1963 and to over $15 billion in 1965.[54]

But what of the more publicized Kennedy Administration interventions in the economy? Did these, in fact, curtail corporate power? Liberals and conservatives alike have usually assumed government intervention in the American economy during the twentieth century to be a "progressive" step, a public check upon private power. Yet, as Gabriel Kolko has indicated in *The Triumph of Conservatism,* such an assumption is unwarranted. Kolko shows that in the "Progressive" era in American history, 1900–1916, federal intervention in the economy served, not to restrict corporate power, but to stabilize and rationalize the economy in a manner favored by the most influential of the corporate elite. He argues that the great landmarks of Progressive economic legislation—regulation of railroads and the meat-packing industry, the creation of the Department of Commerce and the Federal Reserve System, the Clayton Act and Federal Trade Commission—emerged largely in response to a series of corporate complaints: "unfair" competition to the established companies from new entries into the market, burdensome regulation by populist state legislatures, a generalized disorder and uncertainty pervading the economy. Playing a key role in initiating such legislation, and lobbying for its enactment, business leaders such as George Perkins of the House of Morgan turned to the federal government, Kolko suggests, for a rationalization of the national economy which could not be accomplished by economic means alone.[55]

There are some suggestive parallels between this earlier Progressive period and Kennedy's "progressive" economic policy. Kennedy suffered from a stormier relationship with the business community than either Theodore Roosevelt or Woodrow Wilson. Nonetheless, several of his major economic programs, like theirs, followed closely along lines that had already been marked out by business. His wage guidelines, and other efforts at terminating labor-management conflict over the distribution of income, fit neatly with business's long-standing objective of holding wage costs steady. His liberalization of depreciation allowances furnished business with a tax break which it had sought unsuccessfully from the Eisenhower Administration. His proposed reduction in corporate income taxes and personal income taxes in the higher brackets approached tax reductions earlier proposed by the National Association of Manufacturers and the U.S. Chamber of Commerce.[56] Corporate executives may not have had Kennedy's ear, but the functional result was not so different than if they had. Economic doctrine and political calculation were enough to make him respond more often to business desires than to those of the economic constituencies that actually supported him.

Kennedy's policies adhered in these respects to corporate doctrine, though businessmen were loath to admit it. Further, his policies served in significant ways—acknowledged by the business community only in retrospect—to stabilize and rationalize the corporate economy at a time when it needed help. With labor costs rising and industry hindered by excess capacity, we have seen how the Kennedy Administration sought to hold wages down and underwrite new corporate investment. Its efforts were generally successful; corporate investment picked up in 1962–63, and average wage-rate increases were lower during Kennedy's Presidency than during any other comparable postwar period.[57] Shortly we shall observe how the Administration's 1963 tax program aimed, as its fundamental objective, at ending years of sluggish demand and ensuring a continuously thriving market for corporate output. And here, too, we shall encounter a record of success. The Kennedy Administration was ahead of all but the most sophisticated businessmen in comprehending the requirements of a rationalized corporate economy. Businessmen might complain of how Kennedy's economic intervening inhibited their market freedom; it would take them a while to understand that what was lost in market freedom was more than made up for in stability and profit.

The foregoing pages have portrayed John Kennedy as an architect of a newly buttressed corporate capitalism. This role was not, it should be pointed out, unprecedented for a twentieth-century President. Mention has already been made of some of the contributions Theodore Roosevelt and Woodrow Wilson made to the stability and rationality of the corporate economy. Franklin Roosevelt, despite his bitter feuding with the "economic royalists," saved that economy in its darkest period. The alliance between business and government which Kennedy was urging had actually been growing, fitfully, for most of the century, whatever the fulminations of businessmen and the rhetoric of Presidents.

But if Kennedy's economic role was not unique, still it was noteworthy. For his administration brought the most sophisticated reasoning and the most modern techniques yet to the partnership with business. And with that reasoning and those techniques, it lifted the corporate giants out of the doldrums of the 1950s. It helped pump fresh vitality into the corporate structure, shoring up some of its weaknesses while underwriting its expansion. It even criticized the corporations' critics, confronting those who wished to sustain the consciousness of inequities and irrationalities in the American economy with a promise of economic abundance sufficient to do justice to all. If the corporate economy seemed more productive and more rational by the mid-1960s, if its fundamental deficiencies were, for the time being, largely out of sight, a not inconsiderable share of the credit should go to John Kennedy.

The question naturally arises at this point: did Kennedy intend to serve the business community so well? The answer, I believe, is no. His main objective was to promote economic growth, not to strengthen the corporate system. But the two ends could not be separated. It did not matter greatly how

Kennedy felt about this fact—although the evidence suggests that it troubled him very little. For the results of his economic program were shaped less by his intentions than by the inherent contradictions of liberal reform within the framework of corporate capitalism.

It is time to return to the narrative and take up an account of Kennedy's most "progressive," Keynesian innovation: the 1963 tax bill. That account will confirm the conclusion which has so far emerged: that Kennedy's progressivism in economic affairs was really no more than an enlightened conservatism. For if prior to the campaign for the tax bill the majority of the business community failed to grasp how Kennedy had strengthened and rationalized the corporate structure, the bill —and its results—at last drove the lesson home. Kennedy's 1963 tax bill was to be the device that finally raised corporate consciousness and cemented the then-fragile alliance between government and business. Hence, it would not take long before his "liberal" economics was to become accepted corporate doctrine.

During the latter half of 1962, the animosity of the business community was not the only economic worry that plagued the Kennedy Administration. After a renewal of vigorous expansion in 1961, the American economy was again beginning, in mid-1962, to display signs of sluggishness. Unemployment had leveled off at a disappointing 5.5 percent. Corporate investment, prior to feeling the stimuli of the new depreciation allowance and tax credit, remained hesitant. Private consumption lagged. When the stock market plummeted dramatically late in May, it was viewed by many as the herald of a Kennedy recession.

His economic advisers pressed the President for immediate action to forestall the threat. Walter Heller, chairman of the Council of Economic Advisers, led the fight for a temporary

emergency tax cut to pump money into the languishing economy. But Kennedy, backed by Treasury Secretary Dillon, resisted this scheme. He argued that the economic indicators
were, in fact, " 'a mixed bag,' some down, some up, some
steady." [58] And in the absence of overwhelming evidence,
Congress was unlikely to agree to the existence of an emergency.
Kennedy, therefore, remained unconvinced that an immediate
tax cut was either essential or feasible. Events were to prove him
right; the situation was not as bleak as his economic advisers
imagined. Yet the debate over a "quickie" tax cut in 1962 had
its effect. For it helped turn the attention of the Administration
toward the idea of a tax cut in 1963—this time to be more
carefully planned and extensively promoted.

While Walter Heller and his cohorts had lobbied for temporary tax reduction in the summer of 1962—and had lost—
their real goal was a permanent reduction in the tax rates.
Heller's persistent argument was that the high rate of federal
taxes represented a "drag" upon economic expansion. Each
time the economy began to evince signs of health, taxes si-
phoned off from growing personal or corporate income the
funds needed for further expansion. As a result, aggregate
demand was shackled; the inadequate levels of consumption,
investment, employment, and output which the economy
reached in its upward movements all reflected the inhibiting
effect of the federal tax structure. It was not the threat of
recession, therefore, which primarily occupied Heller; it was the
hope of economic growth.

> In 1961, once recession had turned into recovery,
> nothing was more urgent than to raise the sights of
> economic policy and to shift its focus from the ups
> and downs of the cycle to the continuous rise in the
> economy's potential. Policy emphasis had to be
> redirected from a *corrective* orientation geared to the
> dynamics of the cycle, to a *propulsive* orientation
> geared to the dynamics and the promises of growth.[59]

Although Heller's thinking was fairly orthodox within the community of economists, where Keynesianism was the norm, outside that community it was explosively heterodox. For not only would this thinking commit the federal government to the stimulation of growth; it would do so at the cost of planned budget deficits. Heller was advocating a tax cut that would necessitate a deficit, not at a time of economic crisis, but at a moment when the economy was already moving upward. He was advocating a tax cut that would be matched by new federal revenues only when the economy began to fulfill its unused potential. Faced with a long American political tradition proclaiming the dictum (though that dictum was not always followed in practice) that budgets must be balanced at all accounts, Heller was proclaiming the then-startling Keynesian concept that the federal budget could properly be balanced only in a "balanced economy." [60]

The head of Kennedy's Council of Economic Advisers was thus seeking, in the fall of 1962, to extricate Keynesian theory and method from the textbooks and install them at the center of American economic policy. He was calling for what enthusiastic Kennedy chroniclers would later term a "revolution in fiscal policy." [61] And in John Kennedy he had found an increasingly receptive listener.

Heller's claim to economic innovation did not, however, go unchallenged within the Kennedy Administration. He had a rival, whose position within the Administration was weak, but whose voice was provocative: the Ambassador to India, John Kenneth Galbraith. Galbraith too spoke, in Keynesian terms, of accelerated economic growth—but he insisted that the proper tool of Keynesian fiscal policy should be public spending.

> The expansion produced by tax-cutting, he argued to Kennedy toward the end of 1962, would be an expansion of consumer goods; and these the American people already had in abundance. But it was

"in the area of public needs, notably schools, colleges,
hospitals, foreign policy that our need for growth is
greatest." Tax-cutting, as he later put it, was
"reactionary" Keynesianism, providing the things the
country least needed at the expense of the things it
most needed. "I am not sure," he said, "what the
advantage is in having a few more dollars to spend if
the air is too dirty to breathe, the water too polluted
to drink, the commuters are losing out on the struggle
to get in and out of the cities, the streets are filthy,
and the schools so bad that the young, perhaps
wisely, stay away, and hoodlums roll citizens for some
of the dollars they saved in taxes." [62]

Kennedy reportedly sympathized with Galbraith's view-
point; he had himself defended it on several occasions since the
publication of Galbraith's *The Affluent Society* in the late 1950s.[63]
But Heller had a superior vantage point over Galbraith in the
economic debates. And political considerations were on his side.
Congress seemed to be resistant to any new ventures in social
spending. The business community, which Kennedy was then
actively wooing, could be counted upon to oppose such spending, especially since it would, like the tax cut, mean a substantial deficit. So the President stifled whatever qualms he had,
and ruled out the possibility of a new spending program. If he
believed public spending to be preferable to tax reduction, he
kept that preference to himself.

Heller's brand of Keynes triumphed over Galbraith's—but
for a while it appeared that Kennedy might decide he was not
ready for any brand of Keynes at all. Occupied with Cuban
missiles and congressional elections through the fall of 1962, the
President was, Sorensen relates, unenthusiastic about the tax
bill to be presented to Congress the following January. With the
stock market again climbing, and corporate investment perking
up under the twin incentives of liberalized depreciation and a 7
percent tax credit, the danger of recession had diminished.
Unemployment remained high, aggregate demand sluggish—

but still it did not appear to Kennedy a propitious moment to sell Congress and business the concept of a planned deficit. Figuring that the political costs might be too great, Kennedy was perhaps on the verge of abandoning Heller's Keynesian innovation. Significantly, his support for that innovation was renewed when he received a hint that it might actually produce political benefits.

The occasion was Kennedy's appearance on December 14 before the Economic Club of New York. This was to be the grand test of business's reaction to innovative tax legislation. In his Economic Club speech the President attempted to make his Keynesian proposal sound respectably conservative. He boosted the tax cut by contrasting it to reckless public spending: "To increase demand and lift the economy, the Federal Government's most useful role is not to rush into a program of excessive increases in public expenditures, but to expand the incentives and opportunities for private expenditures." [64] Further, he called attention to his administration's past record of limiting public spending; the increases in federal expenditures during his term, he noted, had gone almost entirely for defense, space, and servicing the national debt.[65] Kennedy skillfully appealed to the self-interest of these New York businessmen, by indicating the rewards tax reduction promised to the private sector, and to their patriotism, by suggesting that the resulting economic growth would strengthen the Free World against the communist onslaught.

Although Galbraith grumbled about " 'the most Republican speech since McKinley,' " and even *Time* magazine remarked that it sounded "like that of an officer of the National Association of Manufacturers," [66] Kennedy and his aides were jubilant about the highly favorable reception accorded the Economic Club speech. The 1963 tax bill, the President now realized, need not estrange him further from the corporate community, whose partnership he still sought; it might even turn out to be an asset in building that partnership. Having obtained evidence of business approval, his doubts about tax reduction vanished. After the Economic Club speech, Sorensen informs us, Kennedy was "fully enthusiastic"[67] about tax cutting.

In the Economic Club speech Kennedy had played down an important aspect of his program: tax reform. The tax legislation under preparation took the form at that point of an omnibus bill, incorporating a number of measures to close loopholes as well as a series of cuts to stimulate private spending. The inclusion of tax reform in the bill was suggested by several factors. Tax reform had long been championed by the Treasury Department and its chief, Douglas Dillon. It was likewise a cherished goal of the Chairman of the House Ways and Means Committee, Wilbur Mills, whose support and influence were critical if the House was to approve tax reduction. Finally, it was considered consoling to old-line liberals, who would invariably be upset about the bonanza tax reduction offered to the wealthy. Despite inevitable business opposition, reform thus appeared politically necessary—and economically desirable as well. The closing of tax loopholes promised to bring in substantial revenues, thereby partially offsetting the drop in federal revenue due to the tax cut.

Kennedy introduced his tax bill to Congress and the public with the kind of rhetorical flourish he reserved for foreign affairs and his annual number-one legislative priority. For the continued growth of the American economy, he declared in his 1963 State of the Union Address, "one step, above all, is essential—the enactment this year of a substantial reduction and revision in Federal income taxes."[68] Walter Heller had pinpointed high federal tax rates as a drag upon economic expansion; Kennedy now excoriated those same rates as the prime source of America's economic maladies:

> Our obsolete tax system exerts too heavy a drag on
> private purchasing power, profits, and employment.

> Designed to check inflation in earlier years, it now
> checks growth instead. It discourages extra effort and
> risk. It distorts the use of resources. It invites recurrent
> recessions, depresses our federal revenues, and causes
> chronic budget deficits.[69]

After this catalogue of ills, the urgency of Kennedy's tax package appeared self-evident. "The enactment this year of tax reduction and tax reform overshadows all other domestic problems in this Congress." [70]

Tax reduction was sought in both individual and corporate rates. Personal income tax rates were to be lowered from the existing range of 20 to 91 percent to a range of 14 to 65 percent. This $11 billion reduction was scheduled to be stretched out over three years, in order to cushion its impact on the federal deficit; still it was expected to release about $6 billion into the hands of consumers in the second half of 1963 alone. Corporate income tax rates were to be lowered from 52 percent to 47 percent, a return to the pre-Korean War level. To aid small businesses, the tax rate on the first $25,000 of corporate income was also lowered, from 30 to 22 percent. On the heels of liberalized depreciation allowances and the investment tax credit, which together had reduced corporate tax liabilities by approximately $2.5 billion in 1962, this new tax cut would eliminate another $2.5 billion from what the corporations annually owed to the federal government.[71]

According to Keynesian theory, the beneficial effect of these cuts would not be restricted to the original $13.5 billion released into the economy. Tax reduction would, in fact, initiate a cumulative expansion. Most of the additional dollars left in the hands of individuals and corporations would be spent for consumption and investment purposes. This would stimulate production and employment and thereby generate further income, which in turn would largely be spent. Through various "leakages" (e.g., savings), expansion would eventually reach a limit; but meanwhile, thanks to the above "multiplier process," GNP would have risen perhaps as much as $30 billion.[72]

Economic growth, by expanding the tax base, would ultimately bring in revenues sufficient to make up for what had been lost due to lowered tax rates. But in the meantime the chief compensatory factor for lost federal revenues was the series of reforms that accompanied Kennedy's proposed tax reductions. Closing tax loopholes would, by itself, produce an estimated $3.4 billion in additional revenues. And, beyond this immediate contribution to holding down the federal deficit, it would greatly improve the equity of the U.S. tax structure.

Most of the reforms were directed at clauses in the tax code which favored the wealthy and the privileged. One proposed change was to set a 5 percent ceiling on deductions for interest payments, medical expenses, and contributions to charity. Another was to tax profits from corporate stock options at ordinary income tax rates, instead of at the prevailing 25 percent capital gains rate. Kennedy's reform package also called for an end to the dividend credit and exclusion, a prize awarded stockholders by the Eisenhower Administration. And it sought to reduce the generous tax writeoffs available to owners of oil wells and real estate. All in all, it was an impressive agenda of reforms. As Robert Lekachman observed, "Most reasonably impartial students of American tax history considered the reforms well conceived and well drawn. If enacted they promised to move the tax code measurably nearer justice and consistency." [73]

Congress, traditionally preoccupied with the size of the national debt, was initially cool to the idea of economic expansion through a planned deficit. Public opinion too—and for the same reason—appeared indifferent to the rewards Kennedy's tax package promised. But the President was not without powerful allies. He obtained an early endorsement for his bill from the AFL–CIO. And, more significantly, influential business groups were lining up behind him. At a news conference in late February, for example, he reported that the National Association of Manufacturers was supporting a tax cut. Corporate backing subsequently crystallized in an Administration-sponsored Business Committee for Tax Reduction, a prestigious assemblage of corporate notables co-chaired by Henry Ford II.

How was a leading segment of the business community so easily mobilized behind a measure which former President Eisenhower was even then denouncing as "fiscal recklessness?" The answer is not far to seek: Kennedy's tax cut brought substantial personal benefits to the men who headed corporations. Kennedy could legitimately argue that taxpayers in all brackets would benefit from his bill, and that the largest proportional reductions would, in fact, go to those in the lower brackets.[74] Still, as Bernard Nossiter has shown, the big monetary gains from lowered tax rates accrued to the wealthy.

> Some 2.4 percent of all taxpayers, those with taxable income of $20,000 or more, stood to pick up $2.3 billion. But the 39.6 percent with taxable incomes of $5000 or less would gain only $1.5 billion. Looking at a more extreme case, the 200,000 wealthiest taxpayers would get an average cut of $4600 and the lowest 20 million about $75 each.[75]

These figures do not include the effects of a reduction in corporate income taxes. Higher corporate profits after taxes would increase dividends and enhance the market value of stocks; here, too, Kennedy's tax cutting promised corporate executives (almost all of them major stockholders, thanks to such devices as stock options) a windfall.

Business's understandable enthusiasm for tax reduction was matched by an equally understandable distaste for tax reform. Corporate executives were hardly eager to watch the loopholes through which they accumulated wealth closed. The Ford Committee and other business backers thus tempered

PRAGMATIC ILLUSIONS

their support for Kennedy's bill with strong opposition to tax reform. Their opposition was not counterbalanced by enthusiasm from those who might be presumed to favor reform. Organized labor, preoccupied with the problem of unemployment, wanted a quick tax cut as a stimulus to production, and feared that consideration of reforms might bog down the legislation interminably. The general public could not get excited about reforms either; most Americans apparently felt, somewhat mistakenly, that the sealing off of tax loopholes was not a matter which affected them.

Kennedy's reform measures thus lacked the boost of a powerful constituency. The only thing that could compensate for this weakness was the strong support of the President himself. But Kennedy did not hazard much of a fight for reform; rather, he made it plain early on, and particularly to business groups, that tax reform must not stand in the way of tax reduction. Robert Lekachman noted that

> in the end, possibly unavoidably, the man who did the most to kill the reform was the President himself. The President had never really concealed his own views. . . . To attentive hearers it was evident that the President was willing, however reluctantly, to accept from Congress tax reduction by itself, if this was the best he could get. It is possible that he might have secured rather more tax reform if he had not revealed his own heart so openly.[76]

Jettisoning tax reform was not the only price that Kennedy paid in steering his tax cut through Congress. In order to placate the various constituencies who were troubled about the burgeoning national debt, the President repeatedly pledged to trim federal expenditures in 1963. He told a symposium of the American Bankers Association in late February: "We have submitted a budget which provides for a reduction in expenditures with the exception of defense, space, and interest on the debt."[77] Rejecting the mantle of a spender, he insisted in an April 3 press conference upon his Administration's frugality: "The fact of the matter is, in nondefense expenditures we have put in less of an increase in our 3 years than President Eisenhower did in his last 3 years." [78]

This was an odd boast for the leader of a party which had long claimed special service to the disadvantaged in American society. Indeed, Kennedy subsequently had to admit to a press conference questioner that the proportionate decline in federal nondefense spending might mean too few funds were flowing into critical areas of domestic need: education, health, the cities, the young, the unemployed.[79] Nevertheless, tax reduction was *the* priority; its beneficial impact upon the economy would prove sufficient, Kennedy assumed, to compensate for any temporary neglect in other areas.

Kennedy's 1963 campaign for tax reduction was basically a repeat of the 1962 drive for tariff reform. Along with the aforementioned lobbying effort aimed at business and labor groups, there was a persistent attempt to win over the largely indifferent public. The President hence plugged his tax cut at every available opportunity. He even turned his nationally televised address after the Senate's ratification of the Nuclear Test Ban Treaty into a lecture on the beneficial results of tax reduction. While tariff reform had been a dubious subject for such an all-out effort, in the case of tax reduction Kennedy's educational barrage made a great deal more sense. The Keynesian logic underlying his bill was newer and more unorthodox to the public, and the bill itself had far greater significance. In convincing the American people of the utility of Keynesian fiscal policy, Kennedy indicated that he possessed substantial abilities as a political educator—when he chose to be one.

Despite the concessions, the lobbying, and the speeches, Congress took its time with Kennedy's tax legislation. The adherents of a balanced budget were in no hurry to vote a planned deficit. And the bill's passage was further complicated by the civil rights turbulence of the spring and summer. But support for tax reduction was deepening, as the Administration's arguments won growing acceptance. On September 25 the House approved the bill by a 271 to 155 margin; while Senate hearings still pended, Administration forces anticipated final passage sometime in the first part of 1964.

Meanwhile, the Administration's elaborate campaign for business backing on tax reduction, following on the heels of Kennedy's numerous gestures to the corporations since the steel confrontation, finally showed signs of overcoming business antagonism toward the New Frontier. Organs of the business community, such as *Nation's Business,* reported a developing sense among executives that the Kennedy Administration was becoming responsive to business needs. Symptomatic of this change in attitude was the statement of Charls Walker, Executive Vice President of the American Bankers Association and a Treasury official under Eisenhower: "Rather than being anti-business, the Administration, except for its actions during the steel price incident, has exhibited a sympathetic and constructive attitude toward the business and financial community." [80]

In view of this new atmosphere of government-business détente—if not yet alliance—Kennedy attempted, in one of his final appearances before a business group, to put to rest any lingering suspicions toward his administration. Addressing the Florida Chamber of Commerce on November 18, 1963, he detailed how well he had served the business community.

> Many businessmen, who are prospering as never before during this administration, are convinced nevertheless that we must be anti-business. With the new figures on corporate profits after taxes having reached an all-time high, running some 43 percent higher than they were just 3 years ago, they still suspect us of being opposed to private profit. With the most stable price level of any comparable economic recovery in our history, they still fear that we are promoting inflation. We have liberalized depreciation guidelines to grant more individual

> flexibility, reduced our farm surpluses, reduced
> transportation taxes, established a private corporation
> to manage our satellite communication system,
> increased the role of American business in the
> development of less developed countries, and
> proposed to the Congress a sharp reduction in
> corporate as well as personal income taxes, and a
> major de-regulation of transportation, and yet many
> businessmen are convinced that a Democratic
> administration is out to soak the rich, increase
> controls for the sake of controls, and extend at all
> costs the scope of the Federal bureaucracy.[81]

Business was not the only constituency that occupied Kennedy in his final months. According to his chroniclers, Kennedy was planning just before his death to move beyond the economic position he had staked out in 1963. Once he had persuaded the business community to resume its profitable partnership with government, and steered his tax legislation successfully through the Congress, Kennedy hoped to shift public attention to a new economic problem: poverty. Having recognized that tax reduction, by itself, was inadequate to eradicate the extensive pockets of poverty which still marred American society, the President was reportedly on the verge of a commitment to a direct struggle against poverty. As Arthur Schlesinger, Jr., relates: "One day in November, musing about the 1964 State of the Union message, he remarked to me, 'The time has come to organize a national assault on the causes of poverty, a comprehensive program, across the board'; this, he suggested, would be the centerpiece of his 1964 legislative recommendations." [82]

After three years of stimulating the economy by pumping money into the hands of corporations and consumers, while limiting federal nondefense expenditures, Kennedy was ready to strike out in a more egalitarian direction. It remains unclear how far he might have progressed in that direction. At the time of his death the antipoverty program was still in a rudimentary state. Neither a theme nor a set of specifics had been adopted. And problems of political strategy had not yet been confronted. After all his 1963 pledges on trimming federal expenditures, after all his 1963 rhetoric on giving private initiative first crack at the nation's economic difficulties, Kennedy was not in the strongest of political positions to carry out a new domestic crusade demanding additional federal spending. It would prove far easier for Lyndon Johnson, in the emotional aftermath of the assassination, to succeed in such a crusade. [83]

Much of President Kennedy's stature in the field of economic policy rests upon the tax cut enacted several months after his death, and the continued economic expansion which extended several years into the term of his successor. It seems appropriate, therefore, to conclude this chapter with a look at the results of his "New Economics."

Kennedy's 1960 campaign pledge to lift America's rate of economic growth up to the 5 percent mark had been fulfilled even before the tax cut was passed early in 1964. From the first quarter of 1961 to the fourth quarter of 1963, the average annual increase in GNP had been 5.4 percent. Thanks largely to tax reduction, even higher figures were obtained during the first two years of the Johnson Administration, with the rise in GNP exceeding 6 percent. Until the escalation of the Vietnam War imposed fresh and unexpected strains upon the Kennedy-Johnson fiscal policy, that policy was responsible for the longest recorded period of peacetime economic expansion in the nation's history.[84]

Kennedy had promised to enlarge the American economic pie; measurably he succeeded. The Kennedy years and the first few Johnson years were a time of prosperity, a period in which the standard of living was demonstrably improving for most Americans. The sluggishness of the Eisenhower years had given way to economic vigor. In place of widespread economic anxiety there was a pervasive optimism. Looked at in these broad terms, Kennedy's economic accomplishments are impressive, and his policy must be accounted a success.

Nevertheless, it is important to ask a question that Kennedy and his economic advisers preferred not to ask: How were the benefits of this new prosperity distributed? If the majority of Americans gained from this economic expansion, what classes or groups gained the most? Here, by comparing the statistics on corporate profits with those on employee compensation and unemployment, a rather different picture of Kennedy-Johnson fiscal policy emerges.

First, let us consider the years 1961–63, before Kennedy's tax cut took effect. How did corporate stockholders (including most of management), employed workers, and the unemployed fare in these years? Corporate profits in this period jumped a spectacular 44 percent before taxes—and 52 percent after taxes, thanks to the tax breaks of 1962. Employee compensation, adjusted for the mild rise in consumer prices, rose only 7 percent in three years; here the effects of the wage guidelines were especially perceptible. Unemployment dropped from 6.7 percent during the 1960–61 recession to 5.6 percent in 1962, but remained near that relatively high figure throughout 1963.[85]

The record for workers and the unemployed was somewhat better in the years 1964–65, a period during which the effects of the tax cut were felt. In 1965, for example, weekly earnings for employees went up 3.5 percent. And on these higher wages they were paying their federal income taxes at a reduced rate. The unemployment situation was dramatically improved; the rate of unemployment stood at only 4.1 percent in December of 1965. As for corporate profits, they continued to skyrocket; for 1965 alone, profits were up 15 percent before taxes, 20 percent after taxes.[86]

The story that these statistics tell is summed up in the figures for the "distribution of gross product originating in nonfinancial corporations." The share of gross product taken by the employees of these corporations as compensation fell each year, from 65.1 percent in 1961 to 62.6 percent in 1965. The share of gross product that went for profits mounted each year, from 14.5 percent in 1961 to 17.0 percent in 1965.[87]

Economic growth policies during the Kennedy-Johnson Administrations were designed to benefit all Americans—and generally they did so. But, as the above statistics indicate, they benefited the prosperous far more than they did people of low or moderate income. The wealthy already owned a disproportionate slice of the American economic pie. From Kennedy's enlargements to the pie, they again received a disproportionate share. Kennedy's impressive record on economic growth hence must be balanced by his record on economic distribution and equity. That record, if judged in terms of Kennedy's expressed sympathies for the underdogs in American society, can only be deemed a sorry one.

The economic stature of the Kennedy Administration does not, however, rest solely upon impressive growth figures. Equally important with the prosperity Kennedy's Presidency produced, his admirers argue, are the methods by which that prosperity was produced. Those methods—devised by Lord Keynes and refined by several generations of American economists—owed little to Kennedy for their formulation; but his sponsorship won them mass acceptance and finally enshrined them as official federal policy. In the eyes of his admirers, the Kennedy years were, thereby, a watershed in American economic history.

> They have borne witness to the emergence, first of all, of a new national determination to use fiscal policy as a dynamic and affirmative agent in fostering economic growth. Those years have also demonstrated, not in theory, but in actual practice, how our different instruments of economic policy—expenditure, tax, debt management and monetary policies—can be tuned in concert toward achieving different, even disparate, economic goals. In short, those years have

encompassed perhaps our most significant advance in
decades in the task of forging flexible economic
techniques capable of meeting the needs of our
rapidly changing economic scene.[88]

It could be argued that this "Keynesian Revolution" (as
some of Kennedy's admirers have called it) was so vital to the
nation's economic health that it justified a skewing of rewards
in the direction of the prosperous. The continuation, and even
intensification, of economic inequality was a price that had to
be paid—along with such short-term sacrifices as abandonment
of tax reform and a freeze upon welfare spending—in order to
modernize American fiscal policy. This argument appears persuasive, as long as it is assumed that the "Keynesian Revolution" has been an unmixed blessing. Yet it is possible to
view that "revolution," at least in the form in which it was
carried through by Kennedy, as of ambiguous value.

Certainly Kennedy's economic achievements represented
an advance over his predecessors. The tenets of modern
Keynesian theory were, under his aegis, substituted for the
hidebound maxims of economic orthodoxy. Flexible tools were
developed to improve the federal government's management of
the economy, to combat its periodic failures and extend its
surges of expansion. The government—to be precise, the President—emerged from Kennedy's "Keynesian Revolution" in a
stronger, and more widely accepted, position as director of the
American economy than ever before.

Yet all this hardly constituted an economic "revolution" (a
word used, as we have already seen in the case of the Alliance
for Progress, rather loosely on the New Frontier). The New
Frontiersmen's excitement over what was essentially an advance in techniques diverted their attention from the fundamentally conservative impact of those techniques. A parallel
might be drawn here with the counterinsurgency fad. The New
Frontiersmen were enthused by the prospect of intervening in

Use of new techniques to maintain established structures of power.

social and economic processes with sophisticated new techniques. They failed to heed the fact that those techniques assumed the maintenance of established structures of power.

The sector of the American economy that Kennedy's "New Economics" techniques served best was big business. His innovations were, in the last analysis, not a threat, but a prop to the established economic hierarchy. And this conclusion—however unpalatable it might seem to the liberal architects of the "New Economics"—was one which even the conservative business community was finally to draw.

Perhaps the most striking feature of Kennedy's "Keynesian Revolution" was the rapidity with which it became the new orthodoxy. Sophisticated leaders of the corporate world had endorsed Kennedy's tax reduction plans from the outset. Once the tax cut actually took effect in 1964, almost the entire business community began to embrace this brand of Keynesian fiscal policy. In the sober language of *Business Week,* "the lesson of 1964 is that fiscal policy needs to be used actively and steadily if balanced long-term growth is to be achieved." [89]

As corporate profits soared, and executive salaries were padded by tax reduction and higher stock dividends, remaining business suspicions of Kennedy's economic program evaporated—particularly since it was now in the hands of the reassuring Lyndon Johnson. Businessmen, Robert Lekachman observed, were at last discovering "that economic expansion was assisted by the termination of the traditional civil war between Democratic national administrations and the business community." The "end of ideology" which Kennedy had called for at Yale had seemingly come. "Business recognition that prudent Keynesian fiscal policies promote larger markets and higher profits has had an unexpected effect. Keynesian prescriptions, the monopoly of reformers and radicals during the 1930's and 1940's, have very nearly become the favorite medicines of the established, propertied interests in the community." [90]

The alliance between government and business which Kennedy had so earnestly pursued thus became firm, reflecting a convergence on economic philosophy as well as a growing recognition of congruent interests. In the next few years this alliance appeared as part of the Johnsonian consensus, its special nature and importance partially obscured by the other linkages within that consensus. And just as in the Kennedy years—when, in spite of its animosity toward the federal government, the business community received a greater largess than Kennedy's political supporters—the principal beneficiary of Johnson's consensus was, once more, business.

Consider, for example, Johnson's economic policy before it reflected the constraints of Vietnam. The much-publicized poverty program did channel new funds into the urban ghettoes and rural wastelands (though some of these funds ended up in the pockets of landlords, construction companies, road builders, etc.). Less publicized, however, was Johnson's continuation of the Kennedy tax program. Corporate and personal income tax rates were, as mandated in the 1964 tax bill, further reduced in 1965. And the Johnson Administration contributed yet another tax boon that year in the form of a reduction or elimination of excise taxes, adding once more to the corporations' swelling profit record. "Like 1964's tax harvest," Lekachman noted, "much of 1965's improvement would be realized by prosperous corporations and wealthy individuals." [91]

Kennedy-Johnson fiscal policy can, in short, best be characterized as "conservative expansionism." [92] While corporate power and profits were blooming throughout the 1960s, social needs continued to go unfulfilled. Despite President Johnson's rhetorical extravagance regarding a "War on Poverty" and a "Great Society," the inadequacy of social services—which John Kenneth Galbraith had vividly underscored during the original debate over the tax cut—was scarcely alleviated by the time Johnson left office.

Once it lost its air of controversy for an increasingly sophisticated business community, the "New Economics" settled
into an ongoing process of economic tinkering which substituted for—and in large part foreclosed—genuine economic and
social change. It had some notable successes in the mid-
1960s—and some important failures later on, as the problems of
maintaining economic expansion with full employment and
stable prices proved more complicated than they had earlier
appeared. Never did it seriously concern itself with the problem
of inequity in the American economy. Nor did it ever confront
the enormity of corporate power. The triumphs of pragmatic
liberalism in the field of economic policy thus masked a deeper
failure, a failure to address the fundamental deficiencies in
American economic life. Those liberal triumphs had, it is true,
won over many conservatives—but only at the cost of ensuring
that the conservative, corporate definition of the American
economy, now decked out in sophisticated Keynesian dress,
remained ascendant.

6

"Listen, Mr. Kennedy": The Civil Rights Struggle

The accelerating civil rights struggle of the early 1960s presented John F. Kennedy with the most difficult political problem of his presidential tenure. It also presents, for any student of Kennedy, the key problem in understanding the character of his political leadership. Against the background of the insistent moral passion of the civil rights cause, Kennedy's mode of pragmatic liberal leadership is sharply illuminated. In the history of his relationships both with the black freedom movement and with a white America confused and troubled by that movement, the capabilities, but far more the limitations, of that pragmatic mode are made apparent.

It may be helpful, before turning to a historical narrative of Kennedy's involvement with civil rights, to set out its central themes. The first is the habit, predominant throughout almost all of Kennedy's Presidency, of defining civil rights in pragmatic terms. By this definition the racial problem was conceived of as politically equivalent to other Kennedy Administration issues, such as trade reform and tax reduction; it competed with them for attention and support, sometimes receiving higher, and often lower, priority. If one considers the institutional constraints and political pressures with which Kennedy had to deal, the handling of civil rights as simply one among several important issues was probably a "realistic" approach. Yet that approach failed to confront the most crucial dimensions of the civil rights struggle—the moral questions it posed and the profound consequences it held for American society. Above all, it lacked understanding of the urgency of the struggle, and of the great passions it brought forth. Faced with a social movement and a moral crisis that transcended the ordinary boundaries of American politics, Kennedy continued (at least until the Birmingham events of 1963) to play politics as usual.

Essential to the pragmatic style is an emphasis upon tangible products. In the case of Kennedy and civil rights the tangible products shifted over time, from an initial focus on litigation and executive orders to a final commitment to legislation. Constant, however, was the downgrading of the intangible—interpretations of and feelings toward the racial question. Kennedy, as will be seen, continually shied away from publicly discussing the *meaning* of the civil rights struggle. If he accepted (sometimes) his presidential responsibility to act, he never fully appreciated the equally important responsibility to educate. On no other subject was political education so vital in the early 1960s; on no other subject did Kennedy prove so deficient as an educator.

True, major costs were involved in serving as an educator on the racial situation in America. A strong public stance on civil rights, Kennedy knew, would antagonize southern Senators and Representatives whose support he hoped to win for various aspects of his legislative program. It also risked alienating a portion of his electoral support, damaging his chances for reelection in 1964. More was at stake for Kennedy, though, than just a loss of votes. The civil rights movement, at least on its more militant side, was overrunning the mainstream of American politics; it sought to redefine the nature of both political action and political ends in America. For Kennedy to respond favorably to that redefinition, he would have had to give up, in part, the political mode of which he was a master. He would have had to enter into an unpredictable and hazardous situation where the familiar tenets of American presidential leadership were of limited value. He would even, perhaps, have had to sacrifice some of his own power in order that American political life could open to new possibilities.

Given these costs, it is hardly surprising that Kennedy eschewed the role of civil rights educator. But one must also consider the costs of his refusal of that role. The black struggle was, in the early 1960s, still in a relatively moderate phase. The goal even of the militants was integration and justice within American society. White Americans might have come to understand, tolerate, even sympathize with that struggle in all its dimensions—if an American President could have portrayed it to them, at that time, with the same urgency and moral force it possessed. The civil rights movement did not need guidance from Kennedy; it needed him, rather, to clarify and interpret its efforts to those whose prejudices might be tempered or overcome by respect for the nation's leader. It needed him, in short, to bear witness to its fundamental righteousness.

The later embitterment of blacks, and attendant backlash of whites, cannot be laid to Kennedy's failure to bear such witness; the social forces at work ran far deeper than the actions of any one man. Yet if the development of black militancy in the mid-1960s was inevitable, and even necessary, the magnitude of racial hostility and misunderstanding on both sides perhaps was not. One cannot help but wonder if a strong and committed educational stance on civil rights, by an American leader such as Kennedy in the early 1960s, might not have tempered blacks' growing anger toward whites and, more importantly, offered white America some chance of understanding the subsequent passions and actions of blacks. Kennedy as educator could not have solved America's racial problems; he might have helped white America to face up to them more wisely and humanely. This was the lost political possibility of the early 1960s—and we are still witnessing its consequences.

The foregoing argument assumes that Kennedy *could* have been such an educator, that his underlying sympathies lay wholeheartedly with the civil rights cause. Actually, the nature of Kennedy's commitment to civil rights was more ambivalent than this. If he wanted to see racial justice attained, he was not so sure he wanted it attained along the lines that the civil rights movement was developing. The movement was perceived by Kennedy to be a rival as well as an ally. For it confronted his mode of politics with the most difficult of all challenges—a different mode of politics.

Kennedy's pragmatic liberalism presupposed a bounded political context within which a plurality of elites competed, bargained, and compromised with one another. The primary skill for an American political leader within this context was the ability to maneuver among and manipulate those elites, so as to achieve the most favorable outcome from the leader's point of view. A corollary to this approach was that, in national politics, the President held a great advantage over other actors—he was expected to be the innovator, the initiator of action. Others in the political elite might resist his aims, but the battle would nonetheless be fought on his terms, according to his definitions.

One of the most striking features of the civil rights move-ment in the early 1960s was its shattering of this context. The movement brought masses of ordinary, nonelite blacks into the political arena and inspired them to new and dramatic forms of "direct action." Sit-ins, freedom rides, mass marches—political action now revolved around the participants in such dramas, ready to back up their commitments with their lives. Their courage and willingness to suffer gave them the initiative on the racial question, made them its definers. A new and democratic mass politics, with different assumptions and rules than elite politics, was emerging among blacks in the early 1960s—and

Kennedy's style of pragmatic liberalism, rooted in elite politics, was hard put to deal with it.

The key, I believe, to the history of Kennedy's involvement with civil rights is this conflict between mass politics and elite politics. Kennedy did not possess the initiative on the subject of civil rights. The issue was out of his control. Its direction, tempo, intensity were defined by others who, while ostensibly his allies, did not always share identical political purposes. Kennedy was not much impressed by the fact that thousands of black people were, for the first time, acting to seize their own freedom. What mattered more to him was that their actions were unpredictable, perpetually threatening to immerse him in situations for which his pragmatic approach was ill prepared. Sometimes, they even intruded on the issues he did control—witness, for example, the manner in which his tax reduction bill was held up by the racial turmoil in 1963.

Kennedy's response was an attempt to reassert the dominance of pragmatic, elite politics. This was reflected in his public pronouncements on civil rights. In the narrative that follows we can observe a pattern of slighting the significance of the civil rights movement, criticizing civil rights demonstrations, and claiming primary credit for his own administration for civil rights accomplishments. In the public interpretation he placed on events, pragmatic politics still held sway; mass politics was given scant recognition. This interpretation amounted to more than merely a failure to educate the American people on civil rights. It seriously distorted the racial and political history of the era.

Parallel to Kennedy's public stance toward the movement were his active efforts to gain control over it and to direct it along lines consistent with his own purposes. I show in this chapter how, at critical junctures in both 1961 and 1963, Kennedy sought to impose his stamp on the civil rights struggle. I indicate how, largely through behind-the-scenes manipulation, he attempted to force that struggle back into the traditional channels of American politics. Each time he was to be partially successful in the short run. Each time, in the long run, he failed; a mass politics of direct action could not be contained within the bounds of Kennedy's pragmatic liberalism.

Prior to his 1960 presidential campaign, John Kennedy owned an undistinguished record on civil rights. Theodore Sorensen concedes Kennedy's lack of involvement as a Senator; Kennedy had not, Sorensen recalls, devoted much thought to the subject in these years or built up many ties to civil rights forces.[1] If Sorensen perceived Senator Kennedy as merely inattentive to racial matters, the civil rights leadership was rather more suspicious of his position. They were unhappy about his wooing of southern support after his unsuccessful run for the Democratic vice-presidential nomination in 1956, especially when that wooing seemed to be reflected in a compromising stand on a key provision of the 1957 Civil Rights Bill.[2] Although this campaign for southern support eventually slackened, by the time of the 1960 Democratic Convention civil rights leaders still greatly preferred Humphrey or Stevenson to Kennedy. Kennedy's weakness in the civil rights camp was underlined by an incident at the Shrine Auditorium in Los Angeles during the convention; appearing there with other candidates before a gathering of black leaders, he was greeted with booing.[3]

During his presidential campaign Kennedy made strenuous efforts to overcome this weakness (which was only intensified by his choice of Lyndon Johnson as a running mate). He began by recruiting a number of aides—most notably Harris Wofford—with far better connections to the civil rights movement than his own. Admitting to these aides that "he understood he was in trouble with the Negroes in this country," [4] he secured their help in devising a campaign pitched to overcome black suspicions and generate black enthusiasm. The quest for black votes became, Sorensen states, "a top priority in his campaign." [5]

Since his own record on civil rights was not particularly favorable, or his opponent Nixon's record on the subject unfavorable, Kennedy's strategy for winning black votes—which might be decisive in several northern states—required him to embrace the civil rights cause. Incorporated into numerous of his campaign speeches was a grim yet moving portrait of the plight of blacks in American society, a portrait replete with statistics on the terrible educational, employment, and health disadvantages the average black had to face. The Democratic candidate additionally pressed hard on criticism of the Eisenhower Administration's activities in the field of civil rights. He repeatedly scored Eisenhower for failing to abolish discrimination in federally financed housing by "a stroke of the Presidential pen," and pledged that he would soon rectify this omission. More important than any of these words in winning black votes, however, was a gesture Kennedy made in the waning days of the campaign. His intervention permitted Martin Luther King, Jr., to be released from a Georgia jail on bail. This was, according to Theodore H. White, one of the actions most responsible for his eventual margin of victory. [6]

Beyond the specific pledges that Kennedy made on civil rights issues during the campaign, there was a promise of a strong and public presidential commitment to the civil rights cause itself. Some of Kennedy's 1960 rhetoric deserves quoting at length here; it can serve as a standard for his subsequent course of action. Speaking in Los Angeles in September 1960, he said:

> When our next President takes office in January, he must be prepared to move forward in the field of human rights in three general areas: as a legislative leader, as Chief Executive, and as the center of the moral power of the United States. . . . As a moral leader, the next President must play his role in

> interpreting the great moral and educational forces
> which are involved in our crusade for human rights.
> He must exert the great moral and educational force
> of his office to help bring equal access to public
> facilities from churches to lunch counters, and to
> support the right of every American to stand up for his
> rights, even if on occasion he must sit down for them.
> For only the President, not the Senate and not the
> House and not the Supreme Court, in a real sense,
> only the President can create the understanding and
> tolerance necessary as the spokesman for all the
> American people, as the symbol of the moral
> imperative upon which any free society is based.[7]

Kennedy's calculated stance as a civil rights advocate during the 1960 campaign was to have important, if unintended, consequences. It helped to create a belief among civil rights forces that the new President would be solidly behind them in their accelerating desegregation drive. Kennedy Administration officials would later chide disillusioned movement activists for their overblown expectations of federal protection and aid. Yet if those activists were naive, it was largely because they had taken Kennedy's original pledge of support at face value.

In his campaign Kennedy had aimed to win over civil rights forces. But in his initial months as President he adopted a different tack. Although extensive black support had been vital to his narrow electoral triumph, the narrowness of that triumph now became an argument for a cautious approach toward civil rights. Black leaders were called to the White House and told not to look for Administration-backed civil rights bills in 1961. Kennedy explained to them that the present Congress would not pass civil rights legislation, and that if he fought for it, his other programs (some, like the minimum-wage increase, of benefit to blacks) would suffer the loss of crucial support. Also postponed was the promised executive order on housing; in response to press conference queries Kennedy replied only that the matter was under consideration. Amid the flurry of excitement surrounding the launching of the New Frontier, the cause of civil rights was conspicuously absent. It was evident that "civil rights was in the rear ranks of the Kennedy Administration's early priorities." [8]

In these early months—and, to a great extent, throughout his Presidency—the power of the white South loomed largest in Kennedy's political calculations. Entrenched in key congressional committees, adept at traditional congressional folkways, southern Democrats were a constant source of worry to a President whose problems in Congress were apparent from the first. Kennedy hoped that he could walk a tightrope between these southern Democrats and his civil rights supporters. But this hope entailed a low-profile stance on civil rights. It required that every presidential comment on civil rights be weighed for its probable reception in the South. It required too a policy of behind-the-scenes maneuvering, of negotiation and conciliation with southern power-holders, rather than any public confrontation of issues. James MacGregor Burns, talking with the President in 1962, found him haunted by " 'this Southern problem.' " [9] It was not the moral problem of the South that haunted Kennedy, but the problem of southern power. Kennedy was a President highly attuned to his own power stakes —and the South meted out power to Presidents largely on the basis of how quiet they kept the issue of race.

The civil rights movement and its supporters in Congress could not, in 1961, hope to match this power. Not only did the movement lack the institutional base of the white South; it suffered as well from internal splits and rents. The more established and conservative civil rights organizations, such as the Urban League and the NAACP (National Association for the Advancement of Colored People), did not always get along with more militant groups, such as CORE (Congress of Racial Equality) and SNCC (Student Non-Violent Coordinating Committee). And even where ideological bonds existed, differences of personality and organizational style often led the various groups to work at cross-purposes. The civil rights movement was hardly a unified pressure group pushing on the Kennedy Administration as a counterbalance to the white South; it was a coalition of diverse, and often deeply divided, elements.[10]

Some civil rights organizations (chiefly the NAACP) tried to be this kind of pressure group. But a crucial side of the movement—its younger and more militant side—was by 1961 moving beyond the whole concept of pressure-group politics. It was beginning to talk not only of civil rights, but of love and community. It was beginning to see political action not only as a means of restructuring power relationships, but as a way of transforming human relationships as well. It was, in short, rapidly leaving the tactics of pragmatic liberal politics behind, while calling the purposes of those politics into doubt with hard and disturbing questions. Although Kennedy's calculations did not fully register these developments in 1961, this side of the civil rights movement would eventually come to perplex him just as deeply as the white South.

Afraid of antagonizing the white South, desiring also to concentrate on foreign policy, President Kennedy delegated most of his responsibilities in the civil rights field to his aides at the outset of his administration. What civil rights strategy the Administration did have at this point largely centered upon the efforts of the Justice Department. Under the leadership of Attorney General Robert Kennedy, a campaign of litigation was mapped out there, aimed at making the voting provisions of the 1957 and 1960 Civil Rights Acts effective across the South. Victory S. Navasky describes the thinking governing this strategy: "forego legislation (which would get bogged down in an unsympathetic Congress), forego executive orders (which might alienate key Southern committee chairmen), and concentrate on litigation specifically aimed at winning Southern Negroes the vote. With the franchise, went the reasoning, the Southern Negro would hold the balance of political power and all other rights and privileges would follow." [11]

The White House itself undertook certain efforts in the area of black employment. Vice-President Johnson was made the chairman of the President's Committee on Equal Employment Opportunity (established by executive order in April of 1961); the committee worked to obtain nondiscrimination pledges from government contractors. Harris Wofford, the President's special assistant on civil rights (until 1962), headed a subcabinet group that concerned itself with equal employment opportunity in federal agencies. He had a mandate from the President to push hard on these agencies to hire and upgrade blacks. But, Wofford recalls, Kennedy "didn't particularly want to hear about it because he was busy." [12]

Both these groups achieved scattered successes, without really breaking established patterns of racial discrimination.[13] Their chief importance was symbolic. They supplied the Administration with concrete results that could be used to placate the restive civil rights movement. But the movement was not as impressed by the statistics on black employment gains in the federal government as was the Administration. Particularly in 1961, these statistics reassured the pragmatists of the Kennedy Administration that they were indeed doing something significant for the cause of racial justice.

While the Kennedy Administration was intent upon maintaining this low-profile stance, the civil rights movement had other ideas. On May 4, 1961, a CORE contingent of seven blacks and six whites departed from Washington on the first of the "freedom rides." Their plan was to challenge segregation in bus terminals and facilities throughout the South. The journey exploded into violence on May 14, outside Anniston, Alabama. A mob burned one of the buses carrying the freedom riders, and beat up several of the nonviolent CORE group on a second bus. When the battered freedom riders arrived in Birmingham another terrifying incident occurred. Young white toughs carrying iron bars savagely assaulted two members of the group; one of them, the veteran civil rights activist James Peck, required fifty-three stitches to close a head wound.

Although the first freedom ride got no farther than Birmingham, SNCC and the Nashville Student Movement quickly moved to start another one. They were determined to prove that violence could not overcome nonviolence. Protection for these freedom riders was requested from the Justice Department. According to Ruby Doris Smith of SNCC, "the Justice Department said no, they couldn't protect anyone, but if something happened, they would investigate." [14] As the riders approached Montgomery, both John and Robert Kennedy attempted behind the scenes to extract from Governor Patterson of Alabama a pledge that order would be kept. After much evasion, such a pledge was seemingly obtained. But when the bus reached the Montgomery terminal, the terminal was occupied by hundreds of angry whites—and no police. A number of the SNCC riders were badly beaten, and John Siegenthaler, the President's emissary to Montgomery, was knocked unconscious when he tried to help one of them escape from the mob.

At this point the Kennedy Administration moved in. Six hundred federal marshals (some specially deputized for the occasion) were immediately sent into Montgomery under the direction of Deputy Attorney General Byron White. A federal court order was obtained, enjoining the Ku Klux Klan, the National States' Rights party, and the police forces of Birmingham and Montgomery from interfering with interstate bus travel. And President Kennedy issued a statement calling for the restoration of order in Alabama.

However, at the same time as the Administration acted to curb mob violence and overcome state dereliction of duty, it also sought to call off the freedom-ride campaign. On May 24, Robert Kennedy appealed to the civil rights groups involved for a "cooling-off period." The appeal was promptly rejected —although two days later Martin Luther King, Jr., of SCLC (Southern Christian Leadership Conference) announced a "temporary lull but no cooling off" in the rides.[15]

In the freedom-rides affair the Administration's actions were belated but effective. Far less satisfactory were John Kennedy's public statements on the rides. It is worth looking at these statements for a moment, for they were to set a pattern for Kennedy's public response to the civil rights movement. The only presidential statement during the height of the mob violence was a terse six sentences, asking Alabama citizens to refrain from provocative actions and local officials to meet their responsibilities.[16] Although most of the nation was shocked, and potentially sensitized, by the violence, Kennedy did not take this opportunity to discuss the moral issue involved—the cruel discrimination, backed by terror, practiced against black people engaged in moving through a supposedly free country. Nor was anything said about the courage of the freedom riders in the face of that terror. The President did not even mention the constitutional rights involved: equal protection of the law and the freedom of American citizens to travel anywhere in the country with full privileges and immunities. Although the freedom rides, by vividly illuminating the nature of southern reality, offered the rest of white America an object lesson in racial oppression, Kennedy, perhaps from a fear of offending southern sensibilities, abstained from giving presidential acknowledgment to that lesson.

This educational failure disappointed civil rights supporters. A racially mixed delegation came to the White House to plead with Kennedy for a stronger presidential statement on the freedom rides. One of the whites, Eugene Rostow (whom Kennedy did not know at that point), argued passionately that the President must say something about the moral issue involved in addition to calling for law and order. According to Harris Wofford, Kennedy was highly irritated by this argument. After the delegation had left, he told Wofford angrily: "What in the hell does he think I should do? Doesn't he know I've done more for civil rights than any President in American history?" [17]

As the freedom rides continued into June and July of 1961,
many white Americans, initially sympathetic, became apprehensive and then negative. A Gallup poll in late June showed 63
percent of those questioned disapproving of the rides. Kennedy
remained silent on the subject until his news conference of July
19. There, asked his views on the freedom riders, he replied:

> In my judgment, there's no question of the legal rights
> of the freedom travelers—Freedom Riders, to move in
> interstate commerce. And those rights, whether we
> agree with those who travel, whether we agree with
> the purpose for which they travel, those rights stand
> provided they are exercised in a peaceful way.[18]

Again Kennedy avoided saying anything about the *meaning* of
black people's search for justice. Insofar as he did give support
to the freedom riders, that support was phrased in a defensive
manner. The statement was reminiscent of earlier liberal defenses of the free speech of communists—as if the freedom riders
were a highly unpopular group of dissidents whose rights had to
be protected despite the group's obnoxious nature.

Finally, there was Kennedy's statement on the aftermath
of the freedom rides. In response to the events in Alabama,
Attorney General Kennedy had petitioned the Interstate
Commerce Commission at the end of May 1961 for an order
banning segregation in interstate bus terminals. The ICC issued
the order in September, and it became effective on November 1.
When, in January of 1962, President Kennedy was questioned
about his administration's rather paltry record in civil rights,
he listed the order, along with voting rights suits and the
appointment of blacks to the federal service, as the primary
accomplishments of 1961. No recognition was given in his
statement to the role the freedom riders had played. In claiming
full credit for desegregating southern bus terminals, Kennedy
was helping to foster a mistaken public impression: that civil
rights movement actions which dramatically and openly con-

[handwritten marginalia at top: The civil rights placed Kenn. Admin in a different position - Chose between alienating S. Dem. or the blacks that were dissatisfied with discrim backed by terror. The concessions made were tentative and designed and self protecting politically]

fronted racial oppression were unnecessary because the federal government could be relied upon to end segregation in a more measured, reasonable, and legal fashion.[19]

The freedom rides had placed the Kennedy Administration in an uncomfortable position, had forced it to abandon its low-key approach to civil rights and take on, at least for the moment, the responsibility for safeguarding constitutional rights in the South. Robert Kennedy's appeal for a cooling-off period was a rather futile attempt to slow down the direct-action campaign before it forced even more discomforting decisions. A more subtle, and more successful, effort at controlling movement energy took place during the summer of 1961. As SNCC activists gathered to plan further action, Tim Jenkins, a young black who was Vice President of the National Student Association, proposed to their June meeting that SNCC concentrate its efforts on the registration of black voters in the South. Jenkins had previously met with representatives of the liberal Taconic and Field Foundations, and they had pledged substantial funds to finance such a voter-registration drive, "on condition that civil rights agencies across the board . . . agree to redirect their energies from buses to ballots." [20] Since Burke Marshall of the Justice Department and Harris Wofford, President Kennedy's special assistant on civil rights, had been present at these meetings, and since the emphasis on voter registration coincided with the Kennedy Administration position, it soon became widely known that the Administration had an important hand in the foundations' offer.

Jenkins' proposal stirred up a major controversy within SNCC. Many SNCC members regarded a concentration upon voter registration as a return to gradualism. They were wary too of the support of white liberals and the federal government; they nourished, Howard Zinn observes, "the suspicion that an attempt was being made to cool the militancy of the student movement and divert the youngsters to slower, safer activity." [21] But another SNCC faction was won over to the voter-registration scheme. The availability of foundation money promised, in their view, an expansion of civil rights activity in the South. Equally important, the impression had been created that if the SNCC workers switched from direct action to voter registration, they would receive "full federal protection of rights and safety."[22] For a movement battered by numerous arrests and beatings, this was no small consideration. At an August meeting at the Highlander Folk School in Tennessee, these opposing arguments resulted in an impasse between the direct-action camp and the voter-registration camp; SNCC seemed, for a moment, on the verge of splitting apart. Ultimately, a compromise was reached. Two arms of SNCC were formed, one for direct-action projects, one for voter registration.[23]

The subsequent engagement of civil rights groups in the Voter Education Project was, in the short run at least, a significant victory for the Kennedy Administration. My point here is not that voter registration was an invalid course for the civil rights movement to follow. A voter-registration campaign in the Deep South was clearly needed. Rather, what must be pointed out is how closely that campaign meshed with the purposes of the Administration. The future rewards were obvious: more votes for the Democratic party and its liberal wing. More important, though, were the immediate rewards. A campaign to register black voters created a less perceptible threat to the southern way of life than the desegregation of schools or public facilities; the danger of the Administration alienating the white South was thereby lessened.[24] Because it involved an established constitutional right rather than a controversial form of racially integrated behavior, the need for Kennedy to take a risky moral stance in public was also avoided. Finally, as the SNCC activists perceived, by diverting black concern and energy from direct action, it seemingly reduced the likelihood that the black movement would create further crises in which the Administration would have painfully to choose between the civil rights cause and southern support.

Beyond all these considerations, the Kennedy Administration's effort to shift the civil rights movement from direct action to voter registration revealed a great deal about its basic attitude toward the movement itself. Kennedy and his associates, their effort shows, believed that *they* should set the direction which the civil rights movement should take. As Arthur Schlesinger, Jr., put it in another context, Kennedy "wanted to keep control over the demand for civil rights." [25] The goal of his administration, in the summer of 1961, was to turn civil rights into an issue like any other in national politics—a subject for presidential prerogative, a matter to be managed by prudent and skillful leadership from Washington.

Presidential management provided no space for direct mass action. Voting was, for the Kennedy Administration, a welcome form of black politics; direct action was not. Direct action was the favorite tactic of the civil rights militants, whose political arguments the Administration never took very seriously.[26] Its vices, in the eyes of the Administration's pragmatic liberals, were many. Direct action did more than simply create unpredictable situations. It violated the sphere of elite politics, introducing into the political arena new actors who often refused to play by the rules of adjustment and compromise. It posed extreme demands—extreme because they invoked justice rather than pragmatic objectives. In short, it made the managerial style of politics unworkable. The Kennedy Administration was thus, by its very nature, opposed to the growth of this new form of mass political participation. It felt threatened by precisely the most novel discovery of the direct-action campaigns—that ordinary blacks might organize and struggle to win their freedom themselves.

As the SNCC cadre moved into their voter-registration drive (concentrating first on McComb, Mississippi), lawyers from the Justice Department conducted a complementary campaign of voting-rights suits. The Kennedy Administration pursued its strategy of litigating the vote vigorously. While the

Eisenhower Administration filed only six suits in accordance
with provisions of the 1957 and 1960 Civil Rights Acts, the
Kennedy Administration in its first two years filed over thirty
such suits. Each involved mountains of work—analyzing
records, obtaining affidavits, preparing briefs—by dedicated
Justice lawyers. Yet the magnitude of the effort could not
overcome the narrowness of the cautious legalistic approach.
The strategy of litigation failed to gain the vote for more than a
fraction of disenfranchised southern blacks. As the Commission
on Civil Rights reported in 1963, "After five years of federal
litigation, it is fair to conclude that case-by-case proceedings,
helpful as they have been in isolated localities, have not provided a prompt or adequate remedy for widespread discriminatory denials of the right to vote." [27]

One of the impediments to the litigation strategy was of
the Kennedy Administration's own making. This was the group
of judges Kennedy appointed to the Fifth Judicial Circuit,
whose jurisdiction included those parts of the South where
racial discrimination was most acute. Of these judges, a full
one-quarter turned out to prefer their segregationist biases over
the law of the land. There was Judge W. Harold Cox of Mississippi, who referred to blacks from the bench as "niggers" and
compared them on one occasion to "a bunch of chimpanzees."
Cox refused to find a pattern of discrimination in existence
anywhere, even in a county where no blacks were registered
though there were 2490 blacks of voting age. There was E.
Gordon West of Louisiana, who called the Supreme Court's
1954 decision outlawing segregated schools "one of the truly
regrettable decisions of all time." There was Robert Elliott of
Georgia, who "found against Negroes in over 90 percent of the
civil rights cases that came before his court during [Robert]
Kennedy's tenure as Attorney General." [28] These (and other)
Kennedy judicial appointees managed, through technicalities,
delays, or extralegal challenges to federal authority, consistently to harass and frustrate both the Justice Department and
the civil rights movement.

Both John and Robert Kennedy have received substantial criticism for these appointments. As Victor S. Navasky remarks, "it was a blatant contradiction for the Kennedys to forego civil rights legislation and executive action in favor of litigation and at the same time to appoint as lifetime litigation-overseers men dedicated to frustrating that litigation." [29] While the reasons for these disastrous judicial selections were numerous, as Navasky indicates in his *Kennedy Justice,* the most important one was obvious: feasance to southern power in Congress. Judge Cox, for example, was the nominee and friend of Mississippi's powerful Senator Eastland. In his and other cases the Kennedys avoided bringing challenges to the judicial choices of southern Senators. They were prepared to trade judicial vacancies—and take a chance on who might fill them—for the hope of future legislative favors from the South.

No doubt it would have cost the Kennedy Administration something to refrain from such trading. But if the cause of civil rights had been important enough to it—and if the Kennedys had fully appreciated what mischief an obstructionist judge could work—judicial appointments in the South might have been handled differently. As several critics have suggested, the Kennedy Administration might have rejected senatorial picks who appeared likely to remain segregationists on the bench, and compelled southern Senators to bargain for more acceptable nominees. If some of those Senators stuck to their original choices, the judicial vacancies at issue might have been left open; in such cases the federal court system provided for the rotation of judges from other districts to occupy the vacancies. Such options were, it would appear, never considered by the Kennedy Administration. Here as elsewhere during these crucial years of the civil rights struggle, Kennedy and his associates remained bound by the logic and dictates of the pragmatic mode of politics.

All the civil rights groups had agreed to concentrate their efforts on voter registration. But their work could not easily be kept within such bounds. A SNCC voter-registration project in

Albany, Georgia, in the fall of 1961 soon burgeoned into a full-scale assault on all forms of segregation. The Albany Movement that emerged to conduct the assault was particularly significant because it involved all segments of the black population. During the sit-ins and freedom rides the old-guard leadership of the civil rights movement had been partially displaced by a new cadre of young black students. Black politics were no longer the exclusive domain of an established black elite—yet the students themselves, although not elitist, formed a kind of elite. With Albany the composition of the civil rights struggle shifted once more. As Howard Zinn notes, Albany "represented a permanent turn from the lunch counter and the bus terminal to the streets, from hit-and-run attacks by students and professional civil rights workers to populist rebellion by lower-class Negroes." [30]

With the first small actions of the Albany campaign in November and December 1961—groups of blacks entering the bus terminal waiting room for whites, and being kicked out or arrested despite the ICC order prohibiting segregated terminal facilities—blacks in Albany, and the movement as a whole, learned a painful lesson about the limitations of the Kennedy Administration. The arrests, ordered by Albany Police Chief Laurie Pritchett, clearly violated the federal order. And yet the federal government would do nothing about them. Again to quote Zinn: "It was the first in a long series of tests for the United States government in the Albany area, in which it proved ineffectual in enforcing federal law." [31] The lesson of Albany was to be repeated over and over again throughout the Deep South: without strong federal enforcement, constitutional rights or federal laws could not protect black citizens from the illicit power of a still-dominant segregationist system.

The bus-terminal arrests were followed by mass protest meetings and marches. Three hundred blacks were arrested by Chief Pritchett in mid-December as they marched to City Hall, for parading without a permit. A few nights later, another 250 (led by Martin Luther King, Jr., and Dr. William G. Anderson,

President of the Albany Movement, who had invited King to the city over the objection of SNCC) were hauled in for the same offense. King's arrest drew national attention to Albany; this and the rising militancy of the black community pushed the city government into a truce with the movement.

The ensuing compromise, unsatisfactory to both sides, quickly broke down in January 1962. A cycle of demonstrations and trials began once again, with young blacks turning some of their attention to yet-untouched bastions of segregation: the city library, park, swimming pool, bowling alley. But the segregationist order in Albany resisted with all the devices at its command, selling, for example, the city swimming pool to a private white group. Although the struggle in Albany went on, most observers had, by late 1962, judged it a defeat for the civil rights movement, particularly for Martin Luther King, Jr.

Throughout this period the preoccupation of the Kennedy Administration was to maintain peace in Albany. Since Chief Pritchett did not employ violence in making his illegitimate arrests, the Administration refused in any way to interfere with those arrests. Indeed, Robert Kennedy at one point sent a telegram to Pritchett congratulating him on keeping the peace. The Administration bestowed its blessings on all efforts at compromise. Robert Kennedy thus telephoned the Mayor of Albany after the December compromise to express his appreciation for the Mayor's part in terminating the conflict.

As was the case with the freedom rides, as would be the case in Birmingham, the Kennedy Administration's highest priority was to keep the lid on the explosive racial situation in Albany. In all these situations, the Justice Department in particular acted as "peace-keeper and cooler-downer." [32] This approach sometimes avoided bloodshed. Still it must be faulted, for, in Victor Navasky's words, it "ended up sacrificing civil rights in favor of civic tranquility." [33] Nor can the suspicion be banished that the tranquility the Administration regarded so highly was, in part, its own.

Although the Kennedy Administration's low-profile stance on civil rights had drawn frequent criticism in 1961, its program for civil rights at the beginning of 1962 was not much improved. Two limited measures on voting were sent to Congress this time: a bill exempting those with at least a sixth-grade education from literacy tests, and a constitutional amendment declaring that poll taxes could not prevent voting in federal elections. The amendment sparked little controversy and was passed by Congress in August. The literacy-test bill, on the other hand, encountered stiff southern opposition. The President did not put up much of a fight for the bill, and by May, a southern filibuster had killed it.

The long-promised executive order prohibiting racial discrimination in federally financed housing was again postponed at this time. According to Sorensen, Kennedy had first delayed issuing the order in 1961 because he had been waiting for Congress to act on his nomination of Robert Weaver (a black) as head of the Housing and Home Finance Agency. His housing bill had then occasioned a further wait. Now there was a new rationale for delay. Kennedy wanted to elevate the Housing Agency into a Department of Urban Affairs, with Weaver as its first Secretary. But he feared that issuance of the housing order would antagonize moderate southern Congressmen whose votes were needed for the Urban Affairs bill. The bill was thus given precedence over the housing order.[34] It was killed in the House Rules Committee, yet the housing order was once more delayed. In July, Kennedy was still telling press conference questioners that he would sign the order at "a useful and appropriate time." [35]

During 1962 (and 1963), as civil rights workers penetrated into the most recalcitrant and dangerous areas of the Deep South, the issue of federal protection insistently came to the fore. Movement activists were under the impression that the Justice Department had promised them protection in return for their 1961 shift to voter registration. And President Kennedy seemed to reaffirm that promise in September 1962:

> I commend those who are making the effort to register every citizen. They deserve the protection of the United States Government, the protection of the state, the protection of local communities, and we shall do everything we possibly can to make sure that protection is assured and if it requires extra legislation and extra force, we shall do that.[36]

Yet, in the face of mounting terror against both civil rights workers and prospective black registrants, the Kennedy Justice Department continued to insist that it lacked the authority to intervene in local matters in the South. Howard Zinn, writing in 1964, captures the civil rights movement's anguish at Justice Department inaction:

> The ordinary citizen of the United States might claim ignorance of what is happening in the Deep South—as many ordinary Germans claimed not to know of the death camps. But the national government cannot say it is ignorant. Hundreds upon hundreds of affidavits have been filed with the Department of Justice, crying out for redress of grievances, with no results. Phone calls have been made again and again to the F.B.I. and the Justice Department from civil rights workers in desperate need of immediate protection, but have gone unheeded. Requests for protection, made in advance of anticipated trouble, have been consistently refused. Justice Department attorneys have watched and done nothing (as in Selma) while local police arrested citizens who were standing peacefully on federal property. Men from the F.B.I. have stood by and watched (as in McComb) while policemen gave bloody beatings to citizens who were breaking no law, while (as on the Freedom Walk) state patrolmen administered electric shocks to men who had committed no crime.[37]

To justify this inaction, the Justice Department employed a refurbished theory of federalism. According to this theory, whose principal exponent was Burke Marshall, the maintenance of civil order depended upon the states' exercise of their police powers. The federal government could not usurp this field of state responsibility without massive damage to the federal system; it had authority to intervene only in extreme cases—and never in advance—where order had broken down.[38] The movement countered Justice's position with a contrary view of federal authority. Supported by a number of leading experts on constitutional law, it argued that the federal government had ample authority to intervene when local or state officials refused to protect or infringed upon constitutional rights. As well as constitutional provisions, it cited Sections 241 and 242 of the U.S. code—making it a crime to deprive a citizen of his rights under color of law or to threaten and intimidate him in his exercise of those rights—as a source of this authority. But Justice Department officials were not impressed; they retorted with arguments against the feasibility of utilizing Sections 241 and 242 in the South.

Feeling both defenseless and betrayed, civil rights workers on the firing line became increasingly disillusioned with the federal government. Their anguish eventually transformed itself into anger. Nothing that the Kennedy Administration did so alienated the young activists (especially the SNCC workers) as this failure to provide protection. It was a crucial factor in destroying their faith in the American political system and, ultimately, in turning a substantial number of them toward the radical and separatist vision of "black power." [39]

For most Americans, the question of protecting thousands of blacks in the South was overshadowed at this time by the drama of protecting one black—James Meredith—as he attempted to enroll at the University of Mississippi. Before turning to the Meredith affair, however, it is important to note a minor but revealing incident that happened at about the same time. A gathering was held at the Lincoln Memorial to commemorate the centennial of the Emancipation Proclamation—and to this gathering Kennedy directed a message that included strong praise for the black struggle for freedom. He said of the hundred years since the Emancipation Proclamation that "the essential effort, the sustained struggle, was borne by the Negro alone with steadfast dignity and faith." [40] On this occasion, before a small and sympathetic audience, Kennedy addressed himself to the true nature of the civil rights struggle. (A similar occasion was the receipt of the Civil Rights Commission's report "Freedom to the Free" in February 1963. In his brief remarks on this occasion Kennedy again gave primary credit where it was due: "It is the Negroes themselves, by their courage and steadfastness, who have done most to throw off their legal, economic, and social bonds. . . ." [41]) Such words—praising black activism and heroism—Kennedy would not utter before the nation, in major speeches or press conferences or during civil rights crises; their educational impact was lost because they were directed only to a safely restricted audience, an audience that already appreciated them.

Like all the other racial crises of the Kennedy Presidency, the "Ole Miss" affair was not of the Administration's making. The federal courts had ordered the admission of James Meredith to the all-white University of Mississippi, and, frustrated by open defiance from state officials, had directed the federal government to enforce the order. President Kennedy and his brother, the Attorney General, were determined upon enforcement—but at the same time committed to a policy of bargaining with or conciliating southern power-holders. Desirous of escaping a confrontation, resolved to avoid the use of troops if at all possible, the Kennedys thus entered into incessant telephone negotiations with Mississippi Governor Ross Barnett. They sought assurances from Barnett that order would be maintained, and Meredith protected by local authorities, during the process of enrollment. After countless evasions and delays, Barnett gave such assurance.[42] But, like the assurances of Governor Patterson of Alabama during the freedom rides, the Mississippi Governor's pledge was not worth much. When

Meredith at last was brought to the Ole Miss campus on Sunday, September 30, the small force of 200 state police Barnett had provided vanished suddenly, at the first signs of violence from a growing crowd that eventually numbered around 2500 angry whites.

This time, however, Kennedy had federal marshals on the scene when they were needed. The 550 marshals faced the mob bravely, obeying orders to use tear gas only and to refrain from returning fire. They could not control the mob—but without their presence things would have been far worse. Throughout that Sunday night rioting raged, leaving two people dead and hundreds injured. It ceased only upon the arrival of a federalized National Guard unit from Oxford and regular army units from Memphis. The next morning Meredith, accompanied by marshals and protected by troops who occupied the university campus, finally enrolled in Ole Miss. The Kennedy Administration had acted somewhat slowly in the Meredith affair, allowing itself once again to be stalled by a southern governor of obvious bad faith. Yet when it did act, the matter was handled well, with a judicious blend of firmness and restraint.

Again, as in the case of the freedom rides, the effectiveness of Kennedy's actions was not matched by an equivalently effective public interpretation of events. In his televised report to the nation on the Mississippi situation the night of September 30, Kennedy's sole concern was to calm irate Mississippians. He reminded them that he was simply carrying out his constitutional responsibility as President in implementing the court order, and appealed—rather futilely as it turned out—to Mississippi traditions of honor, courage, and patriotism (even spending several sentences recalling past Mississippi war heroes). Nothing was said of James Meredith's cause—or of *his* courage. Kennedy's preoccupation in this brief speech with averting bloodshed was understandable. But it was hardly pleasing to blacks, who wondered why all the kind words were directed at white Southerners engaged in the process of defying federal law. Even the black author Louis E. Lomax, a strong supporter of Kennedy, was dismayed by the speech. He wrote:

> What galled us was the image of *our* President bending over backwards to oil ruffled feathers in Mississippi. We flinched and grew angry as the President droned on, calling the names of the great heroes from Mississippi who served the nation well. For many of us—and I am among them—there was an unforgivable gap in the President's speech: he failed to call the roll of the Negroes who had served, and died for, the nation, and he failed to make it plain to Mississippians that they were in the wrong, legally and morally.[43]

The Meredith affair was soon overshadowed in the public mind by the drama of the Cuban missile crisis. With the nation's attention still riveted on Cuba, Kennedy took the opportunity, at his November 20 press conference, to announce that he had signed an executive order banning racial discrimination in federally supported housing. This was apparently the "useful and appropriate time" he had sought for issuing the order—after the congressional elections, to a press and public preoccupied with the withdrawal of the Soviet Union's remaining bombers from Cuba. Not only was the announcement of the order deliberately low-key,[44] designed to attract as little public notice as possible; the order itself fell considerably short of expectations. Most important, it excluded housing facilities already constructed with federal or federally insured funds. To deal with the problem of racial discrimination in existing housing, Kennedy went no further than attaching a vague declamatory phrase to the order, suggesting that government agencies "use their good offices to promote and encourage the abandonment of discriminatory practices." [45] Thus, the long-heralded "stroke of the Presidential pen," having come to be an embarrassment to the Kennedy Administration, was in the end intentionally blurred.

During the winter of 1962–63, the frustration of civil rights forces with the timid policies of the Kennedy Administration was again on the rise. In an article published at this time, Martin Luther King, Jr., characterized 1962 as "the year that civil rights was displaced as the dominant issue in domestic politics. . . . The issue no longer commanded the conscience of the nation." [46] The Kennedy Administration, he complained, refused to recognize the gravity of the racial problem, accepting token victories in place of fundamental changes. Particularly disturbing to King and other black leaders was the Administration's repeated failure to seek new civil rights legislation. But Kennedy was not one to let frustrations build too high. As Schlesinger recounts, "the President, recognizing the discontent and *perceiving a need for new action if he were to preserve his control,* had decided to seek legislation himself." [47] On February 28, 1963, he addressed a Special Message on Civil Rights to the Congress.

In this message Kennedy finally began to speak about racial discrimination in moral terms. The need for the advancement of equal rights was placed above pragmatic considerations. "Let it be clear, in our own hearts and minds, that it is not merely because of the Cold War, and not merely because of the economic waste of discrimination, that we are committed to achieving true equality of opportunity. The basic reason is because it is right." [48] Yet, if in this respect the message was a considerable improvement over Kennedy's previous efforts, in other respects the approach was identical. Great progress in civil rights was claimed for the preceding two years through executive action, litigation, and persuasion; as usual, the achievements of the civil rights movement went unnoticed. Kennedy was calling for an end to racial discrimination but doing nothing to overcome white America's ignorance or anx-

iety about the most effective force seeking that end. The legislative proposals themselves also reflected his familiar caution;
Schlesinger summed them up as "piecemeal improvements in
existing voting legislation, technical assistance to school districts voluntarily seeking to desegregate, an extension of the life
of the Civil Rights Commission." [49] Joseph Rauh, Jr., later
characterized this as "such an inane package of legislation as to
make the movement feel that it wasn't worth going for." [50]
Kennedy had acted in the face of black discontent, but in a
manner scarcely consonant with the strength of black
grievances.

That the President still hoped to keep the civil rights issue
relatively quiet, and to guard his ties with southern Democrats,
was made evident by a controversy that erupted at this time
between the Administration and the independent Civil Rights
Commission. Members of the Commission were upset by the
news they received of segregationist terror in Mississippi, and
consequently decided to hold hearings in that state in the early
part of 1963. The Justice Department, on the other hand,
thought that the Commission's evidence of Mississippi violence
was scant [51] and that its hearings would only cause trouble for
the Administration in the South. So Justice exerted pressure on
the Commission, with Attorney General Robert Kennedy asking its members on three separate occasions to put off their
hearings. President Kennedy too, in less direct fashion, made
plain his displeasure at the prospect of Mississippi hearings.
The Commission finally acceded to the Administration's
wishes; as Reverend Theodore Hesburgh (one of its members)
explained, "one hates to go directly against something that a
President thinks you shouldn't do." [52]

The Administration's tepid civil rights bill was still languishing in the Congress when it was far outdistanced by
events. Early in April 1963 the Southern Christian Leadership
Conference launched a well-planned assault on segregation in
Birmingham, Alabama—termed by SCLC's leader Martin

Luther King, Jr., "the most thoroughly segregated big city in the U.S." [53] SCLC's prime target was Birmingham's downtown business community, which maintained segregated facilities and severely discriminated against blacks in hiring and upgrading. The civil rights organization was bent on confrontation—aimed at compelling Birmingham's white establishment, and beyond it the federal government, to end a palpable state of injustice. King explained the philosophy underlying the SCLC strategy in his famous "Letter from Birmingham Jail": "Nonviolent direct action seeks to create ... a crisis and establish such creative tension that a community that has constantly refused to negotiate is forced to confront the issue. It seeks so to dramatize the issue that it can no longer be ignored." [54]

At the urging of Robert Kennedy, SCLC had postponed its Birmingham campaign until after the April 2 local elections, in which Eugene "Bull" Connor, the ardently segregationist Commissioner of Public Safety, was a candidate for mayor. Connor was defeated and a moderate city administration prepared to take office, but legal wrangling left Connor, for the time being, at the head of Birmingham's police. Hence, Schlesinger relates, "the Attorney General three times counseled the Birmingham [movement] leaders not to force issues while Bull Connor was still in charge. But the movement by now had a momentum of its own. King told Robert Kennedy that the Negroes had waited one hundred years and could wait no longer." [55] Demonstrations on a limited scale were mounted throughout April, with Connor and his police force maintaining a surprising civility. Local authorities obtained an injunction against the SCLC leadership on April 10; King and his colleagues violated the injunction, were jailed, then released on bail. They were given light sentences, since the Birmingham authorities had prudently decided to avoid creating martyrs. By the end of April, the white power structure had managed to keep the situation under control; from the movement point of view, affairs seemed to be approaching a frustrating impasse.

SCLC now put into operation its most dramatic battle plan. On May 2, 6000 children organized by SCLC marched from the Sixteenth Street Baptist Church toward the downtown area; over 950 of them were arrested. Criticism of the movement's use of children was heard from many quarters, including the Attorney General. But it was stilled by the events of the next day. Confronted on May 3 by a thousand demonstrators of all ages, Connor's restraint gave way; the demonstrators were clubbed, blasted with fire hoses, attacked by snarling police dogs. The following days witnessed a repetition of the violence, with thousands of blacks courageously enduring beatings and arrests. Nonviolent discipline was generally maintained, though there were incidents of bottle and brick throwing by a few angry demonstrators. Police violence, on the other hand, was massive and highly visible. News photographs of police dogs attacking marching blacks or policemen ganging up to beat a woman served to shock and outrage the entire nation.

Burke Marshall of the Justice Department arrived in Birmingham during this period to serve as mediator between the black movement and the white establishment. Most of his efforts were directed at a group of white businessmen who possessed the power to grant black demands. Marshall's was not the only behind-the-scenes operation the Kennedy Administration mounted during the crisis. Administration officials, notably Douglas Dillon and Robert McNamara, contacted northern industrialists with business ties in Birmingham and urged them to use their influence to expedite a settlement. The Birmingham business elite held out but was finally swayed by the Administration's efforts, the growing force of the demonstrations, and the ominous turn of one of those demonstrations into a minor black riot. On May 10, a settlement was publicly announced: the white leadership of Birmingham agreed to desegregate lunch counters, rest rooms, fitting rooms, and drinking fountains in the large downtown stores; to expand the hiring and promotion of blacks in commercial and industrial establishments; and to form a biracial committee to facilitate further racial progress. The settlement was nearly sabotaged by the bombing of a black home and motel and ensuing rioting by both blacks and whites. But it held up tenuously, with help from President Kennedy, who publicly praised the Birmingham accord and dispatched 3000 troops to bases near the city to ensure against renewed outbreaks of violence.[56]

The Kennedy Administration displayed, in its approach to Birmingham, an obvious sympathy with the demands (which were quite reasonable) of the civil rights movement. But its highest priority was still the maintenance of peace. In this regard, it set itself against the SCLC leadership. It acted to relax the "creative tension" which the black leaders saw as the essential prerequisite to racial progress. Operating behind the scenes to postpone or prevent demonstrations, it sought to forestall the public dramatization of injustice. Yet if King and his cohorts had reason to complain of the Administration's early efforts at averting a Birmingham confrontation, by the time of the May 10 settlement they were ready to welcome a path to peace. Indeed, by this time all parties were eager for a truce.

The business community was, by May 10, becoming apprehensive over the widening disorder and violence; the situation was clearly bad for business. SCLC too was growing apprehensive, as it began to lose control over Birmingham's black community. Black violence, though largely a retaliation against white violence, was for the first time becoming a significant factor in the racial struggle of the early 1960s. Its chief perpetrators were alienated and embittered lower-class black youths, to whom King's nonviolent appeals were largely irrelevant. If the accord had not been reached when it was, SCLC faced the possibility of losing control entirely, of watching the Birmingham campaign turn into a brutal melee between ghetto blacks and the most intransigent racists from the city's white population.[57]

President Kennedy's fears paralleled those of the SCLC leadership. When members of the Administration warned Southerners who expressed antipathy to Martin Luther King, Jr., that the alternative was extremists such as the Black Muslims, they scared themselves as well. The danger that disciplined demonstrations would deteriorate into violence was real enough in Birmingham. Yet concern with that danger was to mount to almost an obsession for the Kennedy Administration, blinding it to the continuing need for demonstrations and admirable self-discipline of demonstrators in other places. The experience of Birmingham had brought Kennedy closer to the goals of the civil rights movement—but it also hardened his opposition to the movement's foremost tactic.

In the aftermath of Birmingham, as demonstrations spread to other cities, and the racial problem captured the nation's full attention, civil rights at last received top priority from the Kennedy Administration. Discussions began (particularly in the Justice Department) on the subject of new legislation to meet the growing racial crisis. An effort at private persuasion was also undertaken. Prominent leaders in business, labor, education, religion, and the legal profession were invited to meetings at the White House and requested to lend their support to the cause of equal rights. The dimensions of this effort were impressive: "within a forty-day period, there were twenty-one such meetings, attended by some 1700 persons." [58]

Meanwhile, President Kennedy was giving civil rights a prominent place in his public discourse. Speaking at Vanderbilt University in Tennessee on May 18, he proffered an endorsement to the civil rights cause: "No one can deny the complexity of the problems involved in assuring to all of our citizens their full rights as Americans. But no one can gainsay the fact that the determination to secure these rights is in the highest tradition of American freedom." [59] On June 9, before the U.S. Conference of Mayors in Honolulu, he urged local action to promote peaceful remedies for black grievances. His

words on this occasion caught the urgency, and the moral force,
of the black struggle:

> Justice cannot wait for too many meetings. It cannot
> wait for the action of the Congress or the courts. We
> face a moment of moral and constitutional crisis, and
> men of generosity and vision must make themselves
> heard in every section of this country.[60]

On the afternoon of June 11, Alabama Governor George
Wallace stood in the doorway of his state university's registration building and symbolically blocked the entrance of two
black students. As planned, President Kennedy promptly federalized the Alabama National Guard; a few hours later, Wallace yielded to a representative of federal authority. The incident was not a major one, but for once Kennedy seized the
opportunity to speak to a troubled nation on the subject of civil
rights. He went on television that same evening, to deliver what
were to be his finest words ever on the racial crisis during his
Presidency.

The June 11 speech ranged over a variety of arguments in
favor of the civil rights cause. It mixed references to the American tradition of equality with statistics on the grim life expec-
tancies of black people, and suggested that white Americans
imagine themselves in the shoes of blacks. But the overriding
theme of the speech was an appeal to conscience. Kennedy was,
in this speech, ready to confront the issue of civil rights on a
moral plane. His words here deserve to be quoted at some
length, for they show the possibility of rhetoric which could
match the moral power of events.

> It is better to settle these matters in the courts than on
> the streets, and new laws are needed at every level.
> But law alone cannot make men see right.
>   We are confronted primarily with a moral issue. It
> is as old as the Scriptures and is as clear as the
> American Constitution. . . .

> One hundred years of delay have passed since
> President Lincoln freed the slaves, yet their heirs, their
> grandsons, are not fully free. They are not yet freed
> from the bonds of injustice. They are not yet freed
> from social and economic oppression. And this
> nation, for all of its hopes and all its boasts, will not be
> fully free until all its citizens are free. . . .
>   We face, therefore, a moral crisis as a country and
> as a people. It cannot be met by repressive police
> action. It cannot be left to increased demonstrations
> in the streets. It cannot be quieted by token moves or
> talk. It is time to act in the Congress, in your state and
> local legislative body, and, above all, in all of our daily
> lives.[61]

It was an excellent speech—appropriate, timely, eloquent.
Yet there was still something lacking in it. Once again Kennedy
had failed to give the civil rights movement its due credit for
illuminating America's moral crisis, had failed to pay tribute
before the American people to its dedication and courage. Once
again he had passed up an opportunity for creating a positive
appreciation of the movement among white Americans. Indeed, the end of his speech was a veiled warning to militant civil
rights activists: "We have a right to expect that the Negro
community will be responsible, will uphold the law, but they
have a right to expect that the law will be fair, that the Constitution will be color blind. . . ." [62] The coming weeks would
amplify the hint contained in these words—that while the
Kennedy Administration had finally adopted the moral posture of the civil rights movement, it remained a rival to the
movement for control over the direction the civil rights struggle
would now take.

On June 19, the Administration's proposed legislation on
civil rights was presented to Congress in a lengthy Special
Message. The moral tone of the previous week's speech was
repeated, and the warnings of potential racial disaster were
intensified. "The result of continued Federal legislative inaction will be continued, if not increased racial strife—causing the

leadership on both sides to pass from the hands of reasonable and responsible men to the purveyors of hate and violence. . . ."[63] The Administration bill itself was wide-ranging. Its key provision guaranteed equal access for black citizens to public accommodations. A federal suit had to be filed by the aggrieved party in each case where an establishment refused to comply with the law; the Attorney General could intervene, however, when the prospective litigant lacked funds or feared reprisal. Other provisions granted the Attorney General authority to initiate school desegregation suits when parents were unable to undertake litigation themselves, increased funds for programs boosting black employment (such as manpower retraining and adult education), put the President's Committee on Equal Employment Opportunity on a statutory basis, established a Federal Community Relations Service to aid localities in settling racial grievances peaceably, and granted the executive branch discretionary authority to cut off funds from any federal program in which racial discrimination occurred. The voting-rights reforms first sent up to Congress in February were also incorporated into the bill.

The most striking and dramatic passages in Kennedy's message did not concern his legislative proposals, however, but rather the subject of civil rights demonstrations. In unmistakably stern language—which I here quote in full—Kennedy announced to the civil rights movement that the time for demonstrations was over.

> During the weeks past, street demonstrations, mass picketing, and parades have brought these matters to the Nation's attention in dramatic fashion in many cities throughout the United States. This has happened because these racial injustices are real and no other remedy was in sight. But as feelings have risen in recent days, these demonstrations have increasingly endangered lives and property, inflamed emotions, and unnecessarily divided communities. They are not the way in which this country should rid

itself of racial discrimination. Violence is never
justified; and while peaceful communication,
deliberation, and petitions of protest continue, I want
to caution against demonstrations which can lead to
violence.
    The problem is now before the Congress. Unruly
tactics or pressures will not help and may hinder the
effective consideration of these measures. If they are
enacted, there will be legal remedies available; and,
therefore, while the Congress is completing its work, I
urge all community leaders, Negro and white, to do
their utmost to lessen tensions and to exercise
self-restraint.[64]

These paragraphs reflected Kennedy's concern that
further civil rights demonstrations might antagonize Congress
and ensure the defeat of his bill. They reflected, too, his fears of
spreading racial violence, in the wake of the Birmingham
bombing and rioting and the murder of Medgar Evers, a Mississippi civil rights leader, a few hours after the President's June
11 speech. Such apprehensions were understandable, but they
scarcely justified such an unfair and intemperate verbal assault
on the civil rights movement. Kennedy recognized the value
of past demonstrations, but characterized present demonstrations as "unruly tactics or pressures." He ignored the
movement's disciplined employment of the techniques of non-
violence, creating an aura of purposeful violence in his
description of its current efforts. Instead of pointing out to
white America the ugliness of a white racism whose champions
bombed homes and churches and murdered black leaders, he
laid the responsibility for future violence upon the black freedom movement, upon those same oppressed people who had
always been the recipients of violence.
    More than his apprehensions accounted for Kennedy's
attack on demonstrations. Kennedy was also asserting, in these
paragraphs, that the leadership of the civil rights drive had now
passed into his hands.[65] He was arguing, in effect, that once the

federal government took action, through presidential initiative and congressional deliberation, it preempted the political action of black citizens, rendering their further efforts at self-liberation unnecessary. He was telling the civil rights movement to abandon its successful tactics of direct action while Congress was doing its work; knowing that that work always lasted a long time, he apparently hoped that the extended moratorium would turn the movement to lobbying and related tactics, and eventually transform it into one more pressure group associated with the liberal Democratic coalition. A new and powerful form of democratic mass politics was growing up in America in the spring and summer of 1963. But Kennedy, while responding to the grievances which inspired that politics, had little appreciation for the political form itself. In insisting that the black struggle leave the streets and be conducted thenceforth within the restricted forum of legislatures and courts, he betrayed the inherent limitations of his elitist political style. Kennedy's attack on demonstrations was his manifesto proclaiming the continued dominance of elite politics in America—in which, of course, *he* remained the central figure.

Kennedy was scheduled to depart on a European tour a few days after the Special Message was presented to Congress. Martin Luther King, Jr., urged him to cancel this trip abroad in dramatic witness of the growing domestic crisis, but Kennedy went ahead with his plans. The day before his departure he invited the principal civil rights leaders to a meeting in the White House. These leaders had been discussing a march on Washington to mobilize support for the civil rights bill, but at the meeting the President marshaled his arguments against a march. Signs of a "white backlash" against the civil rights movement were already starting to emerge, and Kennedy expressed the fear that a march on Washington would trigger such a backlash in Congress. He predicted that the march would create a dangerous appearance of intimidation, thereby providing wavering Congressmen with a convenient excuse for voting against the civil rights bill.

His opposition to the march was tempered, however, by the persuasive arguments of the civil rights leaders. A. Philip Randolph, who had threatened Franklin Roosevelt with a similar march twenty years earlier, told Kennedy: "The Negroes are already in the streets. It is very likely impossible to get them off. If they are bound to be in the streets in any case, is it not better that they be led by organizations dedicated to civil rights and disciplined by struggle rather than to leave them to other leaders who care neither about civil rights nor about non-violence?" [66] Randolph's point was seconded by Martin Luther King, Jr., and James Farmer of CORE. King added wryly that though the Administration now judged the march to be ill timed, it had previously been of the exact same opinion with regard to Birmingham.

As planning for the march on Washington went forward, Congress took up Kennedy's civil rights bill. What happened to the bill in a House Judiciary subcommittee, which first considered it, was unexpected. Contrary to talk of widespread congressional resistance to the Administration's "progressive" proposals, several members of the subcommittee actually found the bill too weak and decided to strengthen it across the board. Arthur Waskow, who interviewed a number of the participants in the subsequent legislative fray, quotes one of these subcommittee members on the rebellion against the Administration:

> "What we wanted was a real bill, neither just an issue nor just anything with a pretty title on it. We were willing to trade that fake title of the 'Civil Rights Act of 1963' for a real bill in '64. And although Bobby Kennedy publicly insisted we could not get a tough bill passed, the President himself admitted to us in private, at the White House, that there was a good chance we could." [67]

A bipartisan coalition was put together in the Judiciary subcommittee on behalf of a "tough" bill. Traditional political pressures bound several members to this coalition; for most, continuing civil rights demonstrations provoked an awareness of the stakes involved in writing a genuinely good bill. "It was the militant protests that kept some of them conscious of the danger of widespread violence, that brought home to others with great emotional impact (as when the Birmingham Sunday school was bombed or students were jailed in Americus, Georgia, under capital charges) the nature of the resistance to racial integration." [68] Backed by civil rights forces, the coalition redrafted the Administration bill section by section.

Coalition members broadened the coverage of the equal accommodations section and extended the Attorney General's capacity to initiate suits in this area. They dictated a mandatory cutoff of federal funds from state programs in which racial discrimination was practiced. They put teeth into the employment section, one of the weakest parts of the Kennedy bill. The Administration had asked only that the Committee on Equal Employment Opportunity be provided a statutory basis, and had given general support to a fair employment bill then under consideration by another committee. The coalition defined as unlawful racial discrimination in any form by employers, employment agencies, or labor unions involved in interstate commerce, and granted the Committee on Equal Employment Opportunity enforcement power through civil action in the courts. Most controversial of all their additions was the bill's new Title 3. This title authorized the Attorney General to seek an injunction in restraint of any action which denied a citizen his rights under the Constitution or federal law. It thus spelled out the authority the Kennedy Administration was continually resisting—authority to take preventive steps to protect southern blacks and civil rights workers from repression and violence.

Insisting that this "tough" bill could not be passed, the Kennedy Administration continued for several months to plug for milder legislation. Finally, after a complicated series of maneuvers, a compromise was hammered out in late October. Under this compromise the much-strengthened employment section of the bill was retained. The Attorney General's authority to intervene in advance to protect civil rights workers and blacks was truncated;[69] the bill did, however, grant him broad authority to initiate suits in order to desegregate public facilities. Robert Kennedy conceded that this compromise resulted in a "better bill than the administration's."[70]

The coalition had done its job well. As Waskow observes, its efforts "not only guaranteed that the Administration's own proposals would be adopted substantially intact, but set a new standard for federal action so vigorous that even continuous compromise from then on during congressional debate left the Civil Rights Act when passed much more powerful than anything the Administration had asked for, or had thought possible."[71] The compromise was reported out by the full Judiciary Committee on November 20 and approved by the House, in the emotional aftermath of Kennedy's assassination, in January 1964.

Throughout the summer of 1963, the march on Washington, scheduled for late August, was a prime subject of discussion and activity. Kennedy had moved by July from opposition to measured approval. This was due, in part, to an agreement by sponsors of the march to switch its focus from a protest on Capitol Hill to a peaceable gathering at the Lincoln Memorial. In addition, Kennedy recognized that the march could not be halted anyway, and might even boost his program so long as it was both orderly and well attended. At a press conference in mid-July, he characterized the upcoming event as a "peaceful assembly calling for a redress of grievances" and endorsed it as "in the great tradition."[72] He was careful to differentiate it, however, from more militant protests. Following his words in support of the march, he renewed his earlier attack upon demonstrations with some comments upon the struggle in Cambridge, Maryland: "I am concerned about these demonstrations. I think they go beyond information, they go beyond protest, and they get into a very bad situation where you get violence, and I think the cause of advancing equal opportunities only loses."[73]

With considerable help from the Administration (suspicious militants charged that the Administration was running the whole show), the march took place on August 28. A larger-than-expected throng, estimated at 250,000 (about two-thirds of whom were black), descended upon Washington in impressive testimony to the urgency of the civil rights battle. It was a memorable day, blending without contradiction moments of passion, dignity, and humor. The dramatic highlight for most participants was Martin Luther King's "I Have a Dream" speech.[74] But, unbeknown to the crowd, equally dramatic events were occurring behind the scenes.

John Lewis, a young veteran of the toughest southern campaigns of the freedom movement, and the current head of SNCC, was scheduled to be one of the principal speakers at the Lincoln Memorial. But when his prepared text was shown in advance to the other leaders of the march, they demanded that he make major deletions from it. Lewis had gone well beyond the usual attacks on the evils of discrimination and racism, to focus on the failures of the movement's supposed ally, the Kennedy Administration. His text set out forcefully the SNCC indictment of the Administration, and pointed up the contrast between the Administration's old-style politics and the new form of politics that SNCC was discovering in action in the South. Pressures from moderate civil rights leaders and, indirectly, from the Kennedy Administration,[75] forced Lewis to censor his own words. Yet even in the speech he publicly delivered much of the critical thrust remained. From various accounts a number of Lewis's *intended* comments can be pieced together. As the statement of a hope, and an anger, that the Kennedy Administration never could grasp, they are well worth quoting:

In good conscience, we cannot support, wholeheartedly, the administration's civil rights bill,
for it is too little, and too late. There's not one thing in
the bill that will protect our people from police
brutality.

The voting section of this bill will not help
thousands of black citizens who want to vote. It will
not help the citizens of Mississippi, of Alabama, and
Georgia, who are qualified to vote, but lack a sixth
grade education. "One man, one vote," is the African
cry. It is ours, too. . . .

We are now involved in a serious revolution. This
nation is still a place of cheap political leaders who
build their careers on immoral compromises and ally
themselves with open forms of political, economic,
and social exploitation. . . . The party of Kennedy is
also the party of Eastland. The party of Javits is also the
party of Goldwater. Where is our party?

We all recognize the fact that if any radical social,
political, and economic changes are to take place in
our society, the people, the masses, must bring them
about. In the struggle we must seek more than mere
civil rights; we must work for the community of love,
peace, and true brotherhood. Our minds, souls, and
hearts cannot rest until freedom and justice exist for
all the people. . . .

Mr. Kennedy is trying to take the revolution out
of the streets and put it in the courts. Listen, Mr.
Kennedy, listen, Mr. Congressman, listen, fellow
citizens—the black masses are on the march for jobs
and freedom, and we must say to the politicians that
there won't be a "cooling-off" period.[76]

With Lewis successfully muzzled, August 28 became a
high point of unity between the civil rights movement and the
Kennedy Administration. After the day's program had been
concluded, the President conferred with movement leaders in
the White House. Both in this meeting and in the public statement he issued, he was full of praise for the marchers. Noting
their "deep fervor and quiet dignity," he declared that "this
Nation can properly be proud of the demonstration that has
occurred here today." [77] Still, the mutual celebration of a

united front could not totally conceal the ambiguous significance of the march on Washington. As Murray Kempton commented at the time,

> If the march was important, it was because it represented an acceptance of the Negro revolt as part of the American myth, and so an acceptance of the revolutionaries into the American establishment. That acceptance, of course, carries the hope that the Negro revolt will stop where it is. Yet that acceptance is also the most powerful incentive and assurance that the revolt will continue.[78]

Although Kennedy had not departed as far from his earlier caution toward civil rights as his admirers later would claim, his actions during the late summer and the fall of 1963 indicated that there was to be no traveling back over the distance he had come. Signs of a white backlash were perceptible everywhere in these months. Polls showed that a majority of white Americans favored the civil rights bill, yet a majority of whites polled also felt that Kennedy was pushing too fast on the subject of integration.[79] The White House received a great volume of hostile mail, especially after the President's endorsement of the march on Washington. Kennedy, however, refused to renege on his newly strengthened commitment to civil rights. While privately voicing apprehensions about the political costs of his civil rights stance,[80] before the public he maintained that stance in tones of guarded optimism. At his September 12 press conference, for example, he expressed doubts that his legislation, or the civil rights issue in general, would divide the nation along racial lines. "I think the American people have been through too much to make that mistake. . . . Over the long run we are going to have a mix. That will be true racially, socially, ethnically, geographically, and that is, finally, the best way." [81]

But if Kennedy held to the course he had set in June, he was careful not to broaden that course. From the march on Washington to the date of his death, he devoted no more speeches—nor even major portions of speeches—to civil rights. He did respond forthrightly to the horrible bombing of a Birmingham Sunday school that took the lives of four young black girls. Professing a "deep sense of outrage and grief," his brief statement went on to suggest that this tragic event should finally awaken the nation "to a realization of the folly of racial injustice and hatred and violence." [82] His attention, nevertheless, immediately turned away from civil rights to the test-ban treaty and the new atmosphere of détente.

Kennedy was content to let the public's temper cool for a while on the subject of race. This was perhaps a reasonable choice—yet it sacrificed any chance for consolidating or extending the moral and educational position which he had first advanced in June. As A. Philip Randolph pointed out at the time of the march on Washington, one or two speeches were not enough to overcome deeply entrenched racial attitudes: "We have a continuing responsibility to develop the moral climate, the moral order that will serve as the underpinnings of this legislation we seek, which will give it reality and integrity." [83]

Civil rights seemed to have lost some of its urgency for Kennedy by the time he was struck down in Dallas. Yet his assassination was to cement his reputation as a friend and benefactor of the black freedom movement. One of the most common explanations for the assassination, for example, was the "climate of hate" that had sprung up in reaction to the civil rights movement and the President who allied himself with it. There is considerable irony in this view of Kennedy. Legend was to identify him more closely with the black revolt than with any other domestic event during his Presidency. In reality, there was nothing else in domestic politics to which his political style was so ill suited, or which gave him such consistent difficulty.

The foregoing account of John Kennedy's involvement with civil rights may seem somewhat harsh. Certainly much

can be said in his defense. A history of Kennedy's actions in the
civil rights field almost invariably minimizes accompanying
problems in other fields of policy. But these problems, too, had
a call on his time and energy; they restricted the attention he
could devote to the civil rights struggle even at its most critical
junctures. Some of these, in addition, competed with civil rights
in more direct fashion. The magnitude of southern power in the
Congress and racist sentiment in the nation as a whole meant
that any presidential commitment to civil rights jeopardized
other important presidential programs. Education, housing,
fiscal management, even foreign policy—in each of these areas
John Kennedy's task was made substantially easier when he
could pursue a pragmatic, low-visibility course on civil rights.

There was also the question of timing. Kennedy, it has
been argued, could not appeal to the nation's conscience on the
subject of racial justice until events had sufficiently sensitized
the nation to that appeal. Only Birmingham, the argument
goes, made possible the moral plea of his June 11 speech. Arthur
Schlesinger, Jr., puts the case forcefully:

> The timing was a vindication of his approach to mass
> education. He had prepared the ground for that
> speech ever since he became President. His actions,
> his remarks, the concern for Negro rights and scorn
> for racism implicit in his personality and bearing—all
> had subtly entered and transformed national
> expectations and attitudes. He had quietly created an
> atmosphere where change, when it came, would
> seem no longer an upheaval but the inexorable
> unfolding of the promise of American life. Yet he did
> not call for change in advance of the moment. If he
> had made his June speech in February, it would have
> attracted as little attention as his civil rights message
> that month. But Birmingham and the Negroes
> themselves had given him the nation's ear.[84]

Considerations such as these might justify Kennedy's cautious record on civil rights—if civil rights had merely been one
among several important issues of his presidential term. But the

racial question was then, and still is, a crisis of supreme magnitude in the life of the American nation. Kennedy, earlier chapters have shown, was all too eager to proclaim a global crisis at the outset of his Presidency. Foreign affairs were continually pitched at the highest frequency during his administration, often in cases where American policy would have benefited from a lower-key, more restrained approach. Yet the struggle for racial justice, the authentic crisis of the times, was granted full attention only when it imposed itself on the Kennedy Administration with an intensity too great to be ignored. Political leaders must be judged by how well they respond to the *genuine* problems of their time. And by this standard, it seems fair to conclude that John Kennedy's record on civil rights contained failures that ran far deeper than his successes.

This chapter has tried to suggest both the nature and the sources of those failures. From the narrative it should be clear that most of them were rooted in the limitations of Kennedy's pragmatic liberalism. Kennedy and his aides were ill equipped, by their pragmatist background and bias, for coping with a social movement generated out of injustice and striving for a vision of community. Adept at calculating the arithmetic of existing political forces, they had great trouble understanding a struggle which, at its heart, called into question those forces and indicated the need for a new form of politics. Skillful at adjustment and compromise to keep situations cool, management and manipulation to control their course and tempo, perhaps nothing was more foreign to their political style than the passionate, urgent demand of the black movement: "Freedom Now!"

For all his limitations in the area of civil rights, John Kennedy at least was a genuine supporter of racial progress. The civil rights movement in the early 1960s certainly could have fared much worse. It could have been saddled with another Eisenhower, viewing the subject of racial discrimination with a benign neutrality. Or it could have had a Nixon in the White House, callously trading black advancement for a southern alliance.

But the movement also might have fared better. It might have been blessed with a President who placed the search for racial justice squarely at the center of American politics. It might have witnessed a President who came to realize that the civil rights struggle was only a preface to a greater struggle, aimed at bringing social and economic justice to all citizens. It might, finally, have had a President who comprehended the democratic and participatory nature of that struggle, who, instead of warding off threats to his own power, welcomed and fostered the development of new political power among the traditionally powerless. After Kennedy's assassination, his admirers—many blacks numbered among them—were to revere him as just such a President. This view of Kennedy made a beautiful legend, perhaps even a useful one from the standpoint of the civil rights cause, but it bore slight resemblance to the actual history of his Presidency.

7

Reassessing the Modern Presidency

My review of John Kennedy's Presidency has been by no means a comprehensive one. It has primarily focused upon those areas of foreign and domestic policy in which Kennedy was most deeply engaged. The intangibles of his career—style, flair, charisma—which have so delighted his admirers have been treated only in the first chapter, and in a rather skeptical fashion. The popular practice of speculating upon what Kennedy might have done had he not been killed has been avoided as much as possible. I have tried, in essence, to reassess John Kennedy as a political leader, to analyze and interpret what he did (or failed to do) with the power he had sought, and what consequences his actions carried for American society in the 1960s.

That reassessment has been consistently critical of Kennedy's presidential politics. Kennedy's foreign policy has been shown to be neither very progressive nor even very pragmatic. Operating on the basis of a gravely distorted theory of Soviet global aggressiveness, Kennedy spurred the Cold War, seemingly in the process of decline, to new heights of explosiveness. His was the dynamic role, if not the sole blameworthy one, in the confrontations over Berlin and Cuba, confrontations that

271

brought the prospect of nuclear war nearer than any other events of the postwar age. Even when Kennedy turned to a more pacific approach toward the Soviet Union, in the successful test-ban negotiations of 1963, he continued to engage in a global struggle in what he believed to be the chief battleground of the Cold War, the Third World. His program for a "democratic revolution" in Latin America and his counterinsurgency campaign in Vietnam were the two sides of a single imperial project: to deny Third World countries to the forces of communist revolution by extending to them the mantle of American control.

In domestic politics Kennedy's actions turned out to have predominantly conservative consequences. His economic program was founded upon the idea of a rational partnership between government and business which would boost the entire American economy. The majority of Americans enjoyed increased prosperity under this program, and the federal government won general recognition for its Keynesian methods of intervention in the economy, but the greatest beneficiary of Kennedy's "New Economics"—in terms of power, ideological sanction, and money—was an ungrateful corporate community. In the area of civil rights, a far more essential partnership was undermined by both calculations of political advantage and a fear of mass politics. While Kennedy did make some valuable contributions as President to the cause of racial justice, the possibility of a truly creative relationship between the black movement and the Presidency was lost because a political leader rooted in elite values and assumptions could not come to terms with a politics of mass participation.

Kennedy's presidential record cannot, in sum, sustain his reputation as a progressive. Behind the image of the popular hero lies the reality of service to established power and established values. This reality is not a case of bad faith on Kennedy's part, or a sign that he deceived the American public. It *is* a sign that we have misunderstood the nature and functions of the modern Presidency.

Once we set aside the assumption that the twentieth-century Presidency has been a progressive institution, it is possible to see that Kennedy's presidential record is not untypical. Once we take account of the President's role in the maintenance and expansion of the prevailing American order, it is possible to see the continuity between Kennedy and those who preceded or followed him in the White House. In this final chapter I briefly sketch some of the central features of the modern Presidency. I argue that the Presidency, even (perhaps especially) in liberal hands, is best understood as the chief stabilizer—and not the leading force for change—in American politics.

In comparison to the sluggish workings of Congress, and the muffled dealings of private power, presidential actions monopolize the limelight in American political life. Chief Executives have had many allies—especially the media and academics—in fostering the notion that American politics revolve around the President's travails, that his struggles are inherently dramatic and momentous in consequence. But from a critical standpoint, what is striking is how limited recent presidential accomplishments have been, at least in domestic affairs. A great deal of noise and excitement goes on in the political foreground, but the background of American social and economic life has, since the end of World War II, scarcely been remodeled by any occupant of the White House. Indeed, it is hard to find many areas where the Fair Deal, the New Frontier, or the Great Society have brought about significant and permanent alterations in American life.

What tends to be obscured by the emphasis upon presidential action is the extent to which that action is embedded in, and shaped by, an existing context. Students of presidential action are, of course, well aware of a broader institutional context. The checks and balances in the political system, both constitutional and extraconstitutional, are perhaps the most familiar theme in American political thought. So the boundaries for presidential action here are fairly well demarcated.

Those who ignore such boundaries, like Richard Nixon, invite disaster; those who probe their outer limits, like Franklin Roosevelt in his court-packing scheme, risk political disfavor and decline.

Presidential scholars' recognition of this institutional context is seldom accompanied, however, by a like sensitivity to the power of the economic context and the ideological context within which presidential politics take place. The boundaries in these areas are more hazy, but this is largely because they are not often approached. Contemporary Presidents have persistently increased the federal government's role in the economy in order to promote economic growth, combat inflation, encourage foreign trade, or grapple with the balance-of-payments problem. But whatever course they have adopted, they have premised it on a system of corporate capitalism that they assume to be beyond dispute. Some (such as Lyndon Johnson) have worked cordially with corporate leaders; others (such as John Kennedy) have had to struggle against intense business criticism. But none have sought to question—much less assault—corporate power and its extraordinary skewing of resources and rewards. The present structure of the American economy has been accepted by modern Presidents as a given of American life.

The ideological context is similarly fixed in presidential consciousness. There is room here only to specify its broadest features. Corporate capitalism is, of course, a part of this ideological context; its abuses are periodically noted but are quickly forgiven in light of its contribution to American prosperity. The welfare state complements corporate capitalism, with government coming to the aid of those who have somehow been bypassed by prosperity. Liberal values are at the ideological core: equality of opportunity, the power of knowledge, individualism, enterprise, pluralism. Here, too, abuses are dutifully acknowledged—e.g., racial discrimination—but the American social order is seen as basically sound and healthy.

This contrasts with much of the external world, where liberal values have not yet taken hold (the "underdeveloped" countries) or have been destroyed by illiberal ones (communism). America is thereby burdened with global responsibilities. It is committed, by both interest and morality, to providing its beneficent largess and exemplary values to poorer nations; it is committed as well to protecting them from the expansive designs of the communists. For liberals in the White House even more than for conservatives, the Cold War has served as the all-inclusive ideology of presidential politics.

Always operating well within these economic and ideological contexts, the modern Presidency has taken on a characteristic form. Despite differences of personal and partisan emphasis, modern presidential action tends to be modest in its domestic goals, yet assertive once it enters onto the world stage. It does not seek to reshape America; it seeks to shape much of the rest of the world.

The presidential preoccupation with foreign affairs has been recognized by most students of the office. One political scientist, Aaron Wildavsky, has gone so far as to talk of "two presidencies," one for domestic affairs, the other for foreign and defense policy. The domestic President, in Wildavsky's view, is cramped and confined by his power competitors; his political maneuverability is sharply restricted by Congress, interest groups, public opinion. The foreign and defense President, in contrast, enjoys an exhilarating freedom of action. In this area the significant constituencies, such as Congress and the military, are weaker; further, both constitutional powers and public expectations ensure that the President will ordinarily have his way. The disparity between the "two presidencies" can be read in the record of recent Presidents; tabulating congressional action on key presidential proposals from 1948 through 1964, Wildavsky found that "Presidents prevail about 70 per cent of the time in defense and foreign policy, compared with 40 per cent in the domestic sphere." [1]

Wildavsky is correct in insisting that the institutional

context for presidential action favors foreign policy. What is left out of his analysis, however, are the economic and ideological contexts of presidential action. And these favor foreign policy just as much as does the institutional context. The "two presidencies" are not only the result of disparate institutional pressures on the President; they are also the result of disparate presidential functions and goals.

Because of their acceptance of the prevailing social and economic order, even the more liberal of recent Presidents have had little novel or profound that they really wanted to achieve in domestic affairs. Their most controversial domestic proposals have envisioned only modest reforms. Basically, these Presidents have sought to patch up remaining holes in the New Deal, and to stabilize and rationalize the corporate economy. None have acknowledged more fundamental problems in American society; none have proposed anything that resembles a program of social and economic reconstruction. Contrary to the conventional view, it has not been an obstructionist Congress or an apathetic public that has kept Presidents since FDR from major domestic accomplishments as much as it has been the orthodoxy of their own domestic vision.

This conventionality in domestic affairs has already been documented in the case of John Kennedy. But what of other liberal Presidents? Harry Truman and Lyndon Johnson seem, at first glance, to represent stronger reform impulses. Both began their Presidencies with an orientation toward domestic politics that Kennedy lacked; both possessed, in addition, greater aspirations to FDR's mantle as a domestic reformer. If the New Frontier was expressly global, the Fair Deal and the Great Society laid claims to a political transformation at home.

But neither the aims nor the substance of Truman's and Johnson's reforms cut very deep. (Franklin Roosevelt represents a more complicated case—genuine reforms that modified existing power relationships in order to preserve them.) Harry Truman is usually remembered as a game progressive who fought fruitlessly for reform against a hopelessly conservative Congress. But recent scholarship has uncovered considerable evidence that his fight had more to do with political advantage than with a commitment to social change. If Truman attempted to help labor by vetoing the Taft-Hartley bill in 1947, it was largely to placate a constituency he had outraged in 1946, when he asked for legislation empowering the government to draft strikers into the Army.[2] If he pushed public housing, national health insurance, and civil rights programs on a resistant Congress in 1948, it was with an eye to the electoral strategy mapped out by his political counselor, Clark Clifford:

> The Administration should select the issues upon
> which there will be conflict with the majority in
> Congress. It can assume that it will get no major part
> of its own program approved. Its tactics must,
> therefore, be entirely different than if there were any
> real point to bargaining and compromise. Its
> recommendations—in the State of the Union message
> and elsewhere—must be tailored for the voter, not the
> Congressman; they must display a label which reads
> "no compromise." [3]

Lyndon Johnson was more successful than Harry Truman in domestic politics; his War on Poverty is easily the most impressive achievement in domestic reform since the 1930s. Johnson sincerely wanted to help the poor—especially the black poor. But his conception of help bore all the limitations of New Deal politics. If Franklin Roosevelt had left blacks out of his New Deal "concert of interests," Lyndon Johnson would extend his own consensus far enough to incorporate them. If Franklin Roosevelt had responded to the political threats of Huey Long, the Townsend Clubs, and the labor movement by endorsing the Wagner Act, the Social Security Act, and a host of other liberal programs in 1935, Lyndon Johnson would come up with his own panoply of legislative measures to pacify black anger and retain black loyalty to the Democratic party. If Franklin

Roosevelt had understood that the provision of social services to discontented groups and the involvement of their leaders in new public agencies was essential to presidential control over the ultimate shape of domestic politics, Lyndon Johnson would attempt to absorb and delimit the black struggle of the 1960s with similar offerings to the exploding urban ghettoes.[4]

Some genuinely innovative features of the War on Poverty differentiated it from the New Deal: "community action" and "maximum feasible participation" of the poor. But while a number of those in charge of the War on Poverty believed that political action by the poor was the best way to force a reallocation of services in urban areas, there is little evidence that President Johnson shared this view. Johnson seemed to pay scant attention to the more radical features of his own program until they ran into opposition from Congressmen and big-city mayors. Then he began a visible retreat from controversy. Even if Vietnam had not drained potential resources away from the poverty program, it is doubtful whether Johnson would have kept pushing the program in the face of mounting political resistance. He wanted to be a domestic reformer as long as he could operate within a New Deal context and consensus; when that context and that consensus began to crumble, he began to burrow ever more deeply into Vietnam.[5]

Advocacy of mild domestic reforms is expected from contemporary Presidents, but if such reforms are blocked or truncated, Presidents have a host of excuses at their disposal. What is inexcusable for a modern President is the failure adequately to manage the corporate economy. When Franklin Roosevelt propped up a beleaguered American capitalism during the 1930s, until the onset of war could revivify it, he established a presidential responsibility that none of his successors could shirk. Indeed, that responsibility became statutory through the Employment Act of 1946. Moderating economic fluctuations and promoting prosperity were now inescapable executive functions.

Presidential efforts to deal with such problems as unemployment and inflation are obviously of great import to the ordinary citizen. Whether from human sympathy or from reelection calculations, modern Presidents have worked to relieve mass economic worries. They have suffered along with the majority (if only politically) in times of distress, and have basked in the shared glow of prosperity. But while the economic concerns of the majority are never ignored, they seldom serve as the chief basis for executive policy making. Economic management by the White House is, in essential matters, geared to economic power.

The stabilization of corporate capitalism is the paramount domestic duty of the modern Presidency. It has not mattered greatly that recent Chief Executives have been relatively unlearned in economics; the imperatives of the giant corporations who dominate the American economy impose themselves on the Presidency with a force that cannot be misunderstood. As we have seen in the case of John Kennedy, even a President elected by other constituencies, and distrusted by a majority of the business community, is likely to assume that he has no choice except to meet those imperatives. The complex partnership between the White House and the corporate community thus transcends personalities and party lines. Placed in a position where they take the blame if the corporate economy falters, contemporary Presidents shape their economic programs with a careful eye to corporate stability.

While stabilization is a continuous and sometimes routine preoccupation for Presidents, rationalization of the corporate economy represents a notable achievement. A President like Kennedy, who establishes new governmental methods of underwriting investment and expanding markets, plays an important role in the development of corporate capitalism in America. Kennedy's investment credit and tax cut were, in this regard, far more significant than the domestic reforms (such as federal aid to education and Medicare) that he failed to maneuver through Congress. If the modern Presidency does provide opportunity for substantial achievement in domestic affairs, it is largely in this area of rationalization of the corporate economy. It is difficult, however, to characterize such achievement as progressive. Historically, progressivism has claimed to restrict corporate power and to redistribute wealth; the kind of rationalization typified by the "New Economics" serves to solidify corporate power and to sharpen existing inequalities.

In contrast to domestic politics, the social and economic order that emerged from the New Deal and the Second World War has required a wholly different presidential approach to foreign policy. In the ideology of the Cold War the overriding goal of American foreign policy has been the containment of communist expansionism—and the means to that goal has been a corresponding expansion of American power. Since World War II the United States has become the leader in the global capitalist economy; and here, too, an expansion of American power has had to occur apace. Intertwined political and economic motives have thus propelled the United States into an ill-disguised global empire.

We have observed, in the foreign policy of John Kennedy, the kind of thinking that has rationalized the existence of this empire and justified its further expansion. President Kennedy noted with pride in 1963 that one million Americans were serving outside the frontiers of the United States "on a mission of freedom." President Johnson dramatically increased that number—also in the name of "freedom." The growth of freedom was, however, far less noticeable than the growth of American military, political, and economic power. American foreign investments, for example, amounted to almost 60 percent of the world total in this period.[6]

Executive primacy in foreign affairs has situated recent occupants of the White House at the heart of an enormous military, political, and economic apparatus. Strengthening this global apparatus whenever possible, protecting it wherever it comes under attack, the modern President is the dynamic central figure in the American empire. The advance or retreat of that empire seems to ride on the force of his international strategy. Small wonder, then, that the same Presidents who pursue modest policies at home come to nurture ambitious dreams when they go abroad.

The political and economic demands that have called forth activism and aggressiveness in foreign affairs have often been reinforced by inner presidential demands. Kennedy has not been the only recent President to display a thirst for action that can win both present and permanent acclaim. Others, too, have strived for accomplishments that might gain them the cherished title of "great" President. But external constraints and conventional purposes have largely closed off the domestic scene as a field for great action. It is in foreign policy—with its inherent drama, its freedom of action, its momentous consequences—that presidential heroes are made these days.

The tasks that characterize the post–New Deal Presidency have been set by a social and economic order which no Chief Executive has presumed to question. Presidential power has developed in accordance with those tasks. While the precise features of presidential power vary with personality, style, and partisanship, its broader dimensions have been relatively constant since Harry Truman.

In the arena of domestic politics, power is pluralistic; Presidents have to share its precious coinage with a host of competitors. Important Congressmen or congressional committees, agency chieftains, established interests can each contribute to or detract from presidential potency, depending upon their own relative potency. In the process of enacting their programs, Presidents must weigh the preponderant balance of forces, ensuring that the more powerful of those forces are satisfied that their opinions have been considered and that their interests have been at least partially fulfilled. Presidents do not command in this elite realm (a maxim that Richard Nixon fatally ignored). They negotiate and they deal, trading off about as much as they gain in return.

Presidential power has its ups and downs here, its moderate gains and losses. But if the bargaining system itself is challenged, that power takes on a very different aspect. Confronted with a challenge from outside the existing political elite—e.g., from a mass movement—Presidents have acted forcefully to maintain the bargaining system. For a President like Richard Nixon, forcefulness is equated with repression. But for liberal Presidents, the preferred response is to accommodate the more moderate demands and to incorporate the more moderate leaders of mass movements into the existing system. Sometimes, because of strong opposition from conservative segments of the existing elite, this can cost the President considerably. But to keep the boundaries of the elite realm intact, to ensure ultimate control of domestic political life, Presidents such as Kennedy and Johnson have been willing to pay a high price.

Control is only at issue in domestic politics when the elite realm is threatened, but in foreign policy, power has come to mean nothing less than control. The contemporary President would be horrified by Lincoln's judgment of himself toward the end of the Civil War: "I claim not to have controlled events but confess plainly that events have controlled me." [7] Such humility has no place in the contemporary presidential view of international affairs. As the agents of American global power, every President since Franklin Roosevelt (with Woodrow Wilson as forerunner) has interpreted his task as a quest to bring a beneficent American order to a world in dangerous flux. From Europe to Latin America to Asia they have almost ceaselessly labored to construct that order.

Their efforts abroad have suffered from some grievous setbacks—most notably in Cuba and Vietnam. But at home presidential dominance over foreign policy has, until very recently, advanced dramatically. The twin claims of expertise and secrecy have ensured presidential management of foreign affairs information. Increasingly institutionalized deception has woven a cloak of mystification over the executive conduct of both diplomacy and war. Those in a position to challenge the presidential monopoly over foreign policy have largely acquiesced in such developments, settling for the illusion of patriotic duty and the solid rewards of domestic power.

Until the force of the antiwar movement shattered Lyndon Johnson's Vietnam consensus and stayed Richard Nixon's hand in Cambodia, Presidents enjoyed remarkable freedom in their global ventures. They were able not only to make commitments and maneuver troops at will, but to control American foreign policy in an even more basic sense—that of imposing upon the nation their interpretation of the world. While this control finally may have peaked in its growth, it is likely to remain, in the absence of another debacle as enormous as Vietnam, essentially intact.

The modern Presidency, as I have so far sketched it, is best understood through its relationship to the prevailing American order. Having internalized the values of this corporate and imperial order, recent Presidents have found little difficulty in serving its needs. Few of them, however, have recognized or admitted to this kind of service. For they have conceived of their purposes in more immediate and limited terms, and have conceived of themselves as more practical and objective actors. Obscuring Presidents' understanding of their own historical role have been, above all, their pragmatic illusions.

Most modern Presidents have claimed the title of "pragmatist" for themselves. Richard Nixon was just as concerned as John Kennedy and Lyndon Johnson to announce that he was not wedded to dogma, and that his administration would follow a realistic and flexible course. It has chiefly been the liberal Presidents, however, who have captured the pragmatic label for themselves. To understand how deceptive that label has been, a

brief excursion into the subject of liberal pragmatism is necessary at this point. I hope to explain, by means of this excursion,
the illusions that have mystified not only those who observe
presidential actions, but the actors as well.

For liberal Presidents—and for those who have advised
them—the essential mark of pragmatism is its "tough-mindedness." Pragmatism is equated with strength, an intellectual and
moral strength that can accept a world stripped of illusions and
can take the facts unadorned. Committed to liberal objectives,
yet free from liberal sentimentality, the pragmatic liberal sees
himself as grappling with the brute and unpleasant facts of
political reality in order to humanize and soften those facts.

The great enemy for pragmatic liberals is ideology. In
their view, ideology has tormented the world throughout the
twentieth century and, in communist guise, still bedevils much
of the world today. It is ideology too—though of a different sort—
which has hindered American political progress. Herbert
Hoover is perhaps the supreme exemplar of this American
ideology, muddying up understanding and impeding action so
thoroughly with his outmoded capitalist ethic that only a master pragmatist like Franklin Roosevelt could rescue the American political order. Ideology remains a persistent enemy for
pragmatic liberalism. The conservative heirs of Hoover still
battled the liberal heirs of Roosevelt into the 1960s; then, fresh
challenges arose from a long-dormant left. Throughout those
struggles pragmatic liberals have remained resolutely anti-
ideological, asserting their pragmatic credo as a badge of their
freedom from the taint of the doctrinaire.

Shunning ideology, pragmatic liberals turn their attention
toward ideas that they take to be practicable and feasible. They
insist that history is a continuity and that societies cannot be
refashioned to accord with the visions of intellectuals—but that
piecemeal improvements have been made and can be made
again. Within the constraints of the "possible"—which are the
constraints of politics—they labor to make American life, if not

perfectly just and happy, at least fairer and more worthwhile.[8]

In this eagerness to avoid the illusions of a dogmatic political faith, pragmatic liberals have fallen prey to some distinctive illusions of their own. The scorn that they level against ideologues has conveniently taken the place of a self-critical stance. It has obscured the fact that pragmatism has, in a sense, something to hide. And what it has to hide looks suspiciously like an ideology. As Louis Hartz has suggested in *The Liberal Tradition in America,* "American pragmatism has always been deceptive because, glacierlike, it has rested on miles of submerged conviction."[9] Pragmatic liberals have reveled in their freedom to experiment without ever wanting to peer too closely at the traditional liberal faith which sustained and governed their experiments.

This traditional faith has, in the hands of the pragmatic liberals, shed the crudeness which still characterizes the classical liberalism now upheld on the right wing. It appears embodied in theories that bear all the marks of modernity and sophistication. These theories (which we have seen in abundance on the New Frontier) do not, in any significant fashion, depart from the ideology of corporate liberalism. But they succeed in translating ideology into the more impressive language of social science. Ideology thereby becomes doubly difficult to recognize. The pragmatist's pretense to objectivity is now overlaid with the self-celebrated objectivity of the social scientist; certified by the academy, the modern pragmatic liberal faith is seemingly lifted above any ideological contamination.

The extensive reliance upon theory is almost as touchy a subject as ideology for the pragmatic liberal. Academics can play with theories, but executive decision makers are supposed to be oriented toward facts. So the boundaries between theory and fact are rendered indistinct by policy makers, who grow accustomed, in Hannah Arendt's words, to "dealing with hypotheses and mere 'theories' as established facts."[10]

Especially when challenged at their roots, as in Vietnam, pragmatists' theories may be converted wholesale into facts in order to drive out contravening facts (a process Arendt calls "defactualization"). Pragmatic liberals fall back on the facts—their facts—to protect themselves from the chastening experience of theoretical and ideological failure. Vietnam revealed how far this process could go. In this extreme but far from atypical case, pragmatism, a philosophy of experimentation and tentativeness, became scarcely distinguishable from the most dogmatic of ideologies.

An illusory objectivity is one of the pillars of pragmatic "tough-mindedness." The second pillar is the readiness for power. Pragmatists are interested in what works; their prime criterion of value is success. It is the very definition of pragmatism to turn away from a belief in fixed principles toward the truth of concrete results. But as a believer in concrete results, the pragmatist is ineluctably drawn to power. For it is power that gets things done most easily, that makes things work most successfully. Power is the shortest path to effecting things in the world, the supreme tool for those who define themselves by effecting things.[11]

Power is not only useful, in the pragmatist's view; it is also a badge of worth. The readiness to exercise power differentiates the pragmatist from ineffectual idealists and utopians. In describing the intellectuals of the Kennedy years, Arthur Schlesinger, Jr., pressed home the distinction: "The pragmatists accepted the responsibility of power—and thereby risked corruption. The utopians refused complicity with power—and thereby risked irrelevance."[12] The pragmatist, in short, is tough enough, self-confident enough, to face up to the responsibilities and conquer the temptations of power.

The self-confidence of pragmatic liberals in the face of power has been eminently visible in recent history; often, it has taken the form of arrogance. But such self-confidence is only part of the story—the more superficial part. Underneath the tones of self-assurance, one can often detect a note of fear.

The political world that pragmatism inhabits is full of perils. Ideology spreads its illusions and arms its legions under the banner of those illusions. Irrational passion and moralistic fervor propel previously inert masses into movements that scoff at institutional restraints and refuse to acknowledge political limits. At home in a world where the fundamental political questions have been settled, pragmatists are perpetually anxious about threats to that world. The rhetoric of pragmatic liberal leaders is replete with metaphors describing the crumbling of order and the collapse of progress, both abroad and at home. We need not turn to the troubled years of the late 1960s to find examples of such rhetoric; we have discovered them in profusion even in the more peaceful Kennedy years.

From the New Deal on, pragmatic liberalism claimed to be the one political approach that could stave off disorder and keep affairs under control. It achieved its political ascendancy by expressing its own anxieties, relating them to the anxieties of the American public, and claiming that it would conquer both. From FDR's pronouncement that "the only thing we have to fear is fear itself" to John Kennedy's assertion that he was preparing the nation to survive "the hour of maximum danger," the simultaneous immersion in and relief of public anxiety was the core of pragmatic politics. The alternatives were starkly drawn: a liberal power structure—or a world out of control. It was a potent political appeal, fading only when, under Lyndon Johnson, the world *did* go out of control. Then the conservatives rode to power with an almost identical argument.

However successful pragmatic liberal Presidents were in relieving public anxieties, their own anxieties did not yield so easily. FDR, it is true, possessed a supreme self-assurance, derived in large part from his patrician heritage. But his successors were not so fortunate. They were nagged by an uneasy sense that the forces of disorder (which are often, it should be noted, the forces of change) were too strong for their pragmatic politics. So they became preoccupied with proving their own strength, and the strength of their politics, in order to quiet such doubts. In foreign affairs this meant "tests of will": Berlin, Cuba, Vietnam, the Dominican Republic. At home it meant a strong reaction to any political movement perceived as a challenge to presidential authority. Kennedy's harsh response to militant civil rights demonstrations, Johnson's growing fury at antiwar protestors—these reflected the heightened anxiety of pragmatic leaders when their control over affairs seemed to be slipping away. (Liberal pragmatists have not had a monopoly on anxiety. Richard Nixon topped both of his predecessors in his obsession with crises and fury at dissenters.)

Power is at the heart of pragmatic politics. But the belief that power is sought only as a means for producing concrete results is another pragmatic illusion. The pragmatist's quest for power is rooted, ultimately, in anxiety. Power maintains a settled political order, in which everything is under control. It preserves the pragmatist's carefully delimited reality. When power begins to slip away, when the defenses against anxiety start to crumble, "tough-minded" pragmatists can explode through all the limits they themselves ordinarily uphold. Vietnam is the supreme testament to the potential of pragmatic politics when an anxiety that has become overwhelming is wedded to power that, although challenged, is still immense.[13]

In examining both the functions of the modern Presidency and the illusions which obscure those functions, one important subject has so far been slighted: the President's relationship to the American public. Back in the days (not so long ago) when scholars were uncritical devotees of presidential power, much was made of the President's role as representative of the American people. Not only was he the sole official elected by a national constituency; he also became, by virtue of his position, the sole spokesman for national aspirations. The President was, in Clinton Rossiter's memorable phrase, "the Voice of the People." [14]

Presidents have naturally welcomed such a title, and made the gestures appropriate to it. Every modern Chief Executive has, at some point in his term, echoed Franklin Roosevelt's statement that his office "is pre-eminently a place of moral leadership." [15] Yet such professions of devotion to a moral and educational mission are increasingly out of kilter with the contemporary experience of American politics: Presidents given to profuse rhetoric that tells little and conceals much, citizens accustomed to feeling themselves too uninformed and impotent to have any significant impact upon public affairs. The presidential claim to be the guide and spokesman for the American public can no longer be taken very seriously. The erosion of that claim has revealed a more complex—and far less attractive—relationship between Presidents and the public.

Recent Presidents and their advisers, armed with the findings of public-opinion surveys as well as their own political experience, have assumed that there is a critical gap between the general populace and the political elite. This gap is partly one of information, but also one of emotion; ordinary citizens, in this view, compound their political ignorance with a passionate attachment to the products of that ignorance. They possess enough knowledge, certainly, to make broad electoral choices, but valid judgments about the complex options involved in presidential decision making are taken to be beyond the scope of most citizens in the American polity. Thus did President Kennedy stress the irrelevance of "passionate" popular movements to the difficult, technical questions of economic and foreign policy. Thus did President Johnson dismiss out of hand even the more moderate of popular arguments against the war in Vietnam.

What ordinary citizens lack, and what members of the political elite (whether top officials in the executive branch, Congressmen, state and party leaders, or political illuminati outside government) possess, is best summed up by the word "sophistication." Sophistication involves a certain style and mode of judgment: experienced, reasoned, sober, practical. Not all members of the political elite are considered equally sophisticated; Presidents and their aides, for example, tend to look down on the parochial views of most Congressmen. Still, this is a realm where what people think has weight. It is the domain where political rationality resides; indeed, some recent Presidents have come perilously close to equating reason with the state.

The public, then, is perceived by Presidents only as "public opinion"—broad, amorphous, setting general parameters for action yet hardly guiding or directing it. Ordinary citizens are polled, but they are not really listened to; Presidents want to know what they will or won't accept, not what is truly on their minds. They are regarded, on the one hand, as a constraint upon presidential action, sometimes accessible to manipulation, often simply immovable. But they are also the essential audience for presidential action, the audience from which every President tries to coax approval.

To gain that approval Presidents have an array of weapons at their disposal, ranging from honest argument to the most subtle of public relations techniques. They also have the power of the deed; nothing is better guaranteed to rally popular support to the Presidency than forceful action in a situation publicly defined as a crisis. To recent Presidents, almost any method has seemed legitimate to win or hold the support of a public that could not grasp the political realities anyway. Lying—to the public and even to others in the political elite—is only the final stage in the procession of evasions and half-truths that has become increasingly characteristic of the modern Presidency.

Not only the flagrant cases of deception, like Vietnam and Watergate, indicate presidential disrespect for public consciousness. Even when contemporary Presidents are most honest, their aim is seldom to educate the American people. More often, Presidents simply want to win over the public to their own programs, to enlist public opinion in the service of presidential causes lest it be mobilized in opposition to those causes.

For this purpose specific issues are raised, argued, and encased in a rhetoric of historical significance. Then, as the President moves on to other policy areas, they are forgotten; the public is left to slip back into political apathy and private preoccupations. Most Presidents like to talk about education and moral leadership; what their words and their practice usually aim at, however, is not the greater enlightenment of the pupils, but the growing power of the teacher.

While presidential efforts to shape public opinion are generally instrumental, and thereby limited, they do have broader consequences. For most Americans, the statements of Presidents serve to define the significant issues in national politics. Since Presidents almost always stay well within the boundaries of the existing social and economic order, those issues become defined in relatively narrow terms. When, for example, the President appeals to the public to support his economic program rather than that of his opposition in Congress, the impression is conveyed that these two positions constitute the gamut of public options. That Presidents set the agenda for national political discourse is a crucial factor in circumscribing political controversy in America. It is more important in sustaining the prevailing order than all the homilies on free enterprise, individual responsibility, or the American way of life that Presidents ritually recite on dreary ceremonial occasions.

most people want the choices made for them

Presidential "leadership" of public opinion has, in recent years, served mainly to limit public awareness of political possibilities. It has also served to discourage mass action which might open up such possibilities. Most Presidents do pay lip service to the idea of citizen involvement in politics. But as we have seen in the case of John Kennedy, they hasten to remind the public that the important issues are complicated and technical, and best left to the expertise of the political elite—or else explosive and divisive, and best left to the sobriety of the political elite.

In place of genuine involvement, ordinary citizens are

offered presidential drama. They can respond to that drama with pleasure, dismay, boredom—all conveniently measured by the polls. But they are not supposed to seek their own stage for action. To the extent that presidential efforts at shaping mass opinion are successful, the central lesson the public absorbs is its own powerlessness.

The American public is generally a passive audience for presidential drama. Sometimes, however, segments of that audience begin to reject their passive role and to force their way onto the political stage. Mass movements periodically erupt into American politics, to redefine the issues and to raise the stakes of political conflict. Whatever the specific targets of such movements, they represent a problem for the Presidency. For they invariably pose the question of where the President really stands, and what his relationship is to the existing order. No matter how carefully a President has cultivated his image as a reformer or advocate for the disadvantaged, mass movements insist upon testing the reality behind that image.

Ironically, the effect of mass action is often to bring the reality more into line with the image. Most of the historic accomplishments that have bestowed on the Presidency a reputation for progressivism were, in fact, pushed upon Presidents by forceful social movements. Antislavery agitators and their Radical allies in Congress prodded Abraham Lincoln to relinquish his reservations about emancipation. The railroad brotherhoods' threat of a national rail strike (and the intransigence of railroad owners in the face of union demands) drove Woodrow Wilson, in the election year of 1916, to endorse the eight-hour day through the Adamson Act. The swelling tide of labor militancy and discontent with the New Deal (along with the growing hostility of businessmen) left Franklin Roosevelt little choice in 1935 save a belated sponsorship of the Wagner Act. The marches and demonstrations of the black freedom movement impelled John Kennedy and Lyndon Johnson to propose major civil rights legislation in 1963 and 1965. In the absence of mass pressures, Presidents have tended to cling to established arrangements. Because of such pressures, a few of those Presidents have, as Richard Hofstadter remarked of Lincoln, "conducted a brilliant strategic retreat toward a policy of freedom." [16]

In their responses to mass movements Presidents have usually manifested a desire to ease the pressures, and to restore executive control over the definition and disposition of public issues. A few of them, however, have understood that there may be no simple path back to political normalcy. Presidents have, on occasion, themselves been educated by mass action. They have, consequently, realized that the lessons they have reluctantly learned must in turn form the content of their own public discourse. The best moments of the American Presidency have come when Presidents have abandoned their pretensions to superior wisdom and have engaged in a dialogue initiated by others.[17]

It is at these moments, when Presidents express what they have learned from mass action, that they can truly be considered political educators. The actions of mass movements confuse, and often alienate, other sectors of the public. The role of the President, as political educator, is to clarify and interpret such actions to those who do not understand them. It is also to relate the problems of those already engaged in action to the concerns of those who are still politically inert. When Presidents frame their messages solely for their own instrumental purposes, they effectively promote the political helplessness of the American people. On those rare occasions when they address themselves to the aspirations of mass movements, they begin to reawaken in Americans a sense of their own capacity for political freedom.[18]

The Presidency does have some potential for progressive action, some capacity for authentic political education. But they must be drawn out by public action. Even then, there are definite limits to how far Presidents can go. They may respond positively to movements that aim at racial justice or protection for labor, since the goals of such movements are not, ultimately, incompatible with the prevailing social and economic order. But a very different kind of presidential response has been forthcoming when other movements (such as the IWW) have called into question that order itself.

Compared to its infrequent and limited progressive ventures, the overwhelming reality of the Presidency has been as a stabilizing force. Even the most liberal Presidents have done far more to preserve existing patterns of power and wealth than to alter them. When we turn away from their brightest historical moments to the bulk of their administrations' activities, the conservative role played by twentieth-century Presidents is unmistakable.

This role is almost certain to continue. It should be sufficient at this point merely to note the forces that press for presidential continuity. Before current aspirants reach the Presidency, they are extensively screened for its central functions. They have to demonstrate their acceptability to a wide range of established powers: corporate leaders (especially as financial backers), party chieftains, entrenched interest groups. They have to prove their political orthodoxy to those who control the organs of national publicity; otherwise, even a hint of heterodoxy will, as the campaign of George McGovern illustrated, be blown up by the media to disastrous proportions. They have to show, in sum, that their long struggle to rise to the top has formed their political consciousness, that they speak and think in the familiar vocabulary of the prevailing American order.

Socialized well before they reach the White House, Presidents confront an array of pressures which effectively reinforce their orthodoxy. We have witnessed, in the career of John Kennedy, the continuous interplay between political demands and <u>personal desires</u> that typifies the modern Presidency. Thus, proponents of economic, political, and military expansionism find willing agents in Presidents fascinated by their own opportunities for global action. Sophisticated leaders of industry and finance deal with self-proclaimed partners anxious to make the corporate economy thrive on its own terms. Entrenched power-holders bargain with cautious White House politicians concerned, even when responding to the grievances of the powerless, to maintain the dominance of the existing political elite.

The record of the Kennedy Presidency should serve as a warning to those who still believe that major changes in American society can be instituted if only the right liberal makes it to the White House. Liberals will no doubt regain the Presidency in the future. But they will hardly refashion it into an instrument for the progressive transformation of American politics. That transformation can be accomplished only by those who have a stake in change. It is likely to be impeded by Presidents—who are, after all, the most successful products of the existing order.

If it is a self propagating and as locked a system as he makes it
Should his contention that transformation
of Am. politics is possible by those
who take stake in change. Sounds a
bit romantic and unrealistic
Basically incremental gradual institutional change that will be maintained
as long as flexible. Sounds a possible worlds. But the best that can be practically hoped for. Not the best &

Notes

INTRODUCTION

1. Erwin C. Hargrove, *The Power of the Modern Presidency* (New York: Alfred A. Knopf, 1974), p. 9.

2. James David Barber, *The Presidential Character: Predicting Performance in the White House* (Englewood Cliffs, N. J.: Prentice-Hall, 1972).

3. George E. Reedy, *The Twilight of the Presidency* (New York: Mentor, 1971).

4. Arthur Schlesinger, Jr., *The Imperial Presidency* (Boston: Houghton Mifflin, 1973).

5. Ibid., p. 208.

6. In addition to Hargrove, Barber, Reedy, and Schlesinger, "revisionist" presidential writers include Emmet John Hughes, *The Living Presidency* (Baltimore: Penguin, 1974); Philippa Strum, *Presidential Power and American Democracy* (Pacific Palisades, Calif.: Goodyear Publishing, 1972); Dorothy Buckton James, *The Contemporary Presidency* (Indianapolis: Bobbs-Merrill, 1974).

7. Barber, *The Presidential Character*, p. 454.

8. Hughes, *The Living Presidency*, p. 293.

9. Schlesinger, *The Imperial Presidency*, p. 418.

10. Books that effectively undermine the "progressive" interpretation of the Presidency are many. Among the most important are: William Appleman Williams, *The Contours of American History* (Chicago: Quadrangle, 1966) and *Some Presidents from Wilson to Nixon* (New York: New York Review Books, 1972); Gabriel Kolko, *The Triumph of Conservatism: A Re-Interpretation of American History, 1900–1916* (Chicago: Quadrangle, 1967); Paul K. Conkin, *The New Deal* (New York: Thom-

as Y. Crowell, 1967); Bert Cochran, *Harry Truman and the Crisis Presidency* (New York: Funk & Wagnalls, 1973); Barton J. Bernstein, ed., *Politics and Policies of the Truman Administration* (Chicago: Quadrangle, 1970); Frances Fox Piven and Richard A. Cloward, *Regulating the Poor: The Functions of Public Welfare* (New York: Vintage, 1972). Mention should also be made of the numerous "revisionist" histories of the Cold War.

11. See Richard J. Walton, *Cold War and Counterrevolution: The Foreign Policy of John F. Kennedy* (New York: Viking Press, 1972); Louise FitzSimons, *The Kennedy Doctrine* (New York: Random House, 1972); Henry Fairlie, *The Kennedy Promise* (New York: Doubleday, 1973).

12. Barber, *The Presidential Character*, pp. 293 ff.

13. Ibid., p. 342.

14. Hargrove, *The Power of the Modern Presidency*, p. 68.

15. Ibid., p. 64.

Chapter 1   *AN EXISTENTIAL HERO?*

1. Theodore C. Sorensen, *Kennedy* (New York: Bantam, 1966), p. 13.

2. Arthur Schlesinger, Jr., *A Thousand Days: John F. Kennedy in the White House* (Greenwich, Conn.: Fawcett, 1967), p. 618.

3. Ibid., p. 110.

4. Ibid., p. 113.

5. Ibid.

6. "His mind was not prophetic, impassioned, mystical, ontological, utopian, or ideological. It was less exuberant than Theodore Roosevelt's, less scholarly than Wilson's, less adventurous than Franklin Roosevelt's. But it had its own salient qualities—it was objective, practical, ironic, skeptical, unfettered, and insatiable." Schlesinger, *A Thousand Days*, p. 103. Also see James MacGregor Burns, *John Kennedy: A Political Profile* (New York: Harcourt, Brace & World, 1961), p. 262.

7. Power within the Kennedy Administration was closely correlated to proficiency with facts. No presidential adviser was more influential than Robert McNamara, who would overpower any opponent in debate with his immense stockpile of facts. See David Halberstam, *The Best and the Brightest* (New York: Random House, 1972), pp. 213–50.

8. Norman Mailer, *The Presidential Papers of Norman Mailer* (New York: Bantam, 1964), p. 5.

9. As a student at Harvard in the late 1930s, Kennedy took no

part in liberal or radical politics. He was not, either then or later, attracted by causes; he never felt their power or emotional challenge. His wartime experiences did move him—but not in any political direction. When he ran for a House seat in 1946, it was not from commitment to an idea or program, but because he had little else to do with his life at that point. See Burns, *John Kennedy*, pp. 31, 57, 58.

10. Schlesinger's contention that Kennedy concealed emotions too strong to be expressed in public cannot, of course, be disproven. The minor debate among students of Kennedy over the state of his inner feelings ultimately trails off into trivia, such as the President's reputed fondness for sentimental Irish songs. Perhaps the most acute observation on the matter is that of James MacGregor Burns, whose early biography of Kennedy portrayed him lacking deep moral and emotional commitments (for which Burns drew the eternal ire of Kennedy's aides). Burns asks: "Is a man a man of great emotional feeling who never shows it?" James MacGregor Burns, Oral History Interview, 14 May 1965, Kennedy Library, pp. 1–15.

11. Throughout this book I shall be concerned with the role of various New Frontiersmen in shaping (or reflecting) Kennedy's thinking. Obviously there were substantial divergences among these men, and between each of them and Kennedy—yet I think it is more important to understand what they shared in common. This is particularly true in light of the treatment of this subject in Kennedy hagiography. In recent years (i.e., since the Vietnam War became unpopular) Kennedy's defenders have tried to dissociate the President from many of his top aides. This was not always the case; originally these men added luster to Kennedy's reputation, and emphasis was placed upon their kinship with him. Here, for example, is Sorensen: "The men he picked were for the most part men who thought his thoughts, spoke his language and put their country and Kennedy ahead of any other concern. . . . They were, like him, dedicated but unemotional, young but experienced, articulate but soft-spoken. There were no crusaders, fanatics, or extremists from any camp." Sorensen, *Kennedy*, p. 287.

12. A. Alvarez, *Under Pressure* (Baltimore: Penguin, 1965), p. 108.

13. Schlesinger, *A Thousand Days*, pp. 683–84.

14. See G. William Domhoff, *The Higher Circles: The Governing Class in America* (New York: Vintage, 1971), pp. 131–34.

15. Ronald Steel, "The Kennedy Fantasy," *New York Review of Books* 15 (19 November 1970): 3.

16. James Reston, "What Was Killed Was Not Only the President but the Promise," in *John F. Kennedy and the New Frontier*, ed. Aida DiPace Donald (New York: Hill & Wang, 1966), p. 229.

17. I. F. Stone, *In a Time of Torment* (New York: Vintage, 1968), p. 13.

Notes

18. Schlesinger, *A Thousand Days,* p. 81.

19. Ibid., p. 104.

20. Garry Wills, *Nixon Agonistes* (New York: Signet, 1971), p. 210.

21. John F. Kennedy, *Profiles in Courage* (New York: Harper & Row, 1964), p. 49.

22. John F. Kennedy, *Public Papers: 1961* (Washington, D.C.: Government Printing Office, 1962), pp. 22–23.

23. Ibid., p. 19.

24. John F. Kennedy, *Public Papers: 1962* (Washington, D.C.: Government Printing Office, 1963), p. 15.

25. John F. Kennedy, *The Strategy of Peace* (New York: Popular Library, 1961), p. 5.

26. Ibid., p. 73. For the parallels with Churchill, also see pp. 38–39, 235.

27. As President, Kennedy invoked Churchill less often in his speeches. He no longer needed, as he had as a young Senator, to enhance his stature by such historical identifications. Still, Schlesinger informs us, "Churchill remained his greatest admiration." Schlesinger, *A Thousand Days,* p. 84.

28. Kennedy, *Profiles in Courage,* p. 1.

29. Kennedy, *Public Papers: 1961,* p. 534.

30. The original source for this interpretation appears to be James Reston, who had talked with Kennedy at Vienna. It is discussed in several accounts of Kennedy's foreign policy; see, for example, Louise FitzSimons, *The Kennedy Doctrine* (New York: Random House, 1972), pp. 70–71; and Halberstam, *The Best and the Brightest,* pp. 75–77.

31. Walt W. Rostow, *View from the Seventh Floor* (New York: Harper & Row, 1964), p. 43.

32. Christopher Lasch has brilliantly captured the idea of "tough-mindedness" and its historical appeal to American intellectuals. See his *The New Radicalism in America (1889–1963): The Intellectual as a Social Type* (New York: Vintage, 1967), pp. 289–90, 308–10.

33. Kennedy's widely reported enthusiasm for the James Bond novels might also be mentioned in this regard. That enthusiasm might have been partly a publicity device, but it is still nicely symbolic. For the Bond books—and even more the American-made Bond films—depict the triumph against incredible odds of the unique Anglo-American combination of toughness and technology. They are a vivid expression of the fantasies of omnipotence of an imperialist nation.

34. Sorensen, *Kennedy,* p. 713.

35. Ibid., p. 714.

36. Halberstam, *The Best and the Brightest,* p. 300.

37. Halberstam suggests that Kennedy was moving away from most of these advisers in 1963 on the subject of Vietnam; as support for

this view he cites the rise of Roger Hilsman in Washington's Vietnam bureaucracy. Ibid., pp. 254–57. But Hilsman was never an opponent of the Vietnam commitment itself. He was pushing instead for a change in the American strategy, a shift of emphasis from conventional military methods to a counterinsurgency approach centering on the concept of strategic hamlets. Hilsman was, in his own way, just as much of an enthusiast for Vietnam as Robert McNamara or Maxwell Taylor.

38. Mailer, *Presidential Papers*, pp. 26–27.

39. Ibid., p. 7.

40. Reston, "What Was Killed Was Not Only the President but the Promise," p. 229.

41. Schlesinger, *A Thousand Days*, p. 662. For Schlesinger's defense of Kennedy as educator, see pp. 655–77.

42. Schlesinger was disappointed when Kennedy eschewed such conflicts. He thought that they were "the best way to break national apathy and communicate the reality of problems." Ibid., p. 664.

43. Theodore H. White, *The Making of the President, 1960* (New York: Signet, 1967), p. 158. Also see Burns, *John Kennedy*, p. xi.

44. Richard E. Neustadt, *Presidential Power—With an Afterword on JFK* (New York: John Wiley & Sons, 1968), p. 206.

45. In pointing out that Kennedy possessed an elitist bias, I do not mean to suggest that he—or his aides—were motivated by petty selfishness or arrogance. As a matter of fact, the New Frontiersmen were notably free of self-seeking. Unlike either its predecessors or its successors, there were no scandals in the Kennedy Administration.

46. Walter Lippmann, Oral History Interview, n.d., Kennedy Library, p. 8.

47. Kennedy, *Public Papers: 1961*, p. 3.

48. Ibid., p. 377. Also see pp. 154, 450.

49. Kennedy, *Public Papers: 1962*, p. 533.

50. Ibid., p. 422.

51. The widely held belief that Kennedy inspired young people to become involved in politics rests more upon developments after his assassination than it does on examples of participation during his Presidency. It is no doubt true that some young people were moved to political action by the memory they carried of Kennedy. But the moral appeals of the civil rights movement and later the antiwar movement were, I believe, far more important in creating the participatory politics of the 1960s. There is, too, a certain irony in the notion that Kennedy's untimely death launched many young people into politics. For if he had not been killed, they might not have acted; their action only became necessary because their hero, Kennedy, was no longer there to run affairs.

52. Sorensen, *Kennedy*, p. 436.

53. Ibid.

54. For these and other reasons, Neustadt expressed marked admiration for Kennedy in a 1968 afterword appended to a new edition of *Presidential Power.* Neustadt thought Kennedy had everything it took to be a strong President; in addition, he seemed to have that special quality which Neustadt had identified as the mark of a potentially great President—the sensitivity to and desire for power.

55. John F. Kennedy, Foreword to Theodore C. Sorensen, *Decision-Making in the White House* (New York: Columbia University Press, 1963), p. xii.

56. I do not mean to imply that Kennedy *should* have been expected to alter the political context in which he operated. The point of this discussion is not that Kennedy held attitudes on power that were extraordinary for an American political leader, but that he possessed a conception of power that was all too typical.

57. See FitzSimons, *The Kennedy Doctrine,* pp. 8–9.

58. Sorensen, *Kennedy,* p. 341.

59. John F. Kennedy, *Public Papers: 1963* (Washington, D.C.: Government Printing Office, 1964), p. 894.

Chapter 2   CREATING HISTORY

1. John F. Kennedy, *The Strategy of Peace* (New York: Popular Library, 1961), p. 85.

2. Theodore C. Sorensen, *Kennedy* (New York: Bantam, 1966), p. 573.

3. John F. Kennedy, *Public Papers: 1961* (Washington, D.C.: Government Printing Office, 1962), pp. 2–3. It is worthy of note that Kennedy says "I" instead of "we" in the second sentence.

4. Kennedy, *The Strategy of Peace,* p. 65.

5. Ibid., p. 8.

6. Walt W. Rostow, *The United States in the World Arena* (New York: Harper & Row, 1960), pp. 381–82.

7. Maxwell Taylor, *The Uncertain Trumpet* (New York: Harper & Brothers, 1960), pp. 24–25.

8. Kennedy, *The Strategy of Peace,* p. 8.

9. Ibid., pp. 9–10.

10. Ibid., p. 10.

11. Ibid., p. 35.

12. Ibid., p. 69.

13. Ibid., p. 32. Also see pp. 5–6, 34–35.

14. John Lukacs, *A History of the Cold War* (Garden City, N.Y.: Anchor, 1962), p. 171.

15. Sorensen shows that Kennedy deliberately reached for this effect. Sorensen, *Kennedy,* p. 327.

16. Kennedy, *Public Papers: 1961*, pp. 22–23.

17. Ibid., p. 23.

18. Ibid., p. 27.

19. As Richard E. Neustadt had recommended in *Presidential Power* (New York: John Wiley & Sons, 1968).

20. Walt W. Rostow, *View from the Seventh Floor* (New York: Harper & Row, 1964), p. 152. For a nearly identical enumeration of post-Sputnik Soviet "advances," see Sorensen, *Kennedy,* p. 256.

21. Kennedy, *The Strategy of Peace,* p. 35.

22. Lukacs, *A History of the Cold War,* p. 170. Russian motives are notoriously difficult to ascertain, but other considerations besides Khrushchev's eagerness to talk with Eisenhower support Lukacs' contention that the Soviet leader was seeking, not world dominion, but an accommodation with the United States in these years. Consider, for example, the alleged signs of a Soviet global offensive. Khrushchev's warnings of nuclear destruction wreaked upon the West appear, in retrospect, to have been designed more to cover up Soviet missile shortages than to "blackmail" the Western powers. And the other major "proof" of Soviet aggressiveness—subversion and revolution in Asia, Africa, and Latin America—turns out not to be the result of Russian machinations at all.

This is not to excuse the excesses of Soviet policy in these years. Khrushchev often did adopt a bellicose stance, and Soviet foreign policy under his leadership was calculating and sometimes—as in the case of Eastern Europe—ruthless. But the Soviets did not pursue any grandiose scheme of world mastery, nor did their foreign policy preclude détente with the United States. Indeed, Khrushchev's relationship with a peace-seeking Eisenhower, as well as his eager embracing of détente after the Cuban missile crisis, suggest that such a détente was always a major goal for him.

23. George F. Kennan, Oral History Interview, 23 March 1965, Kennedy Library, pp. 27–33.

24. David Halberstam, *The Best and the Brightest* (New York: Random House, 1972), p. 122.

25. Kennedy, *Public Papers: 1961,* p. 236.

26. Sorensen, *Kennedy,* p. 686. Four years later, in *The Kennedy Legacy* (New York: Mentor, 1970), Sorensen admitted that "much of that build-up appears now to have been unnecessary" (p. 142). Sorensen did not go on, however, to explore the consequences of that "unnecessary" action.

27. See Richard J. Walton, *Cold War and Counterrevolution: The Foreign Policy of John F. Kennedy* (New York: Viking Press, 1972), pp. 61–69; and David Horowitz, *The Free World Colossus* (New York: Hill & Wang, 1971), pp. 358–62.

28. Horowitz, *The Free World Colossus,* p. 356.

29. Kennedy, *Public Papers: 1961,* pp. 305–6.

30. Ibid., p. 336.

31. Ibid., p. 340.

32. John F. Kennedy, *Public Papers: 1963* (Washington, D.C.: Government Printing Office, 1964), p. 728.

33. Kennedy, *Public Papers: 1961,* pp. 725–26, 732.

34. Arthur Schlesinger, Jr., *A Thousand Days: John F. Kennedy in the White House* (Greenwich, Conn.: Fawcett, 1967), p. 338.

35. Ibid.

36. The problem of attributing historical responsibility to one side or the other in this conflict is clearly a complex one; there is room here only for a few considerations on the subject. The standard practice of Kennedy's chroniclers has been to slight the significance of Kennedy's early presidential actions for American-Soviet relations and to view Khrushchev's Berlin ultimatum of June as the catalyst for subsequent crisis. I have attempted in this chapter to point out the dangerous consequences of Kennedy's statements and actions in these months; in the next chapter I shall suggest that while Khrushchev may have set off Berlin tensions, the magnitude of the ensuing crisis is primarily attributable to Kennedy's handling of it. Neither historical interpretation can be conclusively proven; the material presented here seems to me, however, to make a strong case against the orthodox Kennedy interpretation.

Behind that orthodox interpretation lies an assumption that it would be well to bring out. Kennedy and his associates were adherents of the Cold War dictum that the Soviet Union would respond to Western shows of strength with respect and moderation, while gestures of goodwill and a preoccupation with keeping the peace would be taken by the Russians as a sign of weakness and call forth Russian aggressiveness. Following this assumption, Kennedy's tough words and military buildup should have cowed the Soviets. Instead, the Russians reacted aggressively, with tough words on Berlin and a military buildup of their own. It is interesting to compare this to the Soviet reaction to Kennedy's American University speech in June 1963, calling for a thaw in the Cold War. Khrushchev told Averell Harriman that it was "the greatest speech by any American President since Roosevelt" (quoted in Schlesinger, *A Thousand Days,* p. 826), and the long-snarled test ban negotiations were soon afterward brought to a successful conclusion.

37. George Kennan, Kennedy's Ambassador to Yugoslavia, was troubled by the American role in these months. Kennan suspected that Khrushchev was struggling with hard-line opposition in the Kremlin—and getting little help from the Americans in his struggle. "One of the objections I had to our policy from the time of the U-2 on was that I felt that we did not dangle enough in the way of favorable prospects

before the Soviet government to support Khrushchev in his co-exis-tence line with us, and that *we created a situation in which he had to scurry for cover by talking a very, very tough line toward us.*" Kennan, Oral History Interview, pp. 131–32; emphasis added.

38. John F. Kennedy, *Public Papers: 1962* (Washington, D.C.: Government Printing Office, 1963), p. v.

39. Kennedy, *Public Papers: 1961,* p. 205.

40. Kennedy, *Public Papers: 1962,* p. 10.

41. Kennedy, *Public Papers: 1961,* p. 397.

42. Kennedy, *Public Papers: 1962,* p. 265.

43. Rostow, *View From the Seventh Floor,* p. 25.

44. Walton, *Cold War and Counterrevolution,* p. 207.

45. The AID figures are cited in Harry Magdoff, *The Age of Imperialism* (New York: Monthly Review Press, 1969), p. 137.

Chapter 3 *"THE HOUR OF MAXIMUM DANGER"*

1. John F. Kennedy, *Public Papers: 1961* (Washington, D.C.: Government Printing Office, 1962), p. 625.

2. Ibid., pp. 368–69.

3. Hugh Sidey, *John F. Kennedy, President* (New York: Atheneum, 1964), p. 225. Also see James MacGregor Burns, *John Kennedy: A Political Profile* (New York: Harcourt, Brace & World, 1961), p. xii; and James Reston, "What Was Killed Was Not Only the President but the Promise," in *John F. Kennedy and the New Frontier,* ed. Aida DiPace Donald (New York: Hill & Wang, 1966), p. 225.

4. For the following historical account I have drawn heavily on Phillip Windsor, *City on Leave: A History of Berlin, 1945–1962* (London: Chatto & Windus, 1963); and John Mander, *Berlin, Hostage for the West* (Baltimore: Penguin, 1962).

5. "There is no indication that after a peace treaty the Western leaders would ever have been willing to contemplate a neutral great power in the center of Europe; and whenever they discussed German reunification they did so on the assumption that the whole country would be under Western control." Windsor, *City on Leave,* p. 181. Also see pp. 182–88.

6. Ibid., pp. 204–11.

7. John F. Kennedy, *The Strategy of Peace* (New York: Popular Library, 1961), p. 256.

8. Ibid., p. 255.

9. Arthur Schlesinger, Jr., *A Thousand Days: John F. Kennedy in the White House* (Greenwich, Conn.: Fawcett, 1967), p. 355.

10. Ibid.

11. Ibid., p. 354.

12. Theodore C. Sorensen, *Kennedy* (New York: Bantam, 1966), p. 658. Acheson did not deliver his final report to Kennedy until three weeks after Vienna, but by the time of the Vienna meeting Kennedy was already familiar with the substance of his position.

13. These motives were recognized at the time by many Western commentators. See, for example, Geoffrey Barraclough, "Berlin: Background to Crisis," *The Nation* 193 (15 July 1961): 23–25; and John R. Dornberg, "Berlin: Consequences of Crisis," *The Nation* 193 (2 September 1961): 111–13. Nor was it only liberal journalists who understood Soviet aims in the new Berlin crisis to be basically limited and localized; there were even those in the Kennedy Administration who shared this view. Thus, Llewellyn Thompson, American Ambassador to the Soviet Union, suggested after Vienna that "the predominant Soviet motive was the desire to improve the communist position in Eastern Europe rather than to achieve the world-wide political humiliation of the United States." Schlesinger, *A Thousand Days,* p. 356.

14. Schlesinger, *A Thousand Days,* pp. 345–46.

15. Ibid., p. 346.

16. Ibid., p. 348.

17. Kennedy, *Public Papers: 1961,* p. 476. That Kennedy favored a hard line at this point was evident in his selection (late in June) of Curtis Le May as the new Air Force Chief of Staff.

18. Schlesinger, *A Thousand Days,* pp. 358–59.

19. Richard J. Walton, *Cold War and Counterrevolution: The Foreign Policy of John F. Kennedy* (New York: Viking Press, 1972), p. 80. Walton's account of the Berlin crisis is excellent.

20. Schlesinger, *A Thousand Days,* p. 363.

21. Sidey, *John F. Kennedy, President,* pp. 230–31.

22. Kennedy, *Public Papers: 1961,* p. 533.

23. Ibid., p. 534.

24. Ibid.

25. Ibid., pp. 536–37.

26. Ibid., p. 538.

27. Ibid., p. 539.

28. Schlesinger, *A Thousand Days,* pp. 364–65.

29. Ibid., p. 367.

30. Sidey, *John F. Kennedy, President,* p. 245.

31. Ibid., p. 238.

32. Walton, *Cold War and Counterrevolution,* p. 92.

33. Schlesinger, *A Thousand Days,* p. 372. Significantly, once the atmosphere of crisis had vanished, the Kennedy Administration was able to conduct Berlin negotiations in a more moderate and conciliatory fashion. By the spring of 1962, the United States was displaying far more interest in reaching a Berlin settlement than either its French

or West German allies. Kennedy could pursue realistic diplomacy—
when he was not imprisoned by the atmosphere of crisis.

34. For the "insiders' " account of the Cuban missile crisis, see
Robert F. Kennedy, *Thirteen Days: A Memoir of the Cuban Missile Crisis*
(New York: Signet, 1969); Roger Hilsman, *To Move a Nation* (New
York: Delta, 1967); Sorensen, *Kennedy;* Schlesinger, *A Thousand Days.*
For detailed studies by writers with an orthodox (pro-Kennedy) view
of the crisis, see Henry M. Pachter, *Collision Course* (New York: Praeger,
1963); Elie Abel, *The Missile Crisis* (New York: Bantam, 1966); Gra-
ham T. Allison, *Essence of Decision: Explaining the Cuban Missile Crisis*
(Boston: Little, Brown, 1971). For critical views of Kennedy's actions,
see I. F. Stone, *In a Time of Torment* (New York: Vintage, 1968); Ronald
Steel, *Imperialists and Other Heroes: A Chronicle of the American Empire*
(New York: Random House, 1971); David Horowitz, *The Free World
Colossus* (New York: Hill & Wang, 1971); Louise FitzSimons, *The
Kennedy Doctrine* (New York: Random House, 1972); Walton, *Cold War
and Counterrevolution.*

35. Horowitz, *The Free World Colossus,* pp. 363–64.

36. See Hilsman, *To Move a Nation,* pp. 163–64.

37. Ibid., p. 164.

38. Horowitz, *The Free World Colossus,* p. 365.

39. John F. Kennedy, *Public Papers: 1962* (Washington, D.C.:
Government Printing Office, 1963), p. 190. Sorensen freely admitted
the importance of nonmilitary factors: "Political factors entered in,
worldwide as well as domestic political factors. I think, probably,
whatever that analysis [of the Soviet test series] had shown, the President was leaning toward a resumption of atmospheric tests on the
ground that his posture as the political leader of the free world and the
U. S. did not permit him to do anything else." Theodore C. Sorensen,
Oral History Interview, 15 April 1964, Kennedy Library, p. 78.

40. The analogy between the two situations has been noted by
Horowitz, *The Free World Colossus,* pp. 373–74; and Abel, *The Missile
Crisis,* pp. 38–39.

41. Of the studies cited above (note 34), Hilsman, Abel (in part),
Allison, Stone, Steel, Horowitz, and FitzSimons all share the view that
the Soviet move was primarily based upon strategic considerations.

42. Sorensen, *Kennedy,* p. 756.

43. Kennedy, *Public Papers: 1962,* p. 674.

44. Hilsman, *To Move a Nation,* p. 172.

45. Sidey, *John F. Kennedy, President,* p. vi.

46. Abel, *The Missile Crisis,* p. 46.

47. Sorensen, *Kennedy,* pp. 762–64.

48. Ibid., p. 764.

49. Ibid., pp. 769–70.

50. Schlesinger, *A Thousand Days,* p. 741.

51. Ibid., pp. 734–35.

52. Quoted in Sorensen, *Kennedy,* p. 772. Also see Robert F. Kennedy, *Thirteen Days,* pp. 38–39.

53. Sorensen, *Kennedy,* p. 776.

54. See, for example, Pachter, *Collision Course,* pp. 86–87.

55. Kennedy, *Public Papers: 1962,* p. 807.

56. Ibid.

57. Sorensen, *Kennedy,* p. 795.

58. Kennedy, *Public Papers: 1962,* p. 898.

59. Pachter, *Collision Course,* p. 84. Also see Stone, *In a Time of Torment,* pp. 19–20. Metaphors of toughness were common among the Kennedy insiders during the crisis. There was, for example, Dean Rusk's remark when the Russians failed to challenge the American naval blockade: "We're eyeball to eyeball and I think the other fellow just blinked." Quoted in Abel, *The Missile Crisis,* p. 134.

60. Such a line of interpretation was advanced during the crisis by *New York Times* analyst C. L. Sulzberger. The day after Kennedy's "quarantine" speech, Sulzberger wrote in the *Times:* "The new trend in United States policy . . . has now culminated in a showdown with Russia. That is the real meaning of the Cuban crisis. President Kennedy decided to move against Khrushchev's cold war offensive at a time and place of his own choosing . . . Washington seems to feel that this is the time to check and reverse Khrushchev's cold war offensive. We have opted to force the issue ourselves without prior approval of our allies." Quoted in Horowitz, *The Free World Colossus,* p. 382. Variants of this argument can also be found in Pachter, *Collision Course,* pp. 52–53; and Walt W. Rostow, *View From the Seventh Floor* (New York: Harper & Row, 1964), pp. 9–10.

61. Abel, *The Missile Crisis,* p. 158.

62. Ibid., p. 148.

63. Quoted in ibid., p. 161.

64. Kennedy, *Thirteen Days,* p. 94.

65. Ibid., p. 109.

66. Quoted in Abel, *The Missile Crisis,* p. 172.

67. Louise FitzSimons argues that if Kennedy had handled the situation differently from the outset he may not have suffered at all in the upcoming elections: "He could have told the people that the missiles were not a new and unprecedented threat. By a careful leading of public opinion, he might have made the country understand that the main difference was that we now were in a position similar to that of the Europeans, who had lived for years with Soviet short-range missiles next door. . . . There would have been some partisan objection. Yet a sober, reasonable, responsible President, who had refused to risk nuclear war unless the republic's survival was truly at stake, would have afforded a sharp and effective contrast to shrill opposition warmongering." FitzSimons, *The Kennedy Doctrine,* pp. 171–72.

68. Kennedy, *Thirteen Days,* p. 109.

69. Kennedy, *Public Papers: 1962,* p. 815. As we saw in the last chapter, Kennedy would not be adverse later on to claiming an American victory in the missile crisis.

70. Stone, *In a Time of Torment,* p. 18.

71. Schlesinger, *A Thousand Days,* p. 769.

72. Nixon, it should be noted, had more reason than Kennedy to believe that the Russians would not challenge his blockade. For he was, at that moment, engaged in negotiating with the Soviet Union agreements on arms limitations, trade, and credits. For their abandonment of their North Vietnamese allies, the Soviets were apparently to be well rewarded. See I. F. Stone, "Why Nixon Won His Moscow Gamble," *New York Review of Books* 18 (15 June 1972): 9–10.

73. Sorensen, *Kennedy,* p. 822.

74. John F. Kennedy, *Public Papers: 1963* (Washington, D.C.: Government Printing Office, 1964), p. 461.

75. Ibid., p. 462.

76. Ibid., p. 602.

77. Ibid., pp. 602–3.

78. Ibid., p. 524.

79. Schlesinger, *A Thousand Days,* p. 836. There is little reason to doubt Khrushchev's eagerness for détente. It was a goal he had been intermittently pursuing for at least five years. Now it made even greater sense than previously. Khrushchev's gamble to redress the strategic imbalance at minimum expense by placing IRBMs in Cuba had failed; creation of an atmosphere of détente promised to safeguard Russian security at even less cost, thereby permitting a badly needed redirection of resources to the domestic economy. Further, a détente with the United States aided Khrushchev in the bitter ideological struggle with China; the test-ban treaty was heralded as a victory for his line of "peaceful coexistence."

80. Sorensen, Oral History Interview, pp. 85–86.

81. The analysis which follows draws heavily upon a brilliant article by I. F. Stone, "The Test Ban Comedy," *New York Review of Books* 14 (7 May 1970): 14–22. Italics in original.

82. Ibid., p. 15.

83. Ibid., pp. 17–18.

84. Schlesinger, *A Thousand Days,* p. 833.

85. Stone, "The Test Ban Comedy," p. 21.

86. Kennedy, *Public Papers: 1963,* p. 694.

87. Ibid., p. 709.

88. Ibid., pp. 727–28.

89. Ibid., p. 796.

90. Ibid., p. 876.

91. Ibid., p. 894.

Chapter 4   *GLOBAL LIBERALISM*

1. John F. Kennedy, *The Strategy of Peace* (New York: Popular Library, 1961), p. 92.

2. Ibid., p. 93.

3. John F. Kennedy, *Public Papers: 1961* (Washington, D.C.: Government Printing Office, 1962), p. 172.

4. Ibid., p. 175.

5. Ronald Steel, *Pax Americana* (New York: Viking Press, 1967), pp. 215–16.

6. Kennedy, *Public Papers: 1961,* pp. 10–11. Kennedy's foes in the Third World—e.g., Castro and the Viet Cong—were frequently characterized as puppets. But the CIA-organized Cuban invasion force or the Ngo Dinh Diem regime set up and financed by the United States were lauded for their independence and commitment to self-determination. For men as deeply immersed in the Cold War as Kennedy, it seemed both a psychological and ideological necessity to project onto one's enemies one's own manipulations.

7. This was true even of Arthur Schlesinger, Jr., who had been opposed to the invasion scheme from the beginning. He thought it a bad idea, but "not because the notion of sponsoring an exile attempt to overthrow Castro seemed intolerable in itself. As my memorandum said, 'If we could achieve this by a swift, surgical stroke, I would be for it.' " Arthur Schlesinger, Jr., *A Thousand Days: John F. Kennedy in the White House* (Greenwich, Conn.: Fawcett, 1967), p. 237. Schlesinger's opposition was that of the good pragmatist—the plan was, by his analysis, simply impractical.

8. Ibid., p. 243.

9. Ibid., p. 251.

10. Kennedy, *Public Papers: 1961,* p. 304.

11. Ibid., pp. 548–49.

12. Ibid., p. 549.

13. John F. Kennedy, *Public Papers: 1963* (Washington, D.C.: Government Printing Office, 1964), p. 617.

14. Ibid., p. 873.

15. Susanne J. Bodenheimer, *The Ideology of Developmentalism: The American Paradigm-Surrogate for Latin-American Studies* (Beverly Hills, Calif.: Sage Publications, 1971), p. 13.

16. See Jerome Levinson and Juan de Onis, *The Alliance That Lost Its Way* (Chicago: Quadrangle, 1970), pp. 8–13. Lyndon Johnson and his chief Latin American aide, Thomas C. Mann, shifted the emphasis of the Alliance away from social reform toward a narrow concern with economic development. They also abandoned Kennedy's notion of "democratic revolution" and adopted a hard-line anticommunist

stand that included overt acceptance of military dictatorships. Part of the weakness of the Alliance after 1963 can be attributed to this Johnson-Mann line. Yet it would be wrong to shift most of the blame for the Alliance off of Kennedy and onto Johnson; its pattern of failure was already set, as this chapter demonstrates, in the Kennedy Administration.

17. Tad Szulc, *The Winds of Revolution: Latin America Today—and Tomorrow* (New York: Praeger, 1965), p. 239. For a statement of the same complaint by a former Alliance official, see Herbert K. May, *Problems and Prospects of the Alliance for Progress* (New York: Praeger, 1968), pp. 71–76.

18. Kennedy, *Public Papers: 1961,* p. 814.

19. John F. Kennedy, *Public Papers: 1962* (Washington, D.C.: Government Printing Office, 1963), p. 223.

20. Kennedy, *Public Papers: 1963,* p. 184.

21. Kennedy, *Public Papers: 1961,* p. 814.

22. Rodolfo Stavenhagen, "Seven Fallacies about Latin America," in *Latin America: Reform or Revolution?,* ed. James Petras and Maurice Zeitlin (Greenwich, Conn.: Fawcett, 1968), p. 25. For related comments on the political role of the middle class, see Jose Nun, "A Latin American Phenomenon: The Middle Class Military Coup," and Glaucio Ary Dillon Soares, "The New Industrialization and the Brazilian Political System," both in the same volume. Dillon Soares notes the overwhelming support given by Brazil's middle class to the 1964 coup that established a military dictatorship.

23. Kennedy's reactions to military coups often revealed a great deal about the kind of Latin American leadership for which he hoped. When the Peruvian military intervened in July 1962 to prevent Haya de la Torre, winner in a disputed election, from assuming power, Kennedy angrily broke off relations with Peru. Haya de la Torre, thirty years before a fiery nationalist, was now backed by the business oligarchy and overtly friendly to the United States. He told John Gerassi in an interview: "Imperialism is a form of development in underdeveloped countries. Imperialism is necessary for Latin America's development." John Gerassi, *The Great Fear in Latin America* (New York: Collier, 1965), p. 137.

In March 1963 the Guatemalan military ousted the conservative government of Manuel Ydígoras. The immediate cause, according to observers, was Ydígoras's decision to permit former President Juan Arevalo to return from exile and begin campaigning in the upcoming elections. Arevalo, who had initiated the reformist era in Guatemalan history which the military and CIA had terminated in 1954, was expected to win the Presidency with labor-left support. The new military junta canceled the elections; Washington gladly went along. As Levinson and de Onis comment, "the Kennedy Administration would not risk its prestige and influence on a reformist leader whose political base seemed too radical, even if the only alternative was a right-wing military regime." *The Alliance That Lost Its Way,* pp. 83–85. On the Guatemalan coup, also see Edwin Lieuwen, *Generals Vs. Presidents: Neomilitarism in Latin America* (New York: Praeger, 1964), pp. 37–45, 117–18.

24. Oscar Delgado, "Revolution, Reform, Conservatism," in Petras and Zeitlin, *Latin America: Reform or Revolution?,* p. 390

25. Gerassi's *The Great Fear in Latin America* presents a damning indictment of Betancourt. For his discussion of repression under Betancourt, see pp. 155–66. Robert J. Alexander defends Betancourt's record on civil liberties in *The Venezuelan Democratic Revolution: A Profile of the Regime of Rómulo Betancourt* (New Brunswick, N.J.: Rutgers University Press, 1964), pp. 118–35. Alexander admits Betancourt's suspensions of civil liberties but justifies them on the grounds that his leftist enemies refused to confine themselves to constitutional methods and the role of a "loyal opposition."

26. Steel, *Pax Americana,* p. 217.

27. Schlesinger, *A Thousand Days,* p. 699. The architects of the Alliance certainly did not fear the word "revolution"; instead, they used it in ways that were sometimes perverse. Thus, for Lincoln Gordon, Kennedy's Ambassador to Brazil, the 1964 military coup which overthrew the "leftist" Goulart was a genuine revolution. "In Brazil I would say that the Alliance for Progress may have come alive, not of course with the death of Kennedy but with the revolution." Lincoln Gordon, Oral History Interview, 30 May 1964, Kennedy Library, pp. 70–83.

28. Delgado, "Revolution, Reform, Conservatism," pp. 384–94.

29. The source of this story is Charles Burrows, American Ambassador to Honduras under Kennedy. Charles Burrows, Oral History Interview, 4 September 1969, Kennedy Library, pp. 5–16.

30. Lieuwen, *Generals Vs. Presidents,* p. 124.

31. Szulc, *The Winds of Revolution,* p. 21. Also see Lieuwen, *Generals Vs. Presidents,* pp. 124–26.

32. James Petras, "Revolution and Guerrilla Movements in Latin America: Venezuela, Colombia, Guatemala, and Peru," in Petras and Zeitlin, *Latin America: Reform or Revolution?,* p. 350.

33. On the civic-action program, see Michael T. Klare, *War Without End: American Planning for the Next Vietnams* (New York: Vintage, 1972), pp. 287–95. President Kennedy was highly enthusiastic about the concept of civic action. Much of that enthusiasm may have come from listening to General Maxwell Taylor, who had experimented with civic action in Korea, and who remained one of its leading advocates.

34. Lieuwen, *Generals Vs. Presidents,* p. 127.

35. Robert A. Hurwitch, Oral History Interview, 24 April 1964, Kennedy Library, p. 179.

36. Schlesinger, *A Thousand Days*, p. 717.

37. Quoted in Gerassi, *The Great Fear in Latin America*, p. 277.

38. Walt W. Rostow, *The Stages of Economic Growth: A Non-Communist Manifesto* (New York: Cambridge University Press, 1960), p. 139.

39. Ibid., p. 162.

40. Ibid., p. 156.

41. Teotonio Dos Santos, "The Changing Structure of Foreign Investment in Latin America," in Petras and Zeitlin, *Latin America: Reform or Revolution?*, p. 97.

42. This figure is from the May 1963 report of the United Nations Economic Commission for Latin America, cited in David Horowitz, *The Free World Colossus* (New York: Hill & Wang, 1971), p. 228.

43. Levinson and de Onis, *The Alliance That Lost Its Way*, p. 144.

44. See Harry Magdoff, *The Age of Imperialism* (New York: Monthly Review Press, 1969), pp. 142–48.

45. Levinson and de Onis, *The Alliance That Lost Its Way*, pp. 138–39.

46. Ibid., pp. 134–36.

47. Schlesinger, *A Thousand Days*, p. 724.

48. Kennedy, *Public Papers: 1963*, p. 299.

49. Ibid., p. 875.

50. Phillip Chodur brought this Kennedy letter to my attention. A copy of it can be found in the Lyndon B. Johnson Library, White House Central File: Executive FO 3-2-1, 22 November 1963–30 May 1964. David Rockefeller sent the copy to President Johnson in beginning a similar correspondence. At Rockefeller's urging, Johnson met with members of the Business Group in January 1964.

51. Richard J. Walton, *Cold War and Counterrevolution: The Foreign Policy of John F. Kennedy* (New York: Viking Press, 1972), p. 162.

52. Kennedy, *Public Papers: 1962*, p. 210; *Public Papers: 1963*, pp. 324, 894.

53. Kennedy, *Public Papers: 1963*, p. 501.

54. Modernization and counterinsurgency were closely interwoven in New Frontier ideology. Walt W. Rostow was a key figure here in establishing the linkage. The Administration's leading theoretician of economic development and modernization, Rostow was also one of its most fervent proponents of counterinsurgency. He considered counterinsurgency an integral branch of modernization; hence, he told a graduating class of Green Berets at Fort Bragg in 1961: "Your job is to work with understanding with your fellow citizens in the whole creative process of modernization. From our perspective in Washington you take your place side by side with those others who are committed to help fashion independent, modern societies out of the

revolutionary process now going forward. I salute you as I would a group of doctors, teachers, economic planners, agricultural experts, civil servants, or those others who are now leading the way in fashioning new nations and societies." Walt W. Rostow, "Guerrilla Warfare in Underdeveloped Areas," in *The Viet Nam Reader*, ed. Marcus G. Raskin and Bernard B. Fall (New York: Vintage, 1965), pp. 115–16.

55. Quoted in Klare, *War Without End*, pp. 40–41.

56. Kennedy stated, in a speech at Philadelphia on 30 October 1963, that military growth during his administration had been as follows: 100% in available nuclear weapons, 45% in combat-ready Army divisions, 175% in airlift aircraft, 500% in counterinsurgency forces. Kennedy, *Public Papers: 1963*, p. 823.

57. Ibid., p. 98.

58. Quoted in Klare, *War Without End*, p. 49.

59. Robert S. McNamara, "Response to Aggression," in Raskin and Fall, *The Viet Nam Reader*, p. 197. The authors of the Pentagon Papers themselves use the test-case notion. "Vietnam was the only place in the world where the Administration faced a well-developed Communist effort to topple a pro-Western government with an externally aided pro-Communist insurgency. It was a challenge that could hardly be ignored." Neil Sheehan et al., *The Pentagon Papers* (New York: Bantam, 1971), pp. 87–88.

60. Schlesinger, *A Thousand Days*, p. 497.

61. Sheehan et al., *The Pentagon Papers*, p. 88.

62. Ibid.

63. Ibid., p. 90.

64. Ibid., p. 91.

65. Ibid. Italics added.

66. Staley is another example of the confluence of modernizing and counterinsurgency impulses on the New Frontier. This builder of strategic hamlets was the author of one of the standard texts on economic and social development, *The Future of Underdeveloped Countries* (New York: Praeger, 1961).

67. Ralph Stavins, "Washington Determines the Fate of Vietnam: 1954–1965," in Ralph Stavins, Richard J. Barnet, and Marcus G. Raskin, *Washington Plans an Aggressive War* (New York: Vintage, 1971), p. 39.

68. Sheehan et al., *The Pentagon Papers*, p. 143.

69. Ibid., p. 146.

70. Ibid., p. 145.

71. Ibid., p. 104.

72. Stavins, "Washington Determines the Fate of Vietnam," p. 51.

73. Cited in ibid., p. 50.

74. Sheehan et al., *The Pentagon Papers,* p. 149.

75. Ibid., p. 108.

76. Ibid., p. 107.

77. Theodore C. Sorensen, *Kennedy* (New York: Bantam, 1966), p. 739.

78. Stavins, "Washington Determines the Fate of Vietnam," p. 54

79. Sheehan et al., *The Pentagon Papers,* p. 108.

80. Sorensen, *Kennedy,* p. 738. Ralph Stavins seeks to refute the notion that Kennedy was fighting an "unconventional" or "brushfire" war in Vietnam. But I find his arguments unpersuasive on this point. He notes that only a handful of advisers favored a counterinsurgency strategy (notably Hilsman and Thompson), while "the dominant positions in the Kennedy Administration were held by exponents of conventional war." Stavins, "Washington Determines the Fate of Vietnam," p. 83. The problem with this argument is that it ignores Kennedy's own passion for counterinsurgency—e.g., his far greater interest than, say Rusk and McNamara in the strategic hamlets. Stavins also focuses on the Kennedy Administration's employment of heavy firepower in Vietnam as a signpost of conventional warfare. But his distinctions regarding weaponry are somewhat overprecise; the use of armed helicopters, which he cites as a mark of conventional warfare, fits perfectly well with a counterinsurgency strategy. Certainly Vietnam was not a case of a "pure" counterinsurgency campaign, whatever that might mean; still, despite elements of conventional warfare, it remained, at least for President Kennedy, essentially an exercise in "unconventional" warfare.

81. Roger Hilsman, *To Move a Nation* (New York: Delta, 1967), p. 426.

82. Sheehan et al., *The Pentagon Papers,* p. 110.

83. George McTurnan Kahin and John W. Lewis, *The United States in Vietnam* (New York: Delta, 1967), p. 139.

84. Stavins, "Washington Determines the Fate of Vietnam," p. 71.

85. Pierre Salinger, *With Kennedy* (New York: Avon, 1967), p. 398.

86. Ibid., p. 399.

87. The proponents of the strategic-hamlet system were confident that theirs was the correct strategy for Vietnam, since a similar strategy had defeated communist insurgents in Malaya. But as a study by Milton Osborne (cited in Kahin and Lewis, *The United States in Vietnam,* pp. 140–41) has shown, the Malayan experience was not really analogous to the situation in Vietnam. In Malaya the British had relocated recently settled Chinese squatters, with few ties to the land. In Vietnam, on the other hand, it was a case of compelling indigenous peasants to vacate their ancestral homes; not surprisingly, there was considerable resentment generated toward the Diem regime. The New

Frontiersmen's ignorance of Asian conditions, and their excitement over their own bold theories, were far more evident here (as throughout the planning for Vietnam) than their supposed objectivity.

88. Hilsman, *To Move a Nation,* pp. 431–32.

89. Kahin and Lewis, *The United States in Vietnam,* p. 140.

90. The creators of the strategic-hamlet program were not adverse to portraying themselves as founders of political freedom. Here is Roger Hilsman, approvingly citing R. K. G. Thompson: "A strategic hamlet program of this kind, Thompson argued, could create the physical security the villager must have before he could make a free choice between the Viet Cong and the government. The primary role of the strategic hamlet was to provide that free choice." Hilsman, *To Move a Nation,* p. 432. Neither Thompson nor Hilsman ever explained what would happen if a villager chose the Viet Cong—though the consequences are not hard to guess.

91. Stavins, "Washington Determines the Fate of Vietnam," p. 67.

92. Hilsman, *To Move a Nation,* p. 456. Also see pp. 464–65.

93. Kennedy, *Public Papers: 1963,* p. 11.

94. Ibid., p. 652.

95. Ibid.

96. Ibid., p. 659.

97. Ibid., p. 660.

98. Ibid., p. 673.

99. See Stavins, "Washington Determines the Fate of Vietnam," pp. 93–94.

Chapter 5 *CORPORATE POWER AND THE "NEW ECONOMICS"*

1. Arthur Schlesinger, Jr., *A Thousand Days: John F. Kennedy in the White House* (Greenwich, Conn.: Fawcett, 1967), p. 579.

2. Theodore C. Sorensen, *Kennedy* (New York: Bantam, 1966), p. 441.

3. Ibid., p. 208.

4. Bernard D. Nossiter, *The Mythmakers: An Essay on Power and Wealth* (Boston: Beacon Press, 1967), pp. 8–9.

5. The sharpest of the critics was Oscar Gass. For his comments on these early months, see "Political Economy and the New Administration," *Commentary* 31 (April 1961): 277–87.

6. John F. Kennedy, *Public Papers: 1961* (Washington, D.C.: Government Printing Office, 1962), p. 86.

7. Ibid., p. 87.

8. See Jim F. Heath, *John F. Kennedy and the Business Community* (Chicago: University of Chicago Press, 1969), pp. 42–44. Heath's book contains a useful compendium of business reactions to the Kennedy Administration.

9. Quoted in Nossiter, *The Mythmakers,* p. 33. For an excellent account of Kennedy's 1961 tax reforms and their subsequent fate, see Nossiter, pp. 28–34.

10. See Heath, *John F. Kennedy and the Business Community,* 29–30.

11. Ibid., p. 30.

12. Walter W. Heller, *New Dimensions of Political Economy* (New York: W. W. Norton, 1967), p. 43. Heller's book is more than a celebration of the "New Economics." It also celebrates the New Economist, whose expertise has become indispensable to Presidents, whose professional credentials, if mixed with a proper degree of pragmatist acuity, now lead directly to the centers of political power.

13. Nossiter, *The Mythmakers,* p. 17.

14. President Kennedy had strong words of criticism for unions that spoke the language of income redistribution. As Seymour E. Harris notes, Kennedy argued that "fights to secure a larger slice of the economic pie 'by forcing wages up ahead of productivity can only weaken our efforts to expand the economy.'" Seymour E. Harris, *Economics of the Kennedy Years* (New York: Harper & Row, 1964), pp. 140–41.

15. Nossiter, *The Mythmakers,* p. 16.

16. Sorensen, *Kennedy,* p. 501.

17. Ibid., p. 502.

18. John F. Kennedy, *Public Papers: 1962* (Washington, D.C.: Government Printing Office, 1963), pp. 315–16.

19. Ibid., p. 331.

20. Sorensen, *Kennedy,* p. 516.

21. Grant McConnell, *Steel and the Presidency, 1962* (New York: W. W. Norton, 1963), p. 114.

22. Kennedy, *Public Papers: 1962,* p. 422.

23. Ibid., pp. 470–71.

24. Ibid., p. 473.

25. Ibid.

26. Nossiter, *The Mythmakers,* p. x.

27. Edmund S. Phelps, *The Goal of Economic Growth* (New York: W. W. Norton, 1962), p. viii.

28. Gabriel Kolko, *Wealth and Power in America: An Analysis of Social Class and Income Distribution* (New York: Praeger, 1962), p. 13.

29. Schlesinger, *A Thousand Days,* p. 595.

30. In this attempt to conciliate business Kennedy was following a

long-standing Democratic tradition. Woodrow Wilson, for example, had charted an identical course during the economic recession of 1913–14. As Arthur S. Link recounts: "In the spring of 1914 the President embarked upon a campaign calculated to win the friendship of businessmen and bankers and to ease the tension that had existed between the administration and the business community. The accommodation of the anti-trust program to the desires of the business world was the first step, along with Wilson's repeated expressions of confidence in and friendship for businessmen. Next the President began to welcome bankers and business leaders to the White House. . . . Wilson climaxed his little campaign to win the friendship of the business classes by turning over control of the Federal Reserve Board, in effect, to their representatives, as if he were trying to prove the sincerity of his recent professions." Arthur S. Link, *Woodrow Wilson and the Progressive Era, 1910–1917* (New York: Harper Torchbooks, 1963), pp. 75–76.

31. Sorensen, *Kennedy,* p. 450.

32. The figures are from ibid.

33. According to Senator George McGovern, "because of steady reductions in the taxable base over the past twenty years, the effective corporation income tax rate has been cut in half." To restore a balance between personal and corporate taxation, McGovern proposed that "the actual corporation income tax be returned to its 1960 level by the elimination of the special loopholes that have been opened since then." George McGovern, "On Taxing and Redistributing Income," *New York Review of Books* 18 (4 May 1972): 8.

34. See Heath, *John F. Kennedy and the Business Community,* pp. 75–76; Sorensen, *Kennedy,* pp. 522–23; Schlesinger, *A Thousand Days,* p. 598.

35. John F. Kennedy, *Public Papers: 1963* (Washington, D.C.: Government Printing Office, 1964), p. 69.

36. Ibid., p. 214.

37. Sorensen, *Kennedy,* p. 460.

38. Kennedy, *Public Papers: 1962,* p. 14.

39. Ibid., pp. 69–74. In characterizing a burgeoning foreign trade as a decisive factor in America's future prosperity and political health, Kennedy was echoing a long line of American leaders. For a seminal treatment of the role of foreign trade and overseas economic expansion in American political thinking since the 1890s, see William Appleman Williams, *The Tragedy of American Diplomacy* (New York: Delta, 1962).

40. Schlesinger, *A Thousand Days,* p. 774.

41. Spokesmen for industries particularly fearful of tariff reduction continued to oppose the bill—but "most of the special interest lobbying in 1962 was for trade liberalization, not protection." Ray-

mond A. Bauer, Ithiel de Sola Pool, and Lewis Anthony Dexter, *American Business and Public Policy: The Politics of Foreign Trade* (New York: Atherton Press, 1963), p. 422.

42. According to Sorensen, Kennedy did express an interest in such restrictions, but was held back by resistance within his administration, particularly from the Treasury Department. Sorensen, *Kennedy*, pp. 457–59. While internal opposition may have influenced him on this issue, Kennedy could hardly have been unaware of the potential for political controversy in any proposal to limit corporate investments abroad.

43. Kennedy, *Public Papers: 1961*, p. 777; *Public Papers: 1962*, p. 350.

44. Harris, *Economics of the Kennedy Years*, p. 174.

45. See Sorensen, *Kennedy*, pp. 525–26; Nossiter, *The Mythmakers*, pp. 21–22.

46. Kennedy, *Public Papers: 1962*, p. 352.

47. John Kenneth Galbraith, *The New Industrial State* (Boston: Houghton Mifflin, 1967), pp. 74–75.

48. Kennedy, *Public Papers: 1961*, p. 708.

49. Quoted in Schlesinger, *A Thousand Days*, p. 588.

50. Nossiter, *The Mythmakers*, p. 41. At times Kennedy perceived the flaw in his conciliatory posture. Schlesinger recounts that the President confided to journalist Hugh Sidey: " 'I think maybe I ought to get a little tougher with business. I think that may be the way to treat them. They understand it. When I'm nice to them, they just kick me. I think I'll just treat them rougher. Maybe it will do some good.' " But Kennedy never followed through on this insight; as Schlesinger notes, "publicly he continued to be nice." Schlesinger, *A Thousand Days*, p. 589.

51. Quoted in Sorensen, *Kennedy*, p. 521.

52. The economic advantages that business derived from Kennedy's policies were more apparent to the corporate community by the time Johnson took office. In this regard Kennedy's suffering at the hands of business cleared the way for his successor's easy treatment. But the vastly different emotional reactions to the two Presidents on the part of businessmen cannot be accounted for simply on the basis of their growing economic sophistication. Political imagery played a vital part; the same particulars of Johnson's public personality and style that alienated Kennedy liberals endeared him to the business community.

53. See David T. Bazelon, *The Paper Economy* (New York: Vintage, 1965), pp. 221–28; and Grant McConnell, *Private Power and American Democracy* (New York: Vintage, 1970), pp. 129–34, 249–54.

54. William D. Phelan, Jr., "The 'Complex' Society Marches On," *Ripon Forum* 5 (January 1969): 9–20. Also see Richard J. Barnet,

The Economy of Death (New York: Atheneum, 1969), pp. 79–125.

55. Gabriel Kolko, *The Triumph of Conservatism: A Reinterpretation of American History, 1900–1916* (Chicago: Quadrangle, 1967). Support for Kolko's thesis is provided by James Weinstein, *The Corporate Ideal in the Liberal State: 1900–1918* (Boston: Beacon Press, 1968), which analyses this period along similar lines, though with more attention paid to corporate ideology. In contrast, Robert H. Wiebe's *Businessmen and Reform: A Study of the Progressive Movement* (Cambridge, Mass.: Harvard University Press, 1962) emphasizes the fact that different sectors of business divided on almost every issue in the Progressive era, that to understand the nature of Progressive policies one must take into account the splits between eastern and midwestern and between giant and middle-size businesses in these years. Yet Wiebe, too, concludes that "in all, the business community was the most important single factor—or set of factors—in the development of economic regulation. And a significant portion of this influence supported reform." Wiebe, *Businessmen and Reform,* p. 217.

56. Nossiter, *The Mythmakers,* pp. 6–7, 13–17, 24–42.

57. Sorensen, *Kennedy,* p. 493.

58. Ibid., p. 477.

59. Heller, *New Dimensions of Political Economy,* pp. 61–62. Italics in original.

60. Ibid., p. 39.

61. Schlesinger, *A Thousand Days,* p. 914.

62. Ibid., p. 596.

63. Ibid., pp. 596–97.

64. Kennedy, *Public Papers: 1962,* p. 877.

65. Ibid., p. 879.

66. Sorensen, *Kennedy,* p. 483.

67. Ibid., p. 482.

68. Kennedy, *Public Papers: 1963,* p. 12.

69. Ibid.

70. Ibid., p. 13.

71. Ibid., pp. 61–63.

72. For the Administration's Keynesian reasoning and calculations, see *Economic Report of the President with Annual Report of the Council of Economic Advisers, 1963* (Washington, D.C.: Government Printing Office, 1963), pp. 43–52.

73. Robert Lekachman, *The Age of Keynes* (New York: Vintage, 1968), pp. 277–78.

74. Kennedy, *Public Papers: 1963,* p. 62.

75. Nossiter, *The Mythmakers,* pp. 35–36.

76. Lekachman, *The Age of Keynes,* p. 281.

77. Kennedy, *Public Papers: 1963,* p. 215.

78. Ibid., p. 308.

79. Ibid., p. 386.

80. Quoted in Nossiter, *The Mythmakers,* p. 41.

81. Kennedy, *Public Papers: 1963,* p. 863. Later in his speech Kennedy apprised the assembled Florida businessmen of whom to thank for their burgeoning prosperity: "The key to this prosperity has been the fiscal and monetary policies of the Kennedy Administration."

82. Schlesinger, *A Thousand Days,* p. 923.

83. Johnson was particularly enthusiastic about the War on Poverty concept because it was *not* associated with the Kennedy Administration; he wanted a large and dramatic poverty program in 1964 that would bear *his* distinctive imprimatur (even though it drew heavily on staff work done during the Kennedy Administration). See John C. Donovan, *The Politics of Poverty* (New York: Pegasus, 1967), pp. 17–38. Also see James L. Sundquist, *Politics and Policy: The Eisenhower, Kennedy, and Johnson Years* (Washington, D.C.: Brookings Institution, 1968), pp. 111–54.

84. The GNP figures for 1961–63 are from the *Economic Report of the President with Annual Report of the Council of Economic Advisers, 1964* (Washington, D.C.: Government Printing Office, 1964), p. 34. The figures for 1964–65 come from the *Economic Report of the President with Annual Report of the Council of Economic Advisers, 1973* (Washington, D.C.: Government Printing Office, 1973), pp. 193–95.

85. The figures are from the *Economic Report, 1964,* pp. 35–36.

86. *Economic Report of the President with Annual Report of the Council of Economic Advisers, 1966* (Washington, D.C.: Government Printing Office, 1966), pp. 3, 7.

87. *Economic Report, 1973,* p. 37.

88. C. Douglas Dillon, quoted in Schlesinger, *A Thousand Days,* p. 924.

89. Quoted in Lekachman, *The Age of Keynes,* p. 270.

90. Ibid.

91. Ibid., p. 294.

92. Ibid., p. 301.

Chapter 6 **"LISTEN, MR. KENNEDY":**
        THE CIVIL RIGHTS STRUGGLE

1. Theodore C. Sorensen, *Kennedy* (New York: Bantam, 1966), p. 529.

2. See James MacGregor Burns, *John Kennedy: A Political Profile* (New York: Harcourt, Brace & World, 1961), pp. 200–204. Kennedy voted in favor of the "jury trial amendment" to the 1957 Civil Rights Act. This amendment, by providing a jury trial in criminal contempt cases involving voting rights, vitiated the possibility of obtaining convictions in the South.

3. David L. Lewis, *King: A Critical Biography* (Baltimore: Penguin, 1971), p. 124.

4. Harris Wofford, Oral History Interview, 29 November 1965, Kennedy Library, pp. 7–8.

5. Theodore C. Sorensen, Oral History Interview, 3 May 1964, Kennedy Library, p. 120.

6. Theodore H. White, *The Making of the President, 1960* (New York: Signet, 1967), pp. 363–64. John Kennedy personally called Coretta King, then six months' pregnant, to tell her that he was endeavoring to help her husband, who faced the prospect of four months' hard labor at Reidsville State Prison in rural Georgia. Robert Kennedy phoned the judge in the case to request bail; the next day King was released. For an interesting account of the affair, see Lewis, *King*, pp. 126–29.

7. Quoted in Harry Golden, *Mr. Kennedy and the Negroes* (Greenwich, Conn.: Fawcett, 1964), p. 125.

8. Victor S. Navasky, *Kennedy Justice* (New York: Atheneum, 1971), p. 97.

9. James MacGregor Burns, Oral History Interview, 14 May 1965, Kennedy Library, p. 71.

10. The importance of these splits in the civil rights movement was pointed out to me by Victor Navasky.

11. Navasky, *Kennedy Justice*, p. 98.

12. Harris Wofford, Oral History Interview, 22 May 1968, Kennedy Library, p. 58.

13. While the Kennedy Administration continued to issue its statistics showing impressive gains in black employment in the federal government, by 1963 the accelerating thrust of the civil rights movement had caused some New Frontiersmen to reexamine their own achievements. According to Burke Marshall, Robert Kennedy (and others in the Justice Department) discovered at that point that the federal government still possessed a rather poor record on equal employment, that many federal agencies still employed very few blacks. Burke Marshall, Oral History Interview, 19–20 January 1970, Kennedy Library, p. 24.

14. Quoted in Howard Zinn, *SNCC: The New Abolitionists* (Boston: Beacon Press, 1965), p. 44.

15. Zinn's *SNCC* presents a strong account of the freedom rides; see pp. 40–57. A chronology of the rides is contained in Louis E. Lomax, *The Negro Revolt* (New York: Signet, 1963), pp. 147–56.

16. John F. Kennedy, *Public Papers: 1961* (Washington, D.C.: Government Printing Office, 1962), p. 391.

17. Wofford, Oral History Interview, pp. 66–68.

18. Kennedy, *Public Papers: 1961,* p. 517.

19. John F. Kennedy, *Public Papers: 1962* (Washington, D.C.: Government Printing Office, 1963), p. 21. The Kennedy Administra-

tion deserves credit for obtaining the ICC order. But a fair and accurate account required crediting the freedom riders too, for courageously exposing the conditions which made such an order necessary.

20. Navasky, *Kennedy Justice,* p. 21.

21. Zinn, *SNCC,* p. 59.

22. Pat Watters and Reese Cleghorn, *Climbing Jacob's Ladder: The Arrival of Negroes in Southern Politics* (New York: Harcourt, Brace & World, 1967), p. 58. Also see Navasky, *Kennedy Justice,* pp. 117–18. The SNCC activists thought the Justice Department had made protection part of the bargain. The Justice Department position later on was that no pledges had been given on the subject of protection. From the rather scanty evidence available, it is impossible to tell exactly who promised what; certainly SNCC *believed* protection had been promised, and the Justice Department did nothing at the time to counter that belief.

23. See Zinn, *SNCC,* pp. 58–59.

24. Arthur Schlesinger, Jr., makes the same point: "Negro voting did not incite social and sexual anxieties. . . ." Arthur Schlesinger, Jr., *A Thousand Days: John F. Kennedy in the White House* (Greenwich, Conn.: Fawcett, 1967), p. 853.

25. Ibid., p. 850.

26. Navasky, *Kennedy Justice,* pp. 192–93.

27. Quoted in Watters and Cleghorn, *Climbing Jacob's Ladder,* p. 213.

28. Navasky, *Kennedy Justice,* pp. 245–47. Also see Alexander Bickel, "Civil Rights: A New Era Opens," in *John F. Kennedy and the New Frontier,* ed. Aida DiPace Donald (New York: Hill & Wang, 1966), pp. 156–64.

29. Navasky, *Kennedy Justice,* p. 244.

30. Zinn, *SNCC,* p. 123.

31. Ibid., p. 127.

32. Navasky, *Kennedy Justice,* p. 205.

33. Ibid.

34. Sorensen, *Kennedy,* pp. 540–42. Civil rights supporters argued to Administration officials that the order had long been expected, even in the South, and would thus raise little controversy when issued.

35. Kennedy, *Public Papers: 1962,* p. 544.

36. Ibid., pp. 676–77.

37. Zinn, *SNCC,* p. 193.

38. On the Kennedy Justice Department's theory of federalism, see Navasky, *Kennedy Justice,* pp. 159–242, for a penetrating account and analysis. Navasky notes that while the Justice Department cited the necessity of deference to local officials on civil rights matters, it simultaneously asserted the primacy of federal action in its fervent campaign against organized crime.

39. See Watters and Cleghorn, *Climbing Jacob's Ladder,* pp. 55–58, 284–85. Ironically, after the process of disillusionment had long since set in, the Justice Department began to do haltingly what it before had said it lacked authority to do. For instance, the FBI arrested three white men in Itta Bena, Mississippi, in June 1964 for interfering with voter-registration workers; the arrests were made under Section 241, whose use the Justice Department had until then declined. Ibid., p. 228.

40. Kennedy, *Public Papers: 1962,* p. 702.

41. John F. Kennedy, *Public Papers: 1963* (Washington, D.C.: Government Printing Office, 1964), p. 160.

42. For a transcript of Robert Kennedy's frustrating and often ludicrous phone conversations with Ross Barnett, see Navasky, *Kennedy Justice,* pp. 165–66, 167–69, 178–81, 186–91, 199–204, 209–17, 223–25.

43. Lomax, *The Negro Revolt,* p. 255.

44. See Sorensen, *Kennedy,* p. 542.

45. Kennedy, *Public Papers: 1962,* pp. 831–32.

46. Quoted in Schlesinger, *A Thousand Days,* p. 867. While movement activists were unhappy with Kennedy's performance, many blacks outside the movement still placed great faith in Kennedy even in this period. What inspired that faith was not so much what Kennedy had already done for blacks, but the sense—perhaps deriving originally from the 1960 campaign—that at last a President was on their side.

47. Ibid. Italics added.

48. Kennedy, *Public Papers: 1963,* p. 222.

49. Schlesinger, *A Thousand Days,* p. 868.

50. Joseph L. Rauh, Jr., Oral History Interview, 23 December 1965, Kennedy Library, p. 106.

51. Memo from Burke Marshall to John Kennedy, 8 April 1963, Papers of Burke Marshall, Kennedy Library.

52. Reverend Theodore M. Hesburgh, Oral History Interview, 27 March 1966, Kennedy Library, p. 12. The Commission also suggested to the President a cutoff of federal funds to segregated programs in Mississippi—a recommendation Kennedy publicly repudiated.

53. Quoted in Sorensen, *Kennedy,* p. 549.

54. Martin Luther King, Jr., "Letter from Birmingham Jail," in *Freedom Now: The Civil Rights Struggle in America,* ed. Alan F. Westin (New York: Basic, 1964), p. 13. In the same letter King developed a powerful critique of white moderates. Although the specific target of his words here was white Birmingham clergy, the critique is not without relevance to Kennedy and his aides. "I must confess that over the last few years I have been gravely disappointed with the white moderate. I have almost reached the regrettable conclusion that the Negroes' great stumbling block in the stride toward freedom is not the

White Citizens' 'Councilor' or the Ku Klux Klanner, but the white moderate who is more devoted to 'order' than to justice; who prefers a negative peace which is the absence of tension to a positive peace which is the presence of justice; who constantly says, 'I agree with you in the goal you seek, but I can't agree with your methods of direct action'; who paternalistically feels that he can set the timetable for another man's freedom; who lives by the myth of time and who constantly advises the Negro to wait until a 'more convenient season.' " Ibid., p. 16.

55. Schlesinger, *A Thousand Days,* pp. 874–75.

56. For a fairly detailed account of the Birmingham conflict, see Lewis, *King,* pp. 171–209.

57. My analysis here owes a great deal to Rick Busacca, who showed me the depths of the Birmingham crisis.

58. Harold C. Fleming, "The Federal Executive and Civil Rights: 1961–1965," *Daedalus* 94 (Fall 1965): 943.

59. Kennedy, *Public Papers: 1963,* p. 407.

60. Ibid., p. 458.

61. Ibid., p. 469.

62. Ibid., p. 471.

63. Ibid., p. 484.

64. Ibid., p. 493. The importance Kennedy placed on these words is underlined by Sorensen's comment that "probably no paragraph in the message which he sent to the Congress was reworked more often —in consultation the night before it went up between the President and the Attorney General—than the paragraph which referred in general terms to civil rights demonstrations and acts of violence." Sorensen, Oral History Interview, pp. 141–42.

65. Schlesinger's words give credence to this interpretation. In writing of the events of May and June 1963, he states that "Kennedy now responded to the Negro revolution by seeking to assume its leadership." Schlesinger, *A Thousand Days,* p. 881.

66. Quoted in ibid., pp. 884–85.

67. Arthur I. Waskow, *From Race Riot to Sit-In: 1919 and the 1960's* (Garden City, N.Y.: Anchor, 1967), pp. 248–49.

68. Ibid., p. 250.

69. While most of the Administration's arguments against the subcommittee bill were based upon the dangers of congressional opposition, its case against Title 3 rested, not on a lack of votes, but on the Justice Department's continuing reluctance to possess the authority granted. Clarence Mitchell, Oral History Interview, 23 February 1967, Kennedy Library, pp. 41–42.

70. Quoted in Schlesinger, *A Thousand Days,* p. 888.

71. Waskow, *From Race Riot to Sit-In,* p. 251.

72. Kennedy, *Public Papers: 1963,* p. 572.

73. Ibid., pp. 572–73.

74. It would, of course, have been highly dramatic for President Kennedy to have addressed the marchers. His reasons for dismissing this possibility are interesting: "The President's feeling was that he did not want to address the march group itself because his political intuition told him that the chances of getting an adverse reaction from that kind of crowd are very great. And particularly if he made remarks—as a President must make his remarks—conform to a nationwide audience rather than to an immediate audience." Sorensen, Oral History Interview, p. 142.

75. According to Victor Navasky, Lewis went along with the demands for moderating his text "at the urging primarily of A. Phillip Randolph (who was urged by Walter Reuther, who was urged by Robert Kennedy)." See Navasky, *Kennedy Justice*, p. 226.

76. Lewis's remarks are cited in Leslie W. Dunbar's Foreword to Watters and Cleghorn, *Climbing Jacob's Ladder*, pp. xiv–xv; and in David Lewis, *King*, pp. 223–24.

77. Kennedy, *Public Papers: 1963*, p. 645.

78. Murray Kempton, "Marching on Washington," in Westin, *Freedom Now*, p. 272.

79. Sorensen, *Kennedy*, p. 567.

80. Sorensen recalls that Kennedy told one black leader: "This issue could cost me the election, but we're not turning back." But in general he evaluated the political costs less dramatically. As Sorensen notes, Kennedy thought that passage of the Administration's bill would ease tensions, whereas presidential inaction might have had disastrous consequences. And he was still reasonably confident of reelection in 1964. Ibid., p. 568.

81. Kennedy, *Public Papers: 1963*, p. 677

82. Ibid., p. 681.

83. A. Philip Randolph, in a television broadcast with March on Washington leaders on August 28, 1963. The transcript can be found in the White House Central Files on Human Rights, Kennedy Library.

84. Schlesinger, *A Thousand Days*, p. 881.

Chapter 7   *REASSESSING THE MODERN PRESIDENCY*

1. Aaron Wildavsky, "The Two Presidencies," in *The Presidency*, ed. Aaron Wildavsky (Boston: Little, Brown, 1969), p. 231.

2. See Bert Cochran, *Harry Truman and the Crisis Presidency* (New York: Funk & Wagnalls, 1973), pp. 198–220. Truman's legislative proposal came during a rail strike which he had failed to forestall. He was so enraged by the strike that he hand-drafted a speech for radio; in

this speech he denounced strikers and their leaders as unpatriotic loafers, and called upon veterans to help him "put transportation and production back to work, hang a few traitors and make our own country safe for democracy" (quoted in ibid., p. 206). Truman's advisers dissuaded him from going on the air with these remarks; the speech he did deliver was, however, still a strong blast at the unions.

3. Memo from Clark Clifford to President Truman, 19 November 1947, quoted in ibid., pp. 217–18. For an analysis of Truman's civil rights record, see Barton J. Bernstein, "The Ambiguous Legacy: The Truman Administration and Civil Rights," in *Politics and Policies of the Truman Administration,* ed. Barton J. Bernstein (Chicago: Quadrangle, 1970), pp. 269–314.

4. For a discussion of the political strategy underlying the War on Poverty, see Frances Fox Piven and Richard A. Cloward, *Regulating the Poor: The Functions of Public Welfare* (New York: Vintage, 1972), pp. 248–82.

5. See John C. Donovan, *The Politics of Poverty* (New York: Pegasus, 1967), pp. 111–41.

6. Kennedy's statement on American personnel abroad was delivered to the American embassy staff in Bonn, West Germany, on 23 June 1963. John F. Kennedy, *Public Papers: 1963* (Washington, D.C.: Government Printing Office, 1964), p. 501. For the figures on American investments abroad, see Harry Magdoff, *The Age of Imperialism* (New York: Monthly Review Press, 1969), pp. 56–59.

7. Quoted in Richard Hofstadter, *The American Political Tradition* (New York: Vintage, 1948), p. 133.

8. Arthur Schlesinger, Jr., has been the most persuasive—and prolific—of pragmatic liberal spokesmen. For a description of the pragmatic mind during the New Frontier, see *A Thousand Days: John F. Kennedy in the White House* (Greenwich, Conn.: Fawcett, 1967), especially pp. 198–202, 679–87. To view the pragmatic liberal hard at work in foreign policy, also see Roger Hilsman, *To Move a Nation* (New York: Delta, 1967).

9. Louis Hartz, *The Liberal Tradition in America* (New York: Harcourt, Brace & World, 1955), p. 59.

10. Hannah Arendt, "Lying in Politics: Reflections on the Pentagon Papers," *New York Review of Books* 17 (18 November 1971): 38.

11. This connection between pragmatism and power can be found in the work of William James, the greatest of pragmatic philosophers. The pragmatist, as James portrays him, turns away from abstractions and systems "towards facts, towards action and towards power." William James, *Pragmatism* (Cleveland: Meridian, 1955), p. 45.

12. Schlesinger, *A Thousand Days,* p. 680.

13. Sheldon S. Wolin has shown that liberalism itself emerged, not as an optimistic vision of progress, but as a philosophy "deeply

shaded by anxiety." Wolin finds that the great liberal philosophers (Locke, Smith, Bentham) were preoccupied with the hostility of nature, the potential explosiveness of a crowded, industrialized society, the fear of loss and attendant desire for security. Sheldon S. Wolin, *Politics and Vision: Continuity and Innovation in Western Political Thought* (Boston: Little, Brown, 1960), pp. 314–31.

14. Clinton Rossiter, *The American Presidency* (New York: Mentor, 1962), p. 29.

15. Quoted in James MacGregor Burns, *Roosevelt: The Lion and the Fox* (New York: Harcourt, Brace & World, 1956), p. 151.

16. Hofstadter, *The American Political Tradition,* p. 130. On Lincoln and the Radicals, see Hofstadter, pp. 124–33, 152–54; and David Donald, *Lincoln Reconsidered* (New York: Vintage, 1956), pp. 103-27. On Wilson and labor, see Arthur S. Link, *Woodrow Wilson and the Progressive Era, 1910-1917* (New York: Harper Torchbooks, 1963), pp. 55–56, 235–37. On Roosevelt and labor, see Burns, *Roosevelt: The Lion and the Fox,* pp. 215–20; William E. Leuchtenburg, *Franklin D. Roosevelt and the New Deal, 1932–1940* (New York: Harper Torchbooks, 1963), pp. 106–14, 150–52; Paul K. Conkin, *The New Deal* (New York: Thomas Y. Crowell, 1967), pp. 35–36, 63–64.

17. For a poignant discussion of Lyndon Johnson's education by the civil rights movement, see William Appleman Williams, *Some Presidents From Wilson to Nixon* (New York: New York Review Books, 1972), pp. 86–89.

18. Mass movements can be intolerant and destructive, rather than progressive. American social science has, since World War II, emphasized precisely this danger. The antidemocratic potential of mass movements is real enough, but after the experiences of the civil rights and antiwar movements of the 1960s, it is the democratic potential of mass politics that appears more essential. Whether masses of people turn toward regressive causes or progressive ones will actually depend on a number of factors: the social strata who are mobilized, the kind of leadership that mobilizes them, the issues around which people are mobilized. The same people who might join authoritarian causes under certain circumstances (e.g., white workers fearing school or housing integration) might also join in progressive movements because of other circumstances (e.g., white workers cooperating with black workers in building a union). Indeed, their antidemocratic or racist attitudes might be significantly modified by their experiences of participation and cooperation. See Michael Paul Rogin, *The Intellectuals and McCarthy: The Radical Specter* (Cambridge, Mass.: MIT Press, 1967), pp. 261–82.

Index

Abel, Elie, 95
Acheson, Dean, 70–72, 74–77
Adenauer, Konrad, 69
Affluent Society, The, 206
Africa, 43, 60, 110
Agrarian reform, in Latin America, 112–13, 119, 129–30
Albany Movement, 242–43
Alliance for Progress, 21, 110–42, 151, 160, 219
American Foreign Service Association, 26
Anderson, William G., 242
Arendt, Hannah, 285–86
Argentina, 118, 124
Arms buildup, 37–40, 49–51, 56, 58, 76, 81, 105–6; Cuban missile crisis and, 83–100; economy and, 174–75
Arosemena, Julio, 124
Asia, 43, 52

Balance-of-payments problem, 171, 192–93
Ball, George, 7
Barber, James David, xii, xiii, xvi–xvii
Barnett, Ross, 247–48
Batista, Fulgencio, 115
Bay of Pigs invasion, xvi, 17, 32, 51–53, 56, 78, 113–17
Belaunde, Terry Fernando, 124
Bell, David, 141
Berlin, 16, 57–58, 64, 88; crisis of 1961, 66, 68–82; Wall, 79–80
Best and the Brightest, The, 19
Betancourt, Rómulo, 122, 124–26
Bethe, Hans, 85
Bethlehem Steel, 179
Birmingham, Alabama, 251–54, 268

Black Muslims, 255
Blacks. *See* Civil rights movement
Block, Joseph, 179
Blockade: of Cuba, 91–92, 96; of North Vietnam, 100
Blough, Roger, 177–80
Bodenheimer, Susanne, 119
Bogotá Conference, 112
Bosch, Juan, 132
Brazil, 63, 124, 139
Brezhnev, Leonid, 46
Brinkley, David, 163
Brizola, Leonel, 63
Bryan, William Jennings, 186
Bundy, McGeorge, 5, 100, 164
Burns, James MacGregor, 31, 231
Business community. *See* Corporations
Business Group for Latin America, 141
Business Week, 220

Canada, 139
Capehart, Homer, 86
Capitalism, corporate, 194–203, 220–22, 274, 279
Castro, Fidel, 32, 56, 86, 113–14, 128, 131, 133
Castroism, 123, 126, 133–35
Central Intelligence Agency (CIA), 31–32, 51, 56, 113–15, 133
Chayes, Abram, 74
China. *See* People's Republic of China
Churchill, Winston, 14–15, 39
Civil defense, 76
Civil Rights Act (1964), 261–63
Civil Rights Commission, 240, 247, 251

DATE DUE